BABIES!

BABIES!

A Parents' Guide to
Surviving (and Enjoying!) Baby's First Year

DR CHRISTOPHER GREEN

Illustrations by Roger Roberts

SIMON & SCHUSTER
A VIACOM COMPANY

Author's Note

I apologise to those who expect a good childcare book to use the words *he* and *she* equally. It is an unfortunate fact that the English language has no polite and neutral term to refer to both boys and girls at the same time.

Juggling the *he's* and *she's* in every chapter seems a bit cumbersome and so I refer to all children by the term *he*. Please interpret this to suit your own little one.

First published in Great Britain by Simon & Schuster Ltd, 1989
This updated edition published by Simon & Schuster UK Ltd, 1998
A Viacom company

Text © Drs Christopher and Hilary Green, 1988, 1998
Illustrations © Simon & Schuster Australia, 1988

5 7 9 10 8 6 4

Simon & Schuster UK Ltd
Africa House
64-78 Kingsway
London WC2B 6AH

Simon & Schuster Australia
Sydney

A CIP catalogue record for this book is available
from the British Library

ISBN 0-684-85121-0

Printed and bound in Great Britain by
Butler & Tanner Ltd, Frome and London

BABIES! could not have been written without
the warmth, wisdom and human touch
of Dr Hilary Green and the editorial input
of Michael Morton Evans.

Contents

Introduction

Not another baby book, I hear you groan. Well, don't close the pages just yet. I think you'll find this is different.

This is not another rigid, frigid this-is-the-only-way-to-do-it book. Nor is it a tome of irrelevant, academic ramblings which tells you the theory of childcare but not the practice. This is a practical, commonsense, up-to-date guide to the everyday concerns of parents facing the first year of their baby's life.

You have probably heard of the change of life child. Well, I believe that every first baby is a change of life child – after this, the parents' lives are never quite the same again. The first year is a time of readjustment with tiredness, uncertainties and many mixed emotions. It is also one of the best years of a parent's life, provided he or she has the confidence, flexibility and sensible expectations to enjoy it.

Twenty years ago I couldn't have written a word of this. I was then a recently qualified, wet-behind-the-ears paediatrician who thought he knew it all. I certainly knew every obscure and irrelevant detail of children's medicine, but I knew nothing about how parents felt, how they worried and what was meant by giving practical help with day-to-day problems. When I saw a child who wouldn't sleep, it was easy – 'Just let him cry all night'. When shown a baby with colic I would tell the parents, 'Don't worry, it can't be important – there's no medical cause for such a condition'. In short, when it came to the things that mattered in childcare, I understood little and helped even less.

This came to an abrupt halt with the arrival of our own first born who had terrible colic. He cried and cried while his parents, both highly qualified doctors, became distraught and bewildered. Within a week we felt incompetent, impotent and utter failures. We found ourselves alone and with little help from childcare books and even less from professional colleagues.

From this experience I became interested in the art of understanding the common concerns of childcare and how to provide high quality practical help. I quickly realised that the feelings of parents had to be respected, that advice had to be extremely down-to-earth and, above all, that confidence must always be given a boost.

And so my first book, *Toddler Taming*, was born. It was written to be practical and entertaining, but now ten years down the track I see that its real strength was something less obvious but far more powerful. It was a book that let parents see that they were not alone, and that they were normal. It boosted confidence and encouraged them to do what they themselves felt was right for their children. I brought back fun to childcare.

Babies! has been written with the same goal. It provides a balanced and accurate view of modern-day childcare for the first year. It aims to reassure parents to trust their own instincts and to do what feels right and works for them.

This book begins at birth and talks about the normal worries parents have adapting to the new human being in their midst. There follow many chapters on the practical day-to-day concerns such as feeding, crying, sleeping, etc., etc. I have included some heavy but important topics, such as postnatal depression, cot death, the handicapped child and what to do when close to child abuse. These are too important to ignore. Flip past what you don't wish to read but, remember, the information is there if you need it. Every chapter stands alone, so you may dip and delve if you wish or go through from start to finish.

Also included are the more humorous, light-hearted moments of family life, for this book is not just about babies, it's also about families and relationships. It is for mothers, fathers, grandparents and anyone who is interested in children.

I must admit that most of the practical ideas in this book are not mine, but those of the many, many parents I have worked with over the last ten years. As you read the text you may chuckle as you recognise yourself, your husband, your mother-in-law or your baby, behaving just as blindly and unreasonably as we all do. Parents need a sense of humour to survive. If you can stand back and laugh at what you and your children get up to, then children can be a lot of fun.

Read on and you'll see what I mean.

Acknowledgements

Thanks to:

My wife Hilary, a long suffering and very special person.

James and Tim, two fun-loving boys who taught their father everything he knows about childcare.

Jon Attenborough, friend and publisher, whose vision created *Toddler Taming* and brought this book into being.

Kirsty Melville, a talented editor, whose red pen has spared the readers from my most outrageous observations.

Roger Roberts, an illustrator with a wonderfully warped sense of humour.

Dr John Yu and the staff of The Children's Hospital, Sydney – a centre of excellence I am proud to be part of.

The staff of Torrens House, Adelaide, Dr Suzette Booth, Marie Anne Waugh and the many, many others who have helped.

1

The Birth – How to Survive Hospital and the 'Helping Professions'

As the forty-week wait grinds to an end, this is where our story really begins. By now the memory of a slim figure and a walk without a waddle will be but a distant memory. Hospitalisation is close and all thoughts will now start to focus on that one major event – giving birth. There will, of course, be a few nagging worries. How will I know when it's time to go to hospital? Will the birth be painful? Will I be sore afterwards? Will I cope with the baby? Who will look after the other children? Will my husband starve to death? What will my home look like when I get back? Will someone have remembered to take the rubbish out? Will the cat be weak with malnutrition? What overgrowth of fungus will be in the fridge? All these questions and more will begin to niggle at you. The secret is to think ahead, plan ahead and (as they say in the boy scouts), be prepared!

The Preparations

A packed bag

First you should pack that little bag of life's necessities which you will take to the hospital with you. You're not packing for a world tour, so keep the contents simple. A couple of nighties, a shawl or bed jacket, toothbrush, toothpaste, hairbrush and comb, make-up and a couple of books – these are the sorts of things you will need. Visitors can always bring what you forget and anyway most hospitals have shops these days and are very keen to accept your money! For those with toddlers, remember to keep the bag well out of reach. Helpful little hands may repack it with personal treasures. The discovery of a much-chewed teddy bear instead of your nightdress is only likely to add to the confusion of your sudden arrival in the labour ward.

Other children

If you have other children, plans must be made for them to be looked after when you go. Fathers or grandparents are usually the best people to look after the children, but if they are not available, anyone the child knows well and feels happy with will do. Children should be told what is about to happen, whether they fully understand the finer details or not. You should be quite open in your talk of babies right from the earliest days. This will help smooth out any problems of jealousy and gives the best chance of producing an enthusiastic little helper. (See Chapter 7 for more on brothers and sisters.)

Malnutrition and husbands

If you are married to a non-cooking male, you had better run a crash course in tin-opening, egg-boiling and bacon-frying or leave a few frozen offerings in the freezer. If you return home to discover these haven't been touched and the family ate out at McDonalds every night, don't worry. What's left will still be extremely useful. This reduction in catering output need only be temporary. As your strength returns, so will a more impressive menu. But be reassured, however much your husband complains, nothing is going to drop off due to malnutrition!

Baby names

It may seem a little premature at this stage, but it does help to consider a few children's names before the event. When you first hold the little one, and your eyes meet, how much nicer to have a name on your lips than to have to say 'it'. On the subject of names, let me just offer a couple of tips. It is generally unwise to resurrect one from an old boyfriend or girlfriend. I

realise that for those parents who led a particularly active life before marriage, this may reduce the available repertoire quite dramatically. Nevertheless it is better to choose elsewhere. Beware of old family names. Great Uncle Ebeneezer may have been very kind to you in his will, but what a name to lumber your son with. Be careful of the names from current TV soap operas. Thirty years on, your favourite TV character's name may seem a bit dated. Also I would plead against those way-out labels favoured in the more trendy quarters. Some children must be severely handicapped by the name attached to them by their parents. Imagine being called Stallone and turning out to be a short, fat, awkward boy with glasses, or being christened Innocence when at eighteen you're out on the town every night. Research has actually shown that children with way-out names more frequently end up in psychiatric clinics, though I suspect that it may be not so much the name as living with the strange people who thought of it in the first place. Life is tough enough without lumbering children with any extra burdens.

The Start

In the final days of pregnancy the baby's head moves down into the pelvis. For some first-time mums this happens late, whilst others feel the pressure so low down that at any moment they expect to see a little face smiling up from below.

The uterus is in a state of constant movement throughout pregnancy which can feel like weak, poorly co-ordinated contractions. When these become strong and regular, this is the real thing. At antenatal classes you will have been told when to ring for advice and when to come in, but if you are in any doubt don't worry yourself – worry someone else! Make the phone call.

Sometimes the baby seems quite content to stay put and the expected day of birth comes and goes without so much as a murmur. If this goes on too long the obstetrician may decide to bring on labour artificially. He can either use an instrument to break the waters or the drug Syntocinon can be dripped slowly into a vein. Both these methods are very common and very safe. Some mothers feel robbed if they cannot go through all the stages of labour naturally, while others don't give a damn for Nature and if things can be easier and more predictable, they are glad to get going.

At the beginning of labour it is normal to have a small show of blood, but if this becomes a flood of blood, you should shout for help at once. The baby has spent nine months floating in a water-filled bag and when this breaks the action begins. This can happen at any time, usually in hospital, sometimes quietly at home or, on rare occasions, one hears tales of a spectacular flood on the supermarket floor. But for most mums there is no bleeding, no great flood, no panic, just regular labour pains which say that it's time to go.

Before leaving home try and have a quick shower in the comfort of your own bathroom. Tell your children that you are going to the hospital and then take off, clutching your little bag. (See Chapter 7 – Before the birth.) Unless things are extremely advanced, drive slowly. Some fathers seem to conceive in a rush and try and end the event with equal speed. Driving from home to hospital like a Grand Prix competitor is unnecessarily dramatic and is likely to cause more problems than it will solve.

The hospital admission

Hospital can be a pretty daunting place. When you first present yourself at the front desk the person who greets you can set the seal on your mood. Try not to be deflated by a bored, cold or harassed receptionist. This is going to be *your* day, so let no-one take it from you. Luckily most receptionists have that knack of receiving you like royalty. They make you feel a most important person and, of course, that's what you are.

Once the admission papers have all been filled in, it's off to the labour ward. Here the contractions will have been timed, the baby's heart checked, your blood pressure taken and an examination given to see how the birth canal is opening. Some hospitals insist on bringing out the Wilkinson's Sword and giving you a quick shave, while others administer an enema, although these days hospitals usually spare you such discomforts. From now on it's a waiting game.

The Birth

Labour can be a long, tedious affair. There will be plenty of time for lying down later, but in the early stages it is best to sit in a chair or walk around. A good book and a good companion close by, make for the best start.

As things progress, relief from pain is freely available either from injected drugs, a self-administered gas mixture or an epidural anaesthetic which numbs all feeling in the lower half of your body. In recent years various groups have campaigned vigorously for less medical interference and more natural childbirth. When all's said and done it's your body, not theirs. You don't have to suffer stoically like a modern-day Joan of Arc. If you want some relief, just ask.

Some health workers now state that proper pain relief may shorten labour and be better for the baby. They claim that pain causes release of adrenalin which interferes with the contractions. Some also ask whether the overbreathing methods used to control pain naturally are good for the baby. I think these questions are interesting but fine-print academia.

Various birth positions are also on offer. You might prefer the usual which is flat on your back and knees bent, or alternatively prefer to lie on your side, as favoured by our Victorian grandmothers. You can also squat, use a birthing chair or choose any other position you like. This is for you, your midwife and your obstetrician to work out.

Episiotomy is where a cut is made to ease the passage of the baby's head through the last stretches of the birth canal. This used to be common practice and then lost some popularity. It is now on the return as refusal to cut in a planned position seems to slow delivery and increase the risk of accidental tearing of the tail, which is to be avoided.

Fathers at birth

As a medical student performing my first deliveries it was a rare occurrence to see a father in the labour wards. They usually stayed at work until the phone call came and then headed for the hospital, probably via the pub. Those who asked to be present were looked upon as some sort of pushy pervert. Everyone seemed to forget that fathers knew their wives quite well and were in fact a 50 per cent shareholder in the baby. Nowadays it is usual to have dads present and enthusiasts have been known to bring in the other children too. Based on the law of natural progression, I suppose we will soon be seeing mothers-in-law in attendance to give the obstetrician some free advice, possibly to be accompanied by the ladies from the bowling club, white hats, thermos flasks and all.

Many first-time dads feel apprehensive about the birth. They may not like hospitals or any thought of blood or pain. They may be the type who faint at the sight of Hawkeye about to perform an operation in M*A*S*H or go into convulsions at the mere thought of the dentist's chair. But be reassured,

very few ever seem to get upset or make fools of themselves when it comes to the real thing.

Sometimes first-time fathers think they can sit and conduct a deep and meaningful conversation with their wife, philosophising about art, culture, politics – or last week's football game – as the baby quietly slips out. The reality is that when the pains start coming, regular conversation becomes very one-sided. It is a presence and support that is needed, not an armchair debate. Dad is the cheerleader, there to urge the home team on to even greater efforts as it pushes hard in the last quarter.

The first hours

When the baby finally squeezes out, the little scrap is usually lifted on to Mum's rapidly deflating abdomen for a cuddle and a bit of closeness and warmth. The umbilical cord is clamped and suction will be applied to nose, throat and possibly lungs to clear out any fluid and establish a good breathing pattern. Having been underwater for nine months it's little wonder he tends to be somewhat choked up at birth. (Most spectators are a bit choked up too!) Don't panic if your potential Einstein seems to be taking an eternity to utter his first cry. About 5 per cent of all babies are very slow to start breathing, which is why most people interested in child development favour hospital rather than home deliveries. In the maternity hospital, expert care and oxygen are always close at hand, in case more major resuscitation is needed.

The obstetrician will tell you the child's sex and assure you that all fingers, toes and other pieces are present. But even before this you will have sensed that all is well. Doctors and nurses are only human and no matter how hard they try, they always let their feelings slip out as you listen to the tone of their voices.

Once all the action is over, it is time for mothers, fathers and babies to have some time alone to carry out their proper introductions. (See Chapter 6.)

The hospital – the staff – the routine

Hospitals, like the armed forces and some stricter schools for aristocratic young ladies and gentlemen, are all run on a hard and fast routine. The day will seem to start at an ungodly hour with the baby at your bedside and a vacuum cleaner roaring in your ear like a 747, as the last speck of dust is sucked from under your slumbering body. All jobs have to be completed before the day staff sign on, so temperatures must be taken, babies fed, beds straightened, and everyone smiling when the senior sister comes on duty. As the day progresses feeds have to be given, physiotherapists come to see if you are moving properly, wounds are examined, babies are checked out and the obstetrician will make a high-speed visitation, whizzing in and out with soothing words like a nun on roller skates. While all this is going on the ward sister is valiantly keeping the whole show on the road, officiating like the *maître d'* of some high-class hotel. Like all good *maîtres d'* she probably has a detached look and a heart of gold. Most in this position are amazing people – a cross between an angel and Florence Nightingale. Occasionally, however, you meet one from the school of hard knocks. You feel sure that if she were a bird she would be of the sort that eats her young!

If you have any queries or doubts ask your obstetrician on one of his fleeting, high-speed visits. If you find it hard to get your thoughts together when faced with such a fast-moving target, do a little homework before his appearance. First be quite sure you know the questions you want to ask. Don't be afraid to write a list and don't let him go until you have all the answers. Doctors are masters in the art of burying patients in a smokescreen of medical terminology. If you don't understand what's being said, for goodness' sake ask for an explanation. Don't allow yourself to be buried in a mound of medical mumbo-jumbo. After all, it's your body we are talking about, so let's ask that a spade be called a spade.

Another important consideration is mealtimes. Some hospitals produce excellent food, whilst others take exactly the same ingredients and produce a meal that would make even the healthy feel sick and the sick feel sicker. If you need a little spoiling get your visitors to snuggle in some take-away food from outside. This alleviates the monotony of hospital diet and reintroduces your tastebuds to that lost ingredient – flavour. In between mealtimes keep nibbling away at the fruit bowl. You don't need this to stop scurvy, but it's refreshing and will help get the sluggish bowel into a state of movement.

Visiting rules have been greatly eased over recent years. Most hospitals provide a general visiting time and then one specifically for Dad so that the three most important people can have time together in peace. Also your other children should be brought in and introduced to the newborn as soon as possible. (See Chapter 7.)

What happens to your body?

Gone now are the prebirth days and waddling like a duck. Now the postnatal mum is moving like a saddle-sore member of the cast from a TV western. Some manage to move with relative elegance, whilst others feel they have given birth to a rhinoceros, horns and all! However, with gentle exercise and bathing such discomfort soon goes.

Feeding your new baby is usually established with ease, but don't be disheartened if you find it difficult at first. No-one expects you to get it perfect on the first day. As you have probably never fed a baby before, don't be afraid to ask for help. And talking of help, watch out for all the experts. With so many changes of staff, you will find different opinions come and go with every new face you see. Don't get worked up over this. Remember, there are many correct ways to bring up a baby, and it's best to latch on to the advice that feels right for you and your style.

At this stage, many mums start to worry about bonding too, particularly with all the opinions floating around about what is supposed to happen! Bonding may be immediate or take some time. Remember, love is something which develops over a long period and lasting relationships are rarely made in minutes. Don't try too hard. Just let Nature get on with it. (See Chapter 6.)

It is usual for new mothers to feel very clingy towards their newborns. You might get upset when a crowd of visitors play pass-the-parcel with the youngster. If you don't want the baby lifted up and passed around, it's your decision and you should let everyone know how you feel. But please give Dad equal access. Hogging the show and telling Dad he is not as good a comforter as you in the early days is unfair, and can set up a pattern where he feels left out – and later opts out! It's better if he can feel involved from the very beginning (you'll appreciate it, later on!).

The days immediately after birth are a time of confusion for your body and brain. All those hormones produced by the placenta reduce sharply after birth leaving muscles, ligaments and many body functions in an unsettled state. Emotions are also very mixed with elation, uncertainty, discomfort, tiredness, lack of confidence and even some tears all vying with each other.

It's a confusing time and although these feelings pass, they can be very bewildering. Not the least of them is wondering just who this little bundle is? And that's the subject of the next chapter.

Going to hospital – what to bring

- Several nighties. These should open down the front for breast-feeding.
- Bed jacket, shawl or cardigan to keep shoulders warm when sitting up in bed.
- Slippers.
- Dressing gown.
- Nursing bras.
- Nursing pads may be needed.
- Sanitary pads (although they are sometimes provided).
- A belt or neat fitting undies to keep pads in place.
- Toilette requirements – toothbrush, toothpaste, nice soap, flannel, shampoo, hairbrush.
- Make-up and perfume – to help you feel more like a person than a patient.
- Some way of relaxing – a good book, Walkman, knitting, crochet, *Babies!*
- A purse with a little money (for the telephone) and a photo of your other children.

Leave ready for husband to bring

- Nappies.
- Nappy pins.
- Plastic pants.
- Stretch suit or some garment to fit any size of newborn.
- Baby blanket.
- Car seat or carry cot.

PS – Don't panic, most hospitals have a shop to buy what you forget.

2

Getting to Know
Your Newborn

A T last the drama of delivery is over. You feel tired, numb and relieved, and somewhat elated at a successful birth. Then you look down at the little bundle in front of you, and out come all sorts of mixed emotions.

He's so small, so delicate, you think, and then, I know so little about babies. How can I ever handle such a fragile little mite!

Well, don't despair, help is there. First of all, despite initial impressions, babies are remarkably unbreakable. They would need to be when you think of all the traumas they endured in the obstacle course of birth (like little marines – they are tough). Of course there will be an awful lot of learning ahead, but if you use commonsense, relax and trust your natural instincts, it all comes together. All you need is a little basic information about what is normal and what to expect and then with a charge of confidence, you can get going.

The first impression

The newborn usually has a small, reddish body, blueish hands and feet, and a head which seems quite out of proportion to the rest of him. He lies with arms and legs flexed up, which is scarcely surprising when you think that for the past nine months he has been all curled up in Mum's tum. In such cramped living conditions there was never enough space to have a good stretch, and certainly insufficient for a daily aerobics workout.

Apart from jumping at loud noises there is no obvious impression of hearing and his eyes drift round in what at first appears to be a purposeless way. Don't be fooled, he sees and hears far more than you realise, being remarkably aware of both your face and voice. In the early weeks he seems to sleep most of the time, completely unperturbed by light or noise.

A little baby can cough and sneeze and often does. His mouth and eyelids may move in sleep as though he is dreaming of some particularly interesting moment of a past existence (for all we know, he is). He will often give a sudden startle in his sleep for a reason which is best known to himself.

He will cry at birth and regularly thereafter. It is a little voice which can come out with amazing intensity. To first-time parents all cries will sound the same, but after a few weeks the subtle differences between boredom, pain and hunger cries become strikingly apparent.

The dimensions

There are several questions friends ask immediately after every birth. How are Mother and Baby? What is the sex? And what about the weight?

Between thirty-eight and forty-one weeks most babies decide they've had enough and deign to appear in this world. But despite many babies having identical gestation periods they somehow manage to come out with a variety of different shapes and sizes.

Weight

The average birth weight is 3.3 kg (7½ lb). In the final months of pregnancy the baby is all tanked up with fluids and kilojoules like a camel preparing to cross the Sahara. These nutrients will fuel him for his strenuous journey into the outside world and keep him going through the first days when breast-feeding gives comfort, but few kilojoules.

These reserves of fuel and fluid are gradually burned up and this explains why the first days are a time of weight loss rather than gain. As a rule of

11

thumb, it is said that a baby can lose up to 10 per cent of birth weight in the first few days to have it all regained by at latest the tenth day.

Once the weight starts to increase it will probably increase by just under 30 g (1 oz) a day for the next four months. This will vary from baby to baby and week to week, so don't become obsessed with each gram of gain. It is health, not the weighing machine we are really interested in. As a student I was taught to allow for the weight gain being just under the ounce or 30 g per day by calculating on the basis of an ounce a day and none on Sundays. This had absolutely no religious significance, but was just a nice Irish rule of thumb, which added up to 6 oz or 180 g per week, which is the average figure.

If your baby is of near average birth weight then this will have almost doubled by four months, and trebled by a year. The actual size at birth bears only a small relationship to the child's weight at twelve months, and almost none whatsoever to his adult weight. It does however exhibit quite a strong family pattern with most brothers and sisters tending to be of roughly the same birth weight. It seems likely that if your first one called for a mighty push, then the chances are that the next will be much the same.

Of course there are medical reasons for some babies being born either very small or particularly large. Mums with high blood pressure, or who have placenta problems tend towards small babies, whilst mums with uncontrolled diabetes may produce larger ones.

Though 3.3 kg (7½ lb) is the average weight, 10 per cent of normal babies will be 4 kg (9 lb) and a further 10 per cent as little as 2.5 kg (6 lb). Right from birth boys tend to be slightly heavier and longer than girls, the difference being on average, 100 g (3.5 oz) in weight and 1 cm (0.4 in) in length.

Length

The average baby at birth has already grown about 50 cm (21 in) all in the nine months from conception. I find this quite mind-boggling. Just imagine a spotty adolescent growing that fast during his puberty growth spurt – you'd be lengthening his blue denims by a centimetre twice a week!

It's also fascinating to realise that at birth a baby has already gained roughly one-third of his ultimate adult height. By two and a half years he has reached almost half his final elevation and close to his eighth birthday, he will have reached the three-quarter mark.

Head size

The head circumference of the average full-term baby is 35 cm (14 in) with a variation of plus or minus 2 cm (0.8 in). Obviously if the head is extremely large, small or changes size unexpectedly, this could be a cause for concern, but slight differences are of little importance.

A big head does not mean a big intelligence. Often it contains just the same amount of cleverness but simply less well packed. Heads are like computers.

TABLE 1: Approximate heights (cm) of children 1–5 years

	Average		Tall Average (Upper 10%)		Short Average (Lower 10%)	
	Girls	Boys	Girls	Boys	Girls	Boys
BIRTH	50	51	52.5	53	47	48
3 months	60	62	63	64	56	57
6 months	66	68	69	71	62	64
9 months	71	73	74	76	67	69
1 year	74	76	79	82	69	71
2 years	85	87	91	95	79	80
3 years	94	95	101	104	87	88
4 years	101	102	109	111	94	95
5 years	107	109	116	118	99	101
ADULT	163.5	177	171	185	156	168

TABLE 2: Approximate weights (kg) of children 1–5 years

	Average		Heavy Average (Upper 10%)		Light Average (Lower 10%)	
	Girls	Boys	Girls	Boys	Girls	Boys
BIRTH	3.2	3.3	3.7	4	2.5	2.5
3 months	5.4	6.0	6.5	7	4.5	5
6 months	7.2	7.8	8.5	9	6	6.5
9 months	8.6	9.2	10	10.5	6.5	8
1 year	9.5	10.5	12	13	7.5	8.5
2 years	12	13	15.5	16	10	10.5
3 years	14	15	18	19	11.5	12
4 years	16	17	21	21.5	13	13.5
5 years	18.5	19	24.5	24.5	14.5	15
ADULT	56.5	69	72.5	87	47	57.5

Note: The ideal relationship of height and weight is to be in proportion, e.g. if the child is of low average height then he should also be of low average weight.

The size of the case that covers all those silicon chips bears no relationship to the complexity of the works.

Please take these figures of dimensions as only a very rough guide. Don't go rushing off to put your baby on the kitchen scales or run a tape measure round him and then worry yourself silly. Each child is an individual and as such some won't match the textbook tables. There are many children who never measure up to average but they are still very normal.

The head

Since it is the baby's top that spearheads his descent into the world, it should come as no surprise to find that the head of this spear has become a pointed tip. This change of shape can occur because the baby's skull at this stage is moveable, being made up of a number of bones held together by a kind of flexible fibrous tape.

At birth, as pressure is placed on the skull, the bones overlap and take on a temporary realignment. They mould into a shape rather like an egg, which greatly eases the slide through the birth canal. After birth it takes a day or two for the normal shape to return, so don't despair, you've not given birth to an egg-head!

Birth may be quite traumatic for Mother, but make no mistake, it's no picnic for Baby either. If you had to spend at least twelve hours standing on your head trying to get out of a confined space, you'd be crying when you got to the other end too.

Where the birth pressure has been on the top of the head a circle of spongy, fluid-filled skin marks the spot for a few days. There is no cause for alarm, this mark is only skin deep and doesn't mean that the baby has been injured in any way. If it has been a breech birth with the baby being round the wrong way the swelling can be on a very different part. Sometimes the nose gets a bit squashed and it is not unusual for a few bruises to show, particularly where instruments were necessary. But don't worry, bumps, bruises and swellings on the outside rarely have any bearing on the state of the important bits on the inside. (See Chapter 3 – Cephalhaematoma.)

There is one spot at the top of the skull where the bones don't quite join. This leaves a little gap known as the 'soft spot' or more correctly as the anterior fontanelle. Don't be frightened of this. It is present in all babies. It is not delicate, painful, nor dangerous to touch. The brain beneath it is well-protected by a tough fibrous covering. By six months it will have almost closed over and certainly all traces will have long gone by two years.

The newborn's head is large and his neck strength almost non-existent. Be careful when you lift up your baby in the early months, as the unsupported head will flop forwards or sideways like that of a rag doll. There's no chance that it will dislocate or fall off, but during the short time that it takes to develop good head control, it's best to be a supporting parent.

The skin

When you are first handed your new born he will not have the clean, sparkling appearance you expect. It's not very surprising – after all, no-one changed Baby's bath water for the last nine months! At birth, when the moisture has been dried off, the skin is often seen to be coated in a creamy, greasy paste called vernix. This disappears with the first bath. But then you may notice the little one is covered in a fur of fine hair. No, he has not regressed to the Stone Age. This is quite normal and will all drop out in the first month.

As for the baby's head of hair, there is a great variation in the luxuriance of growth. Some children are born with a great black mop, whilst most tend towards the Kojak style. If both parents are blonde or red-haired, don't panic and rush to your lawyer when you see a jet-black mat. This colour bears little relationship to the final tint.

The skin of a newborn baby is amazingly red. The reason for this is that at birth the baby's red blood count will probably be 25 per cent greater than Mother's. This explains why he has such a ruddy hue and you look so pale.

One of the greatest miracles at birth is the change in the heart and circulation of a baby. Before delivery the plumbing is all attached to the umbilical cord with various shunts and holes in the heart to keep the flow moving. It's not unlike an astronaut out for a space walk all wired up and connected to a life support system. At birth the umbilical cord is cut, chopping off Baby's supply system. Within minutes the whole dynamics change with the baby rapidly having to become self-sufficient to survive. In the circumstances it's not surprising that the heart takes some time to come to terms with the new order of things, and while this is happening the flow of blood to the skin and extremities can be rather variable. Dusky hands, feet and mottled skin at this stage are very usual.

Until birth the skin has been immersed in fluid and like that of a fish it never gets a chance to dry out. Now out on dry land, it is destined to be sat in dirty nappies, clothed in uncomfortable fabrics which have often been washed in some superblast harsh washing powder. Whereas most skins cope remarkably well with all this, some get rashes, dry out and need a bit of nurturing.

Baby's little fingers can often have remarkably long nails which are fairly lethal when it comes to scratching. They should be trimmed early on before the face gets damaged – something that will probably happen the very day you have made an appointment with the photographer.

Vision and hearing

The newborn spends so much time asleep that his eyes are generally only open for intermittent viewing. When awake his eyes will look around in a seemingly purposeless way, giving no impression of vision. In fact the smallest babies can see, but it takes some patience to prove this. Hold the baby on your knee, well supported and facing you. Get your head in line with his eyes and then move ever so slowly from one side to the other. You will see those little eyes following your face with a jerky, but definitely following, movement.

There is definite colour in Baby's eyes at birth, usually blue, but like the

15

hair this often changes as the baby grows older. So don't count on it to continue. Your blue-eyed little boy may not end up so blue-eyed after all.

When I was a medical student it was fashionable to believe that babies showed no response to normal sound. Certainly they don't turn round and drool when you use words like 'Mars Bar', but they still have ways of showing that they hear.

If you talk soothingly to an upset baby, the crying itself may not cease but its intensity and rhythm usually alters. This shows a definite response to a gentle voice. It has also been shown that as you talk to babies, their arms and legs often move with a body language rhythm which keeps time with your voice. So babies hear plenty at birth. It just takes us to tune in to recognise their response.

The mouth

Little babies prefer not to use their mouths to breathe through. In the early days this opening is reserved for feeding, burping and crying. Consequently if their nose gets blocked and they have to mouth breathe they become extremely unhappy. This we all discover when our little ones have their first cold.

Reflexes

Newborn babies exhibit a number of primitive reflexes which make you wonder if they haven't been here before in another life.

In the first weeks babies have a walking reflex which, on a superficial glance, seems brilliant beyond their age. Hold them upright over a table, tilt them slightly forward and press the soles of the feet firmly down against the surface and off they go in a sort of walk. Unfortunately this does not last. It disappears in three or four weeks and then takes another nine months before the real thing returns.

The feeding reflex is designed as a life preserver. Here you have a baby so delicate and immature, yet if a teat so much as touches the cheek he turns immediately to latch on like a limpet. All a baby needs is to be close to food and feeding will be assured. Sucking is of course another very basic reflex dating back to the earliest days of formation. It's not unusual during a prebirth scan examination to find a baby whiling away the hours to countdown sucking a thumb. As with all these reflexes this disappears as the baby matures. It is probably just as well otherwise every time your cheek was touched you'd flick your head to one side and start sucking on your biro pen or have difficulty applying – instead of chewing – lipstick.

Another lifesaver is the reflex which helps a baby to breathe when the nose is obstructed. If Baby is lying face down on a mattress and the breathing is in danger, Samson-like he will muster amazing strength and lift his head to turn it to one side. This is quite astonishing when you consider that at this stage the head cannot normally be lifted voluntarily at all. Just take my word for this one. It's truly amazing, but certainly not to be tried out by experimenting parents.

The grasp reflex is another interesting one. Babies at birth cannot open or close their hands voluntarily. However, if an object is pressed across the palm the hand will clasp around it. This grasp reflex effectively blocks any useful hand function until at about the age of three months it passes and leaves the hand free to work at will.

There's one other reflex that you will probably see your doctor demonstrate when he examines your baby. With the child lying on his back, the head is lifted slightly and let drop suddenly several centimetres into the examiner's hand. This is known as the Moro reflex. The baby is startled in the Moro reflex and his arms and legs will straighten out and then return to the resting flexed position. This reflex disappears at about three months, but while present it reassures us that the baby is moving all limbs in an equal and normal way.

The umbilical stump

This once great lifeline which nourished the baby for nine months is now left to decay and drop off. The cord contains two arteries and a vein which means that in the first days this has the potential to bleed. At birth it is closed off firmly using a special plastic clip, the design of which ensures that once shut on the cord the arteries and vein are locked, immoveable, don't leak and can only be cut off. The redundant remnant will remain for between five to nine days getting progressively drier until eventually it drops off. Since we have a strange situation where a piece of dying material is attached to a living body, there must be a kind of no man's land where they join. This explains why the stump tends to ooze and remain raw for some time, as it is unsure which way to go.

At bath time the body is cleaned with water, dried and a little bit of surgical spirit is applied to the stump. This dries it up and keeps it clean. Little hernias that bulge from the umbilicus are amazingly common and in most cases disappear. (See Chapter 3.)

The foreskin

The foreskin was put there to protect the delicate and sensitive tip of the penis. During the first few years the skin is still attached to the underlying structures and is not ready to be pulled back. Only after about the fourth birthday will it start to move easily and it should never be forced back before that stage. Thereafter you can start gently retracting it during bath time and it can then become part of the daily wash. (See page 28.)

The stomach and bowels

Before birth the gut is in a state of rest and remains unused until introduced to food. It is one of the great miracles that such an untried piece of equipment can be a useless appendage one day and the next it is providing valuable nutrition. Digestion is a bit haphazard in the early weeks – after all, it's a bit much to expect a perfect performance from the first trial run.

Babies are born with a good load of spare food on board, bringing with them their own haversack of rations into the world. This allows them to cope with the gradual introduction of a decent diet. As a rough rule of thumb they should be offered about one-third of their ideal daily intake on day one. This should be gradually increased until they are given the full amount by the end of the first week.

When Baby takes the first food it may well be returned along with a good deal of mucus which was in the stomach at birth. This is a very common occurrence and though things may be unstable for a short while they usually settle down quickly.

At birth the gut contains nothing more than some debris and fluid which the baby has swallowed before delivery. All of this has to pass through before you will see anything that resembles a proper bowel motion. This debris comes out as a sticky, greeny-black substance which looks foul but has no smell. This is called meconium. By the third day most of this will have passed and partly processed milk products start to appear.

As the gut is trying to come to terms with its new-found function it is not surprising that, initially, motions are poorly digested and pretty loose. Occasionally these motions will be green and watery, giving a false impression of a gut infection. Sometimes the situation is quite explosive with some babies reported to have up to twenty dirty nappies a day while the digestive processes come into balance.

The first motion is usually passed within twelve hours of birth and almost always sometime during the first day. Breast-fed babies tend to have an orangey yellow stool, whereas bottle-fed babies have stools which are pale brown and of a more solid consistency.

It all takes time for equilibrium to set in, so as long as intake is adequate and health appears to be blooming, don't get too worked up about this area of waste disposal.

Conclusion

The newborn bundle in your arms can be quite intimidating the first time round. But if you follow your instincts, use commonsense and have basic information at your finger-tips about what to expect, you'll charge ahead – and enjoy the experience!

3
Imperfections and Common Problems – What to Expect

FOR the new mother, it takes quite a long time before she can relax and know instinctively which are the 'normal, unimportant worries' and which are the genuine problems that need expert help.

This chapter looks at a lot of the common little blemishes and concerns in the hope that many of those unnecessary fears can be diminished. Worrying about real problems is a natural part of life, worrying about non-problems is a futile waste of emotional energy.

Head bruising at birth

When you think of the amount of squeezing that babies have to undergo at birth it's little wonder that sometimes they emerge a little bruised and out of shape. At birth the head is rather like a football which has been moulded into an odd shape as it squeezed through the narrow opening. However, within a day the malleable skull bones will slip back into their normal position. Depending on how difficult the delivery was and other factors such as whether or not forceps were used, there may be bruising which will last a few days. These little blemishes are only very superficial, and the important bits inside are well-protected and unharmed. If your baby is otherwise alert, bright and healthy you can relax. (See Chapter 24 for birth defects.)

Scalp swellings at birth

At the moment of birth it is the skin on the crown of the head which forces the baby's exit, so it is hardly surprising that this can get somewhat the worse for wear. Most newborn babies have a soggy swelling over the part of the head that did the pushing. In medical jargon, this is called the *caput succedaneum*. The name sounds a lot more important than the condition, which will disappear within a couple of days and has no significance other than to remind you which end of the baby came out first.

Cephalhaematoma

This is the medical term which describes a fluid-filled swelling on the baby's head. This is more noticeable and long-lasting than the *caput succedaneum*. During delivery, one of the little blood vessels that lies on the outside of the skull bones ruptures due to the twisting forces. When it bleeds the blood is trapped between the bone and its strong outside covering, which leaves a prominent fluid-filled lump. This occurs in about 1 per cent of all babies. It lasts anywhere from one month to six months. As the fluid gradually reabsorbs, a rim of bone material can temporarily circle the swelling. This can give the impression of a crater in the bone which in fact is not so. The skull is intact, as is all that lies under it. A cephalhaematoma is nothing to worry about. It is quite benign and will go away in due course without any medical interference. Meanwhile the baby will remain perfectly happy and quite unaware of it.

Skin blemishes

It is upsetting when spots and rashes deface our little ones, but such blemishes are normal, benign and of course only skin deep. Let's look at the most common ones.

Milia

In the first few days of life most babies are found to have little yellow pin-head spots, mostly around the bridge of the nose. These are caused by inexperienced skin glands unplugging themselves and getting their act together. Almost all babies have these in the early days and (like your child) they are 100 per cent innocent. They are of no concern, need no treatment and disappear within one week.

Heat rash

This is a term used to describe a vague, though nevertheless common, condition. By heat rash I refer to those tiny, flat, red pin-head spots that appear without warning and often join to make big red patches. Heat is always blamed, but even that is uncertain. Most occur on the face, creases of the neck and trunk. They often seem worse in places where the clothes are tight. They come and go without rhyme or reason, the child being completely symptom-free and oblivious to their presence.

Please don't get into a knot worrying about measles, malnutrition or some obscure allergy. If your baby is happy, healthy and these little blemishes come and go, then relax and ignore them. If you feel compelled to do something, then keep your baby's clothes light, don't let him overheat and allow only cotton or cotton blends close to the skin.

Dry skin

Though it is common to say that something is as soft as a baby's bottom, some babies do have hides on them that are tough, dry and scaly. Dry skin is often hereditary and sometimes is associated with eczema. Whatever the cause, it takes a bit of extra care to keep these little ones comfortable.

For a start, please be sparing with all the washing and scrubbing clean. Avoid those strong soaps that rob the skin of what little natural oil it possesses. After a bath, baby oil, skin lotion or cream will leave the skin soft. A bath oil can also be added to the bath water. Have a chat with your chemist and get a large container of quality skin cream. At our hospital we favour glycerine and sorbolene cream but there are numerous other types.

21

Cradle cap – scurfy scalp

Babies don't get dandruff. That's a condition which is reserved for teenagers, adults and those boring people on the TV hair care commercials. Babies however, do get dry, scaly scalps. If your baby has such a scalp you can either leave it alone altogether, or massage it occasionally with a little oil. In the end the condition will eventually clear itself up whichever way you go. Cradle cap is an extension of this condition which results from the natural oils in the scalp cementing the dry, scaly layers into a brown cap. This does not look too pretty, but it is perfectly harmless. To remove the crusts, massage the top of the head with warm oil (olive or baby oil). Leave it for a couple of hours or overnight and then gently comb the scalp. Continue the process until it's clear. Your chemist can recommend a special product for cradle cap if the oils do not prove to be effective.

Cheek rashes

Some babies are born with the rose petal cheeks of a blushing film-star, whilst others' continually look rough and chapped. The appearance of the skin depends partly on its genetic toughness and partly on what the baby has been lying on. It stands to reason that a delicate cheek which has been lying on a sheet soggy from dribbling, the humidity of breathing and the occasional regurgitation, is bound to be affected. It's best to ensure that whatever Baby lies on, whether a sheet or blanket, is good and soft and not some rough old thing washed and dried to the consistency of sandpaper. It is important to keep the skin as dry, clean and softened as possible. Here again the glycerine and sorbolene type creams are of great value.

If the cheeks are chapped, just be certain that this is not due to the little one rolling around on the carpet. Those floor coverings are made tough to withstand heavy footwork and are none too gentle on a child's delicate complexion. Children with eczema are particularly vulnerable. Cheeks, arms and legs can all become irritated if they come into contact with wool or acrylic.

Skin marks

Skin marks come in a variety of colours and configurations, which is probably why they have been given names that sound like butterflies. The most common ones are known as the *storkbeak mark*, the *strawberry mark* and the *Mongolian blue spot*.

Storkbeak mark

About half the babies I see have a little red mark on the back of their necks. Their mothers look at me in amazement when I tell them that it is a storkbeak mark and begin to wonder if I'm not from the school of thought that babies are found under a gooseberry bush. Nevertheless that's what it's properly called and the mark is due to prominent blood capillaries in the skin. Often the same baby will have little red marks on an eyelid or the forehead as well. Not to worry, these marks are all benign, and usually very temporary.

Strawberry mark

This is less common, but when large it can be unsightly and greatly distress the parents. The mark is produced by a benign growth of the large blood vessels in the skin. There is absolutely no sign of its presence at birth, but within a few weeks a small spot will appear which will gradually grow larger, redder and become raised above the surface. This increases over the first six months then slowly starts its decline. By the time the child is five years old it will be pretty small and will have gone before the age of ten.

At their peak strawberry birthmarks look raised and nasty and it's hard for parents to believe that such a mark could go away without intervention. Generally speaking there is nothing to do but wait patiently and be reassured that it will go away. Nature will heal in her own good time and leave no mark, but if you insist on surgical interference you are guaranteeing a scar.

Mongolian blue spot

I was once threatened with legal action by an Egyptian father who firmly believed that his baby son had been beaten by one of our nurses. It was true that the boy had indeed got large blue marks at the base of his spine and on his buttocks. What the legal profession were not to realise was that this sort of marking is extremely common in newborn babies of southern European, African, Polynesian and Asian descent. These marks have been christened 'Mongolian blue spots' and are present at birth.

Once again there is absolutely nothing to worry about with these. The marks are benign, have no significance whatsoever, and certainly aren't related in any way to mongolism. Most fade in the first year.

Teeth and teething

It is generally about the sixth month that the first little pearl pops through, causing about the same level of parental excitement as would finding the genuine object in your pub-lunch oysters. Early teething does not, I'm afraid, indicate advanced development or super intelligence. If it did all sorts of snappy animals would be telling the human race what to do. Some babies do have teeth at birth; in fact, Julius Caesar, Hannibal and Napoleon were all born with teeth. It's not necessary to be the child of military parents for this to occur, and fortunately for the case of breast-feeding it is rare. If you find such teeth, barely hanging on by a thread, it is better they are removed than possibly swallowed.

When teeth do appear treat them with care, as there will be no replacements for another six years. You can't actually scrub around a baby's gums properly until about two years so I suggest that before then you give him a soft toothbrush to suck so that he can get used to having it in his mouth. Don't bother to use toothpaste at this stage. If you do, just a speck is sufficient, not the extravagant fat worm you see on fresh breath advertisements!

I am a strong believer in the safety and protective effect of fluoridated water. Despite the fact that fluoridating the water supply is accepted internationally, there are still areas where this is not the case. If you are concerned that there may not be proper fluoridation in your water, just ask your health visitor or dentist if extra is needed and how many drops you should add to fluids each day.

When it comes to giving supersweet drinks, start off sensibly. Flavoured milks, blackcurrant health drinks and other very sweet cordial are best avoided. Constant irrigation of developing teeth by sugars leads to decay of the front teeth and bottles should be taken away once Baby has had all the nutrition he wants.

The process of teething usually starts at six months and goes on until the age of twenty. I know that it is fashionable to blame every cold, cough and cry on teething, but you can't do this for twenty years. Teething can certainly cause some pain in the gums, which in turn can increase salivation and dribbling. It may make your little one more grizzly, may change feeding routines and may also affect the bowel exhaust products. On the other hand, teething does not cause vomiting, diarrhoea, fits, fevers, or bronchitis. The main result of teething is teeth!

Most medicos discourage any treatment of teething, but I believe a little paracetamol, a teething ring or your chemist's favourite gum-rub gel never go amiss. (See Appendix, page 243 on teeth.)

Mouth problems

Tongue tie

True tongue tie can happen but it must be as rare as the proverbial hen's teeth. The average baby's tongue is quite tightly strapped to the floor of the mouth. 'Look, the baby's tongue-tied!', shriek the ill-informed relatives. Not so, this is quite a normal state of affairs. Babies can feed, babble and cry very nicely thank you without ever protruding their tongues. It is almost unheard of for tongue tie to cause genuine speech or feeding problems. When your child won't eat his vegetables, the problem is one of behaviour not tongue tie. Nor is speech held back by a tight tongue. As long as the ears can hear and the brain wishes to speak, the tongue is powerless to stop this.

As the tongue grows the tip becomes free, extends and before you know it, Baby's sticking his tongue out at the vicar and you're wishing it was strapped down to the base of his mouth again.

Oral thrush

This is extremely common in babies and usually causes no symptoms at all.

When you look in the mouth there will be little white patches on the cheeks and tongue. At first sight these may look just like milk curds but you'll quickly know that they aren't as they stay put and bleed if you try to remove them.

Thrush is an infection caused by the Candida albicans fungus. It may have been introduced from the birth canal during delivery or later from a contaminated teat, bottle, hand or similar object. No matter how hard you try, total sterility is an impossibility, and Candida is pretty common, even in the most impeccably cared-for child.

Treatment for thrush is simple and usually involves the anti-Candida antibiotic, Nystatin. You apply drops of this suspension to the mouth after feeds. It is clean, easy to take and very effective. Though not used these days, your granny probably used gentian violet. She painted it on the white areas, which were cured safely and efficiently. But when the purple dripped out the corner of the mouth, it was not unlike Dracula around feeding time.

Though thrush is usually symptom free, it can occasionally be painful, cause irritability and feeding problems.

Sucking pads and blisters

During the first weeks, little pads or blisters can often be seen on Baby's lips. These are a reaction to the newly discovered delight of sucking. As the lips toughen up the blisters will disappear of their own accord and no treatment is necessary.

Eye problems

The main eye worries in newborn babies are blocked tear ducts, squints and sticky eye.

Blocked tear ducts

Many babies will have no tears to shed for the first few weeks of life. Mind you this won't stop them crying. They'll be just as noisy but it will be a sort of dry run for later. Once tears are on tap it is quite common to find a baby with one or both of his tear-draining ducts blocked. The result of this is that his eyes look wet and the tears overflow down his cheeks. Usually a blocked duct will clear itself normally within six months, but you can help it along with a bit of gentle massage, as well as making sure the eye is kept clean. As the dampness and the blockage can encourage infection, antibiotic ointment will be needed if this occurs.

If, after six months, the tear duct still hasn't cleared of its own accord then an eye specialist can re-open the offending channel. This is done under a general anaesthetic, and is usually both simple and successful.

Squints

Most babies have two straight eyes which work in tandem as they are supposed to. Some however are born with squints, their eyes intermittently or permanently out of phase. The main reason a child squints is that the tiny muscles which control eye movement have been formed either too long or too short. When this is mild, exercise and use of the eyes can bring a cure. If the squint is more pronounced, however, then a relatively simple surgical readjustment is needed.

It's hard to know when to start worrying about a squinting baby. If the problem is only intermittent and tends only to occur when Baby is tired, then there may not be much to worry about. On the other hand if one eye has a permanent turn then expert help should be sought right away.

An important concern with squinting is the possibility of loss of vision or blindness in one eye. Try and look at this for a moment from the brain's point of view. The brain is receiving two separate pictures which gives double vision. This, the brain reckons, is a pretty uncomfortable situation so it solves the problem by switching off the weakest eye and once more there is single vision. If this continues for many months the brain loses the power to re-engage the eye and eventually it will never see again.

That is why it is important that an eye specialist should look at a permanent squint as soon as practicable and determine which is the weakest eye so that he can either improve its vision with lenses or put a temporary patch over the stronger eye to make the weaker one do more work and build it up that way.

If you have any doubts please seek expert help as soon as possible. Eye specialists can test vision and refraction in extremely small babies and can even give patches and glasses to the smallest children. Whether you can get them to be worn without actually gluing them to your child's ears is, of course, another matter!

Sticky eye

This is an extremely common condition in newborn babies. It looks a bit like an infection of the eyes but is usually just an irritation from some of the fluids and debris encountered at birth. The only treatment required is regular bathing of the eyes. Infection can occur, usually a little later on, and this leaves the eye with red lids and a sticky crust which is generally worst in the mornings. If you have concerns, consult your family doctor who may prescribe special antibiotic drops or ointment which resolves the infection.

Breast enlargement (neonatal mastitis)

At birth, Mother's blood is running high on hormones which are designed to kick start the breasts into action as efficient milk producers for Baby. The placenta protects Baby from most of this abnormal activity but quite often a little will leak through and can cause breast enlargement (neonatal mastitis) in both boy and girl babies. Sometimes small beads of fluid may even appear from the baby's breasts, commonly called 'witch's milk'. It's nothing to worry about, just a natural response to a natural process. Around about day four it will hit its peak and will wane after that. Sometimes enlargement continues for some months and it is often lop-sided. The whole thing is only temporary, needs no treatment and even less concern.

Jaundice

This occurs in all babies to some extent and is caused by an increase in the bile products carried in the blood. These products come from the breakdown of old red blood cells which are then processed by the liver and put out into the gut.

At birth most babies have about a 25 per cent overload of red blood cells. These were required to maintain health in the low oxygen environment of the womb but are no longer needed once Baby has hit the great outdoors. As the red cells reduce they put a lot of pressure on the processing ability of the baby's immature, inefficient liver. The result is that the unprocessed bile builds up in the blood and the baby turns a little yellow!

There's no need for panic. A simple blood test will determine the exact levels and if they are too high, then treatment, usually in the form of shining a bright light on the skin, will be given. Clever midwives have for years known that exposing jaundiced babies to sunlight reduced the levels. The light breaks down some of the bile in the skin and reduces the load on the liver. So a little jaundice is usual for all babies, whilst a lot requires monitoring and treatment.

Circumcision

In this crazy and hypocritical world there are many things we accept as correct just because they have been done for years. But hold it! Just because something is done, doesn't necessarily mean that it's right.

Routine circumcision of babies is one of these accepted things, but it needs to be questioned by all free-thinking parents. In the last ten years most parents have moved away from this, but still some request it to be done.

Of course, there are those who consider circumcision necessary as part of their religious faith and it is not for me to question or criticise this. However, when it is demanded for spurious social reasons – that's different.

Many parents (usually mothers) tell me that it's more hygienic. This was certainly true when living in a desert tribe 2000 years ago. Now that we have showers, baths and running water, however, this just doesn't wash (unless the family don't believe in washing either).

Then others tell me 'His father has been done and he will feel different'. What utter rubbish! In a seventy-year life span there is but a brief passing interest in your dad's anatomical deformities. It may make him like his father, but maybe he will not appreciate it later in life. Who knows what his marriage partner will prefer?

Surely we don't always have to have sons like their fathers. If my nose was broken in my football playing days, I would never want my boys to look the same as their dad.

OK, you have spotted it – I am not a supporter of unthinking baby circumcision. I find it hard to come to terms with the concept of inflicting needless pain on any child, just to satisfy tradition or parental hang ups.

Let's stop and think for a minute. If you were to deliberately and unnecessarily cut off any other bit of your baby you would find yourself before the courts, charged with child abuse and probably lose custody of your child. It is certainly a crazy and hypocritical world we inhabit.

I know that many readers will be unhappy with this view, but all I ask is that parents give some thought before they blindly follow the flock.

The message is – if you don't have a religious reason to dismantle God's handiwork, then I would prefer that you leave it alone.

The umbilical cord

The umbilical cord will shrivel up and drop off somewhere between five and ten days. This leaves a raw stump which won't bleed and doesn't need any supersterile dressings. Just wash it gently at bath times and dry off the wound with a touch of surgical spirit.

Umbilical hernia

It is very common to see a bit of Baby poking out through the navel. This is a hernia. It may look a little strange but it is a harmless condition which will usually go away of its own accord. Most have disappeared before Baby's first birthday, and the ones which hang around longer are generally gone well before he is six. Only very occasionally is it necessary to consult a surgeon. By and large there's nothing you can do to speed things up. These hernias do not obstruct or cause problems. Leave them alone and let Nature do her work.

Groin hernia (inquinal hernia)

Hernias in the groin are equally common, and must be taken seriously. They are due to a defect in the muscles in the abdominal wall and the danger is that part of the bowel can get through which, if it gets stuck, will lead to an obstruction of the gut and eventually serious strangulation. These hernias do not get better without treatment and need safe and simple surgery to put them right. Hernias are caused by a weakness in the design at birth and are not caused by crying, coughing or exertion.

Clicky hips

Congenital dislocation of the hip may be relatively rare but we still take great pains to spot it, otherwise a missed diagnosis can lead to a life-long limp. If the baby has a dislocated hip it means that the top of the femur (thigh bone) is displaced some distance from the socket into which it is meant to fit. Unless the femur head and socket grow in the correct position together it can mean that the two will not fit properly when brought together in the future. This is why your baby's hips will be carefully examined before being allowed to leave hospital. Many newborns will have 'clicky hips' when examined at birth and usually this is of no significance. It's the abnormal 'clunk' of a congenital dislocation that doctors look for and this is taken most seriously. If there is any doubt at this time a temporary splint will be suggested and then the situation reviewed closely until your doctor is completely happy that the hips are normal.

Bandy legs and funny feet

Despite all the kicking, wriggling and crawling that Baby's legs will do in the first year of life there is little or no weight-bearing or upright work. It is therefore hardly surprising that the legs have a strange alignment and the feet flop about a bit. When they start to stand at the age of one, most babies have bow legs and look like professional jockeys. This is a natural occurrence and has nothing to do with being allowed to stand too early. In the strange course of child development it is usual to move from the bends of one year to a fine set of knock knees at two and a half years old before finally straightening up with the legs of an Olympic athlete.

Clubfoot is a fixed deformity which will be spotted immediately at birth. The foot has a limited movement and is turned in. It will need splinting, physiotherapy and, if severe, possibly surgery may be required to resolve it. This must not be confused with the benign inturned foot posture seen in many normal babies. Here the foot may rest in an inturned position, but it can be moved fully in all directions and thus will straighten in time.

Flat feet are also quite usual at this early age and resolve themselves as the muscles and ligaments tone up. That is, unless Mum and Dad have feet like pancakes, in which case the little one may follow suit.

My rule with baby feet is this. If the tone is normal and the foot can be moved fully in all directions, then don't worry. But if you have any doubts, don't hesitate to ask for expert opinion.

Sweaty heads

Some babies seem to have particularly leaky skin on their heads. They lie on their mattress surrounded by a humid halo which leaves them looking like some sort of soggy saint. This is both common and normal and has no significance whatsoever.

Blue hue

As we have seen, the newborn has a great overload of red blood cells which take about a month to reach normal levels. All this super-red blood can give Baby a ruddy hue. In these early days the body's regulating mechanisms are pretty immature and often inefficient, meaning the allocation of blood to different parts of the body isn't always as perfect as it should be. When circulation is slow the red blood will turn to purple, a condition particularly common in the legs. Occasionally the flow of blood to one whole side of the body may be greater than that to the other, giving a momentary two-tone baby, a condition we know as Harlequin baby. Rest assured that blueness and mottled skin in babies is very common and sorts itself out rapidly after birth.

Hiccough

If there's one thing a newborn baby can excel at it's hiccoughing. This is particularly common directly after feeds and is probably due to the pressure of a full little stomach on the diaphragm. It's quite normal.

Snuffles and rattles

These can sound very alarming, particularly in the still of the night. Then suddenly all goes quiet and you start to worry that something fatal has happened. It hasn't. That's just one of the new-found joys of parenthood and one that has no easy answer! Unfortunately babies don't understand that one decent cough or a good blow into a tissue will solve everything. Nose breathing is important to babies and when the nose gets blocked they get upset and cannot feed properly. All you can do is wipe the nose and firmly resist the temptation to stick cotton buds into it. Sometimes a steamy, warm bath helps clear the passages. If things get really bad then obtain some nose drops from your doctor. These are never too popular and can be hard to administer.

Rattly breathing in healthy babies is very normal – they make all sorts of strange noises from the back of their throat at this early age. I wouldn't worry, but if you have any doubts don't hesitate to get it checked out.

Sleep jumps

It is common and very normal for young babies to give sudden jumps in their sleep. These little ones have immature brains, not yet fully adjusted to allowing a smooth slide into slumber. At this age they drop off from fully awake to the deepest of sleep in a matter of minutes. With such speed and

immaturity, it's not unreasonable to expect the odd short circuit and jump. This doesn't indicate epilepsy or any other dire condition. It's benign and perfectly normal. (See Chapter 17 on sleep.)

Gastric reflux

Some babies are notoriously messy. You pick them up for a cuddle and find a mouthful of milk down your front. You can always spot the parents of a messy baby – Mum walks around with an old nappy permanently slung over her shoulder and Dad takes to wearing a cream-coloured business suit!

As human beings we are all built with a valve at the tops of our stomachs which keeps the contents in place. This enables airmen to fly F11s upside-down and Russian gymnasts to stand on their heads without creating international embarrassment.

In all little babies this valve is immature and very unreliable. They tend to bring up a mouthful of milk with each puff of escaping wind. For some this return is occasional, but for others it happens so often as to become a real hassle for parents. Occasionally the baby is so troubled that he fails to gain weight and may even bleed as the stomach acid upsets the oesophagus. Most messy babies are happy, healthy and thriving. For parents the problem is largely one of laundry. With babies who reflux up their food the natural course is spontaneous cure with age. This resolution is helped once solids start as thicker foods are more likely to stay firmly cemented where they belong. Once sitting and the more upright posture starts then gravity will exert a powerful force to keep things in place.

Advice for the mum with a messy baby:

- If the baby is happy, gaining weight, thriving and bringing up no flecks of blood with the milk – relax and be reassured.

- If the problem is major, shows no sign of resolving or has complications then your doctor may suggest:
  - Thicken milk feeds with a feed thickener (one recommended by your health visitor or doctor).
  - Raise the head of the cot on blocks or put a pillow under the mattress.
  - Use paediatric Gaviscon, a medicine that floats on top of the stomach contents and makes reflux difficult.
  - Try an antacid.

- Practical suggestions:
  - Keep Baby in a plastic-backed bib except for special out-to-impress occasions.
  - Wind well after food (with a towel over your shoulder).
  - Start solids early rather than late.

To summarise, gastric reflux is the leaking of stomach contents up the oesophagus. This is extremely common in little babies and is usually harmless and needs no treatment. If your baby is happy, thriving and well, then be reassured. All you need is a good supply of bibs, a towel over your shoulder, an efficient washing machine and patience.

Where the reflux is extreme or very slow to resolve, seek medical advice. If there is poor weight gain, blood flecks in the milk or great irritability, this must be taken seriously and investigated now! Remember that most babies will have got over reflux before their first birthday and very few will need major intervention by the medical profession.

Bowels, constipation, diarrhoea, regularity

For the first month of life the gut is just an unsophisticated, untried tube which produces varied and unpredictable bowel actions. Breast-fed babies tend to have a low residue stool, while bottle-fed babies have stools which are more curdy and solid. With the start of mixed feeding the motions start to firm up and it is now quite normal to find pieces of vegetable which appear to have passed right through without their colour even fading, let alone any digestion having occurred.

Constipation is rare in the totally breast-fed baby, but it can affect a small percentage of bottle and solid feeders. The treatment is by the old-fashioned, well-tried remedies. First, increase the fluid intake, using juice or water. This moistens up the works and may get things moving. Fruit is always good for those on solids and for the really little ones pure fruit juice or the juice of boiled prunes usually guarantees a most moving experience.

There are a number of very normal babies who have been born with a sluggish bowel. They often have a parent who has always tended to constipation and there is obviously a hereditary influence.

Constipation does not lead to bad breath, pallor or the irritability described by your maiden aunts. It does however lead to minor tearing of the tail end, which can cause bleeding or pain on passing. If you're concerned about constipation, please consult your health visitor or family doctor. If increasing the fluid intake and adding fruits does not relieve the siege state then a laxative may be required. This can either be in the form of a baby suppository or a medicine by mouth like coloxy drops. If needed use them and don't listen to those who say that you are producing a lazy bowel. This you have already. It's only by keeping things soft and empty that it will smarten up its act.

Normal bowel movements vary greatly with age, diet and expectations. At six months I would be happy if there was movement somewhere between six times a day and once every three days. It would be unusual for a very, active bowel to be equally active at night. It is lucky for the nocturnal nappy changers that things are usually quieter at that time.

When you start to panic over the bowels, please lift your eyes above the nappy area and carefully observe the whole child. If he is bright-eyed,

33

gaining weight and full of life the liquidity of what lands in the nappy is unlikely to be of importance. On the other hand if he looks dull, sick and unhappy, then it's time to call for help.

Conclusion

All parents worry about these imperfections and illnesses. If you're really concerned, you must speak to your doctor but, remember, if your baby is happy and well, then whatever little problem he has is probably quite normal and nothing to worry about.

4

The Homecoming –
A Shock to the System

AFTER the squeaky cleanness and the sheltered existence of hospital, your home can often seem quiet, isolated and rather lonely. You float out of hospital on your first solo flight, high on a cloud of euphoria, soon to crash land in the real world outside. These early weeks are a time of tiredness and confused emotions. The whole balance of life at home is in for a major shake up. No-one says it is going to be a bed of roses but if approached with commonsense, acceptance of change and a sense of humour it can be a fun time.

A New Lifestyle

The arrival of your first baby is probably the most major and memorable event in your entire life. By comparison, getting married or buying your first home was a mere hiccough. After this birth you, your lifestyle and the whole way you think, will never be quite the same again. Marriage at least has a honeymoon before you hit reality, but parenthood hits with a bang. There are many new features of your changed lifestyle – and they take some getting used to.

Worry

Worry becomes a major part of parenting. I believe most couples only find the true meaning of this word when they have children. It starts with worries over feeding, weight gain and your competence as a parent. Then you have concerns over behaviour, sickness and schoolwork. Worry over children is a part of life and it never seems to cease. Even when they are grown up and have flown the coop you worry about their jobs, their lifestyle, who they're living with, and then the wheel turns full circle and you start losing sleep over your grandchildren.

Becoming number two instead of number one

The self-centred life is past history. Yesterday you were living in 'ancient' times. That was a different existence, BC (Before Children). You were free to go your own way. Now all waking thoughts are focused on a totally dependent youngster.

Spur-of-the-moment decisions which were possible, are now a thing of the past, and excursions into the life outside require planning. Often by the time all the gear is assembled and you've looked at the disturbance to feeding and sleeping routines it hardly seems worth the effort. But it *is* worth the effort. Don't stick in this rut. Don't chain yourself to the home like some oddball recluse. This is never good for Mum's, Dad's or Baby's emotional happiness.

It is particularly important to hold on to some outside social life. Most babies are remarkably portable, especially if they are good, settled sleepers, and they can accompany you in the carry cot. Of course it's hard if you have a colicky, poor sleeper who is resistant to any change. These little ones leave you manacled to the home as if a ball and chain were attached to your left foot. But don't give up. This is when good grandparents and real friends will hopefully come to the rescue to let you out.

Party pooping

Childless friends may feel you are a lost cause. As your friends talk to you they wonder if you really went to hospital to have a baby or to have some essential piece of brain removed. Certainly in their eyes you are not the same carefree, fun-loving person they used to know. When invited somewhere exciting you hum and haw like a politician, never prepared to commit yourself as it all depends on sleep, feeding or whatever. You are now a prize party pooper. At midnight, just when things are really starting to rave you rush off like Cinderella to arrive home before the babysitter puts on an ugly turn. In the past it was all frivolous chitchat about holidays, parties, pop groups and fun times, now life seems stuck in a groove. As you ramble on about the first tooth, baby fashion and the latest baby food, you are surrounded by a sea of yawning faces. Overnight you have become a crashing bore to the childless, but don't worry, one day their turn will also come.

Don't get alarmed. Your real friends will always stay close and as they watch the baby grow they will become quite involved, both emotionally as well as in support and help. Of course you can say goodbye to the beer brigade, the ragers, the eternal Peter Pans and the lounge lizards, but frankly that's no real loss.

The dethroned daddy

When two's company . . .

While you're busy getting used to having Junior around, Dad is being hit with a massive reshuffle of attention in his home life. Often this is not to his liking. Those dads who until recently enjoyed being pampered are in for a shock. The focus of attention suddenly swings away on to the new lodger and it's not surprising that some dads find their noses firmly out of joint. Often there is jealousy of the strong bond between mother and baby, one which is hard to compete with. Suddenly it seems as though there is a new man in Mum's life. This in fact may be true but a happy polygamous existence should still be possible. This readjustment in the equilibrium of the family always happens and, if accepted, husbands can be blissfully happy, whilst if fought against they may become the dethroned dad.

Overpossessive mums

Shared care is important right from the word go. Mothers of the newborn protect their young like a bird in the nest, but this clinginess must not go overboard.

Often I see mums who are so possessive and unsharing that you would think birth had occurred by immaculate conception without any male help. Father does have equal rights and it is a wise mother who tries to involve him in all aspects of childcare right from the start. Dad may be slow and clumsy at what he does, but it's better that he share the load than leave you to do everything. Don't criticise and re-do his less-than-perfect efforts, just be thankful you have such a willing and caring partner.

If approached in the right way there is hardly anything that fathers will not do for their offspring. If you get things off on the wrong footing, you have only yourself to blame when later he refuses to wipe a bottom or bath a baby, and finds it more rewarding to use his talent to support the bar at the club.

Learned helplessness

This is a very special talent perfected by generations of fathers. This selective childcare is a great skill when it comes to changing a nappy, preparing food and working the night shift. The strange thing is that the more enjoyable tasks are often learned with consummate ease. Usually this learned helplessness can be prevented by getting things off to the right start and working out the ground rules of co-operation and shared responsibility from the very beginning.

Sleep deprivation

Sleep deprivation is no fun for anyone but it does seem to be particularly troublesome to dads. From my observations most can put up with cold food, unwashed clothes and reduced attention, but when deprived of sleep, they fall apart. Of course this is not a problem if you have been blessed with a good sleeper, but when darkness is a time of torture then it is so much easier with a team of two involved parents. If Mum is breast-feeding and it's food that Baby is crying for, then obviously Dad won't be able to provide what's required. However, he can offer comfort and deliver the baby to the source of food.

The arsenic hour

With most young children the lowest spot of the day is that arsenic hour between 5 and 6 pm in the evening. This is the time when crying, irritability and colic are often at their peak. Mums are frazzled after a very full day and now they attempt valiantly to cook and at the same time calm, feed, wind and walk around pacifying the baby. This is also the time when most fathers return from work. Instead of a warm cosy greeting, they are met at the door by a screaming baby and an exhausted wife.

This can all come as something of a shock to the unthinking husband, registering somewhere around 10 on the Richter scale. Whether tired or not, dads have to gallop in like the relieving cavalry and take over comfort and care or cook.

The absentee father

The absentee father is pretty common. Some fathers simply never accept their new role and remain a sort of pseudo-single. Life goes on unchanged with the pub, club, sport evenings and weekends with the boys. Such husbands may be good providers of money but they provide little else for their wives and children and provide a very poor example for the next generation. These eternal Peter Pans never like to grow up and shoulder adult responsibilities.

Love and cherishing

In the months immediately following birth many mums feel they have lost their identity as an attractive, independent person. Now is a good time for Dad to love and boost Mum in her own right and not to view her purely as a grumbling, crumbling obstacle who is an unpaid nanny. Now is the time for some love, cherishing and a good cuddle, which never goes amiss. This is probably as intimate as you're going to get as it's sleep not sex that most mums need.

Talking of sex, now's the start of many years of 'constant interruptus'. Babies and children seem endowed with that split second timing that has them demanding immediate attention at exactly the wrong moment. With such a reliable form of contraception one often wonders how parents ever manage to have more than one child.

The New Mum – Different Feelings and Emotions

No-one can ever prepare you for the almighty effect that becoming a mother has on your whole sense of self as well as on your lifestyle. Every new mum experiences a kaleidoscope of different feelings and emotions in the first few months at home.

Tiredness

I realise that this book goes on and on about tiredness but every new mum I have looked after in the last twenty years has suffered from it. Most mums are overwhelmed by tiredness by the end of the day, yet at the same time feel they have achieved virtually nothing.

Husbands find this hard to understand. I can remember when our first baby was born, coming in every evening to our newly purchased home, expecting to find rooms had been painted and renovation projects completed. In my naive state I could never understand how a now full-time housewife was unable to get on with all this extra work. It only takes dads a few days of looking after a little baby to realise that mothering is a very full-time job, leaving little time for anything else.

Once again, at the risk of appearing a bore, be reassured that there is not a new mother in this country who does not sit back in amazement wondering how so little can be achieved when there is apparently so much free time in the day. It took nine months to make this baby and it's going to take at least another three to get the body back into relative equilibrium, and after this between three and nine more before you're firing smoothly on all cylinders again.

Emotional upsets

The early days and weeks after birth are a time for fragile emotions. Tears and confused feelings sneak up like a thief in the night then slip away just as silently. You are not going mad. This is a normal time for delicate emotions. If you feel a little fragile, hang in there. It will all be away in a couple of days. If you are feeling really battered, turn straight to Chapter 5 – The Baby Blues and Postnatal Depression, and get some helpful suggestions.

Isolation

While in that bustling hospital you were surrounded by a safety net of experts always there to support and advise. Now home seems as quiet as the tomb. You are alone and help is far away.

The curse of isolation is its ability to magnify and distort. Small, insignificant problems mushroom out of all proportion. It's not that they are big, it's just that when you have no-one to compare notes with you lose all perspective. Lack of friends and family, unsupportive husbands, and the baby blues can make the crush of isolation all the more savage. There are many mums who feel cut off and isolated, little realising that they are surrounded by other mothers who feel exactly the same.

Isolation, unfortunately, is on the increase as couples move from their close relatives at home and go seeking those far off greener fields with an improved lifestyle. The remedy is to ensure you keep in touch with the real world. Don't sit at home feeding, vacuuming, washing, with your only excitement a much-repeated midday movie on the TV. Get out there into the fresh air and join the rest of us on the living planet. Don't forget the telephone either. You can always pick it up and make contact with a friendly voice.

Keep in touch with family and friends. Visit the baby clinic regularly and talk to other mums. Find a good playgroup – which at this age will do nothing for your little baby, but you'll be with understanding friends and it lets you see you're normal and not alone. With isolation it's all too easy to feel sorry for yourself but that's one luxury you cannot really afford right now.

Identity

The change from working wife to full-time mother does not suit some. One minute you are a respected worker of independent means, the next you are retired and relying on your husband for pocket money. This identity crisis affects many first-time mums, especially those who have pursued a busy career before babies.

In the first three months childcare keeps you too busy for much else but thereafter it's worth taking a stand for identity. You must not be a complete slave to your child. The necessity to be a twenty-four-hours-a-day mother is a popular myth, but all mothers are happier and more effective if they make some time for themselves. Babies have rights, but so have their parents and babies do not have to come first all the time. Please do not feel guilty when you sensibly spare a thought for yourself.

The sort of talk I often hear from my mums sounds like this:

'I used to be my own person. Now I have become just a housekeeper, provider of baby foods and appendage of my husband and child. I feel guilty if I ever consider my own needs, yet my husband comes and goes as he pleases, his life relatively unchanged. I want a life and an identity. I want to be appreciated for being me.'

41

Self image

After birth self image is something else that takes a bit of a battering. Let's face it, it's not easy when you've been used to ordering the latest fashions, to find that just about the only ready-made that still fits is a waterproof car cover. Even those irritating wolf whistles you used to get when passing workmen seem to have stopped. Sleepless nights have left black rings under your eyes and altogether you don't feel very glamorous.

All mums feel a bit vulnerable at this time and it's not helped by some subtle stupidity pushed by the professional purveyors of baby care. As you left the hospital no doubt you were handed a throwaway booklet on babies – your owner's manual. There on the cover is the picture of a glamorous, smiling mum with a crisp laundered outfit, perfect make-up and hair straight from a TV shampoo commercial. Don't despair, she is just a paid model who has been lent a perfect baby. Your dark rings, wrinkles and general disarray are what's normal.

Now I have to be careful what I say here as I don't wish to sound like some militant male chauvinist, but I do believe your self image is worth working at. If you allow yourself to go round looking bedraggled and convinced that you have little appeal, then the chances are your self image will be shot. It's important that you look after yourself and give yourself the occasional treat. For example, you could have your hair done, or if funds allow, buy a new dress. Wearing make-up might also be a boost to your self-esteem.

It's obvious you will get a far better response from those you love when you don't appear at the door, dress covered in milk stains and hair hanging around your face like the sole survivor from a particularly nasty shipwreck. In an ideal world it is the inner person who matters, not the external appearance. Unfortunately the world we all live in is far from ideal and a little bit of sensible psychology is the way to go. But more importantly, you'll feel better about yourself if you make an extra effort.

Self-confidence

It is only natural for new parents to lack confidence in their childcare ability. After all, you've never done anything quite like this before. You need to develop a whole new range of skills, such as recognising what different cries mean, feeding, comforting and solving those difficult puzzles such as how to fasten a stretchsuit so that you aren't left with a popper over at the end. (Don't laugh, after all these years I still get it wrong!)

There are many different theories about the 'correct' way to care for your baby. Some authors believe in the super scientific view of childcare and that trusting your basic instincts is no longer good enough. One expert will tell us we should be playing classical musical to the unborn baby to tone up his developing nerves, whilst another says the birth should be underwater with the lights out with everyone whispering. Another group implies that your baby is deprived unless massaged in oil each day like a Kentucky Fried Chicken. Then there are those who want swimming by one year, reading by two and would like breast-feeding almost until secondary school entry.

All these schools of thought do nothing but generate inside you unrealistic expectations and feelings of utter incompetence. I believe that these experts, with their heads full of learned theories, would very soon come unstuck if they had to join you for a day at the battle front. Treat all the childrearing fashions with the healthy scepticism they deserve. Remember, today's cult message soon becomes yesterday's mistake. Remember, too, that trusting your basic instincts is a good place to start. You'll find when you do, and it all works out, that your confidence will build.

Guilt

Beware of guilt. It is a sneaky enemy which, since Adam and Eve got at the apples, has made countless excellent humans feel miserable. It creeps up on your tired and soggy brain to persuade you that you are incompetent and a disgrace to motherhood. It is your inadequacy that has caused the nappy rash or the failure of breast-feeding. You feel guilty you do not spend enough time with your baby or are not as well bonded as the expert who wrote the latest book tells you you should feel. You wish to go back to work but ill-founded guilt makes this impossible. You have a crier and after a week of sleepless nights you start resenting what this is doing to your life. But real mothers and fathers shouldn't feel resentment, you think. Then you feel guilty at having such feelings and you're stuck on the merry-go-round of guilt and can't get off.

Well, join the club. There is hardly a mother I know who hasn't been on this trip. Unless it's Wonderwoman or Superman who's reading this book I fear this is just the start of many years of self doubt and tarnished self-confidence. The amazing thing is that despite your worries almost all end up with loving and well-adjusted children.

Don't compare – don't despair

You have been given a unique little human being who's been programmed to have a very individual temperament. Don't compare, don't despair when you find he is not identical to 100 million other babies. Don't analyse every behaviour difference in terms of what you have and have not done. Develop your own style of parenting, the one that suits you. There are many different sorts of babies and many different ways to bring up a little one. Some ways may be slightly better than others but few ways are really wrong.

The very best care you can give is to love, enjoy and have fun with your children and then do what feels right and works for you. If this does not happen to coincide with what other people tell you, then just ignore them.

Easy Care Living

Making life easy for yourself when you have a new baby is not selfish, it is just good sense. There are no medals for the martyrs to motherhood. Remember tired, tense parents give inferior care, whilst if you stay on top so do those around you.

The aim in these early days is easy care living, where a minimum of effort is used to produce the maximum of effect. Here's roughly how it works.

Cleaning

At this stage in your life no-one expects your home to look like a *Homes & Gardens* centrefold. You have quite enough work on your plate with the newborn to start worrying about the house. It needs to be sanitary not sparkling, so concentrate on the essentials. Time spent with your baby is far more rewarding than time spent with your vacuum cleaner. I know both pick up a lot of dirt, are noisy and need emptying frequently but it's the baby that needs the attention. These first golden days can never be recaptured while the dirt can be rounded up anytime. If your husband, friends or relatives object to untidiness, hand them an apron and direct them to the workplace. Tiredness and guilt about housework must never stop you enjoying time with your baby in these early days.

Food

If small babies can thrive on plain milk, the rest of the family will do equally well on plain food. Don't feel embarrassed to open a tin, buy some cold cuts or a ready-cooked chicken. When you cook casseroles, cook in bulk and store a reserve dinner in the freezer. With these all you need is time to defrost or a quick burst in the microwave and you have a meal. If your husband feels the need for a four-course dinner, put him in charge of the kitchen, if he isn't already acquainted with it.

Washing and ironing

When it comes to wet nappies it seems unbelievable just how much water can be manufactured by such a small set of kidneys, in one short day. As you have roughly two years of waste disposal ahead of you make sure you have plenty of nappies. Have a large bucket to hide the dirties hygienically and then wash in one large batch, but more of this in Chapter 10.

Encourage the rest of the family to make your life easier. For example, go for easy care clothes and if a shirt looks halfway reasonable, hang it, don't iron it. If funds permit, the neighbour's teenager may like to earn some extra pocket money by helping out with a bit of ironing or cleaning.

Nappy changing

This is going to become one of the more monotonous features of your life for the next twenty-four months, so you might as well make it easy on yourself.

Prepare the area like a little workshop, with a raised roll-proof table where all lotions, wipes, rubbish bins and buckets are close at hand. It's a good idea to make sure that Dad is fully conversant with nappy changing, because his involvement will most certainly be needed. Don't be misled by the view that fathers have some physical or psychological impairment that prevents them from engaging in this activity.

Visitors and relatives

Visitors who offer to roll up their sleeves and help are always welcome, and don't be too proud to accept their offers. If they are just hollow utterances they will learn to be more careful what they say next time. Don't be afraid to subcontract out work like a site foreman. While Grandma is running the washing through, a friend could be collecting the shopping and what a joy are those friends who come bearing a basket of ready-cooked goodies like Red Riding Hood visiting her grandmother. Spongers, nosey-parkers, purveyors of gloom and other assorted pains are unwelcome. After all, you didn't have this baby to provide entertainment for your friends. When it comes to seeking some support you'll soon find out who your real friends are.

If your mother, or mother-in-law, is good company and a reasonably tactful diplomat, having her to stay for the first few weeks is an excellent idea. Be aware that even the most saint-like granny can cause some stress to the established equilibrium of your home. Be particularly careful not to share all the responsibility with Granny so that Dad feels left out and on the opposing team to you when he walks through the door. If he doesn't get on with his mother-in-law before the birth, things are unlikely to alter magically after the event. In this case you'll just have to weigh up the advantages and disadvantages of having a grandmother in the home and be charitable in your behaviour.

Grandparents are often just as elated and involved with the newborn as the parents themselves. The older generation have a fund of excellent help and advice to give but it will fall on deaf ears unless delivered diplomatically. It's jolly hard being a grandparent. You try not to stick your nose in when you see your own children stumbling blindly along into all the same mistakes you made. Good grandparents learn to steer a course of gentle guidance and non-intrusive intervention. Unfortunately at this stage wisdom is not always recognised or welcomed.

Beware of proud, possessive grannies who try to take over the child. Sometimes you might wonder whose baby it is, with Grandma holding on tight like a front-row forward as she hands off all intruders. I saw a baby recently who had two doting Italian grandmothers and bad eczema on the cheeks. Her father was quite convinced the grannies were to blame. 'She has been kissed at least a thousand times a day since she was born. The skin on her cheeks has never been dry. It's all worn away. Mind you,' he said, 'if you were kissed by my mother-in-law I wouldn't be surprised if you got a rash also!'

Getting out

It's all too easy to become house-bound with a newborn. All that paraphernalia which goes to make up the average portable nursery seems such an effort to get together that it hardly seems worth it.

A good way round this is to keep a small bag ready packed with a few nappies and a duplicate set of baby maintenance gear. In this way you can make instant decisions, grab the bag, grab the baby and run for it. Remember to stock the bag up again as soon as you get home or the next time you run for it could be a disaster!

Outside activity helps everyone's physical and mental state. Try and make a point of getting out somewhere each day, even if it's for a quick walk round the block or to go shopping.

With all new mums it's quite natural for them to feel very possessive towards their babies and this makes it hard to leave the child in the hands of even the most competent child minder. But do try. Getting out is a major part of getting yourself together and back to normal again. When it comes to night-life, this depends on the child. If you have been blessed with a remarkably easy, sound-sleeping baby then you can take the child just about anywhere, anytime, all with few problems.

It's not so easy if you have a sensitive screamer who hates any change of routine. If grandparents or a really close friend is prepared to give it a go, then try biting the bullet and leaving Baby for a short time while you get a break in the adult world. If you take an unsettled child out then pick your friends and your venues with care.

Looking after yourself

It is just as important to look after your own wellbeing as it is to look after that of your baby. If you stay on top, so do those who depend on you. If you fall apart they follow you all the way down the slippery slope.

When Junior is asleep, put your feet up, have a coffee, a snooze or a relaxing bath. Take it easy and don't worry about all those half-done chores. Don't be afraid to lift the phone off the hook or put a note on the door to divert disturbance until you return from the land of nod. When feeding your baby, sit in a comfortable chair, perhaps one that rocks. When that night shift is cold and long, rug up and have a flask of coffee or cocoa ready-prepared to pour.

Music can be a great therapy enabling your tired body to soar high with the eagles. If you prefer to get away from all the death, destruction and depression on the radio news, slip on a cassette, and for total escape use the ear phones.

Go gently, especially in the first six weeks. There are no prizes for proving how fantastic you are by being back on your feet and up to all your old tricks the day you return from hospital. Don't let anyone, especially your own conscience, make you feel guilty when you think of Number One. It is vital that you look after yourself properly – everyone reaps the benefits.

Conclusion

With your baby's homecoming you, your lifestyle and the way you think have all undergone massive changes. Patience, flexibility and a sense of humour are needed to survive the shock. It's important that your husband is given equal share and equal care of the baby. It's also important that the two of you have some 'together time'. Above all, mothers must look after themselves!

Babies matter but so do their mothers. So don't feel guilty to put your feet up and ignore the housework. Visitors are welcome as long as they are prepared to pull their weight a little. Family members are always welcome, as long as they are prepared to pull their weight! Try to get out of the house at least once a day, even if it's only a short canter round the block.

Now's the time for getting to know and love your baby. You can resume your love affair with the vacuum cleaner a little later on.

5

The Baby Blues and Postnatal Depression

WHEN you read the biographies of the great world leaders, it comes as a rude shock to realise just how frail some of them were. Mussolini may have made the trains run on time but that doesn't mean that he was happy or confident. He and many others were terribly insecure, lacked confidence and suffered frequent bouts of depression. If the great feel so fragile, then what hope is there for we ordinary people? The reality is that we all have our worries, weaknesses and times of low spirits.

For many mums the time of most confused feelings is just after birth. This may be the happiest day of your life, but somehow you just can't stop crying. Are you losing your marbles and going round the twist? No, this is all part of 'the baby blues' or its more major counterpart, postnatal depression.

In this chapter, let's look at these common conditions and see how to help.

The Baby Blues

This affects about two-thirds of mums in the first ten days after birth. The peak is probably the third day, though some may be teary right from day one. For most this lasts between twenty-four and forty-eight hours and then disappears.

What are the blues? The main outward symptom is generally tears whilst inwardly you may be feeling numb and emotionally fragile. Little triggers can cause great upsets and the most innocent story on the evening news about a baby being injured, malnourished or mistreated starts the tears rolling. As you think of your totally dependent baby you wonder why you decided to bring one so perfect into such a cruel world.

The blues are caused by tiredness, the traumas of birth and the massive reshuffle of hormones that follows delivery. Be reassured that this feeling is extremely common and very temporary. It is not a sign of madness, weakness or that you're an inferior parent. Hang in there for a couple of days. It will go just as fast as it came, soon to be a forgotten part of history.

The baby blues – what to do

The baby blues are so common, so brief and so mild that they require no treatment other than recognition and reassurance. When you realise that you are in the same boat as 75 per cent of all other new mums this removes the fear and lets you see that you are definitely not going round the bend. In two days you should be back on course, so keep moving, keep talking, keep your optimism and be assured that it will soon pass.

Postnatal Depression

This is still a common, though more severe problem. Here there is a degree of true depression which can last for weeks, months or even years.

Now I am not a psychiatrist but I see depression as that sadness which we all get from time to time but increased to such an extent that it flattens your interest in life and immobilises your ability to help yourself. Life seems to hold no joy and there doesn't appear to be much worth looking forward to in the future. For you there seems to be no light at the end of the tunnel and even if a light appears you presume it's an express train coming to flatten you.

Postnatal depression has varied symptoms and severities. Occasionally it can be a long, severe and incapacitating illness. However, usually it is just an overdose of those normal 'flat' feelings most mums have to some degree at birth. You're likely to feel tired, emotionally confused, numb and uncertain where you are heading.

There is a fine line between where these normal feelings merge with a serious state of depression. Often it depends on the length and the severity of the suffering as well as the resilience of the sufferer. No two people are smitten similarly and often the symptoms are subtle and hidden to all but the enquiring eye.

If you are depressed you may feel distant, alienated and numb. You may find it hard to generate enthusiasm for activities that once were fun and even the kilowatts you do manage to produce still seem pretty hollow. You may also find that it's often easier to stay alone than muster the emotional energy to get out and mix.

Above all, confusion reigns supreme. You can't understand it. You should be happy but you are weepy and sad. There is no real optimism or planning for the future. Life is for existing, not for living. Close relationships lose warmth as you do not have enough emotional energy to power your own batteries and certainly have none to spare. Thoughts of sexual activity are often pushed firmly on to the back burner.

For some this is a time of irritability, anxiety, agitation and tension. You may not be sleeping or eating well and your doctor may be hassled over trivial baby worries, which you would normally cope with, in more rational times. Guilt floats to the surface like a dead albatross and hangs round your neck to further weigh down your spirits. You feel weak, a failure and ashamed of the shape you're in.

Some mums are disorganised to the point of despair. To get dressed and moving in the morning seems like a monumental chore. To have a meal on the table at night is nigh impossible. Most overcome this by sticking to a structured routine, performing jobs like nappy changing and clothes washing – anything which does not require emotional input and can be achieved virtually on automatic pilot.

It is estimated that between one-fifth and one-tenth of all new mums experience some minor degree of postnatal depression. If it is so common you might well ask why it isn't more widely talked about? The reason is that most mums feel such a failure that they keep it to themselves, soldiering on, determined not to let those close to them know how much they hurt. Often it is not easy to share these feelings as those physically close can be emotionally distant and deaf to any such talks. Husbands and children may not realise that you're suffering from depression but they can still feel the chill in the air. They may not complain but their way of coping may be to distance themselves from the problem.

The exact cause of postnatal depression is unclear, but as with baby blues it seems to be related to the stresses and hormone changes of birth. This can't be the whole story as it can set in months after birth when your system should have long since settled. There are also reports of adopting mothers and even doting dads similarly smitten.

Other factors are obviously important such as the dramatic change in lifestyle that accompanies birth – tiredness, unrealistic expectations, feelings of failure, doubts about really wanting a baby and a lack of support from those close to you. However, most sufferers have a much-wanted baby and live within a close, supportive family network.

It's important to remember that for most women postnatal depression is a mild irritating hiccough which lasts less than three months. It is only for a few that this condition descends like a black cloud which smothers all sparkle and knocks the joy from the entire first year.

Postnatal depression – what to do

Though postnatal depression can sometimes be severe and serious, most of the time it responds to simple treatment. First you must realise that you are not some off-the-rails oddball. You are suffering from an extremely common condition which affects up to one-fifth of all mothers. It is not necessary for you to display stiff-upper-lip stoicism. You may fool your friends but you won't fool yourself.

As the condition closes in it is all too easy to get immobilised and housebound. Very soon you'll find it is too much hassle to get yourself up and moving. The less you do the less you will want to do. Isolation itself causes further damage. Time spent alone with your sad, under-occupied brain is time spent in bad company.

Part of the process of depression is the great lack of enthusiasm to get up and change the status quo. It is always easier to suffer on alone than to do anything that is going to help. This can lead to a long, lonely haul. Please note:

- Try not to become isolated from your friends and family. It may feel more comfortable to be alone but it's not good for you or your brain.

- Mixing with other mums at the playgroup may be difficult but try to keep in contact. Ask your health visitor about a local group for mothers with postnatal depression. These are invaluable.

- Tell your husband how you feel. Don't feel embarrassed. Your marriage vows said something about loving, cherishing and caring both in sickness and in health.

- You don't have to become a martyr giving all your life to others. What about some time for you? Don't feel guilty about getting out and doing your own thing. You need your own life and identity.

- You may need a professional who understands and will see you through. Don't feel embarrassed to ask someone to help.

I worry a lot about postnatal depression. I worry principally that so many mums suffer in silence and write off this first golden year that should be fun. It seems such a waste of life to be stuck in an emotional desert when things could be so much rosier if help were sought quickly. Another good reason to seek help earlier is for the sake of your family. Emotional deserts are equally arid for babies, children and husbands.

Perhaps the most important thing to remember when you're feeling low is that the sadness will pass. There *will* be a light at the end of the tunnel but you may need help to get there.

Friends and family – please note!

We have been talking about something so common that many who read this will have a loved one who is stuck there right now. Though you are close, usually you have no idea just how sad and upset they are.

If the previous sparkle and enthusiasm for life has gone this may be all you see. Others may slow down, become disorganised, moody, irritable, have disturbed sleep and lose all interest in sex. Some compensate by becoming active and flitting about like a butterfly. They know that if they never stop to think, they never have time to think how rotten they feel.

Don't be fooled by hollow smiles. Prisoners often laugh and joke in front of the firing squad but this doesn't mean that they are happy! Take time to listen and don't change the subject when the talk turns to feelings. Depressed mums can become terribly isolated. They may be ashamed to admit how they feel. They may not wish to burden those they love with their personal problems and suffer alone. But their problems must be your problems. As friends and family do you make time to talk of feelings or is it easier to stay aloof, unsupportive and unable to face up to reality?

A declaration of depression is not a sign of weakness. To admit it is a sign of strength and honesty.

Conclusion

Some degree of baby blues affects most new mothers. The blues go as quickly as they come so give it a couple of days. Postnatal depression is more traumatic and more common than anyone is prepared to admit. This is a reaction to hormones, tiredness and a mammoth change in your life. Talk, time, activity, friends and special groups usually solve the situation. Above all, remember that if you're feeling stuck, you must seek help. There's no point suffering in silence as you become isolated which gets you nowhere fast. Admitting there is a problem is the first step to getting back on your feet. It is a sure sign of sense and sanity.

6

Bonding –
Relax and Give it Time

THE final contractions are over, the nurse whispers softly 'It's a beautiful girl'. As the delicate skin of your newborn baby brushes lightly against yours, from somewhere just behind the anaesthetic machine sweet violins start to play.

Congratulations! Now you have bonded, stuck together for all time as if by superglue. Is it really like that? Well of course it's not.

This natal nonsense is for doves, dicky birds and True Romance comics. Long-term relationships are not made in minutes. Eyes don't meet across the dance floor and together you stay forever. Lasting relationships take time to develop and refine and the process is very much a two-way street. So what is this thing called bonding that gets so much popular airplay?

Bonding refers to that unique relationship which develops between parents and their child. This is a special brand of love. Historically the talk has always been of mother-child bonding. No-one ever seemed to consider Dad very much in this process. Mum was said to hold the key to all emotional development while Dad's role was that of sire and breadwinner. If things went wrong in any way, all the blame was placed unfairly and squarely on one set of shoulders – Mum's! Some cynics refer to this old-fashioned idea as 'mal-de-mer childcare'. Of course it's nothing to do with sea-sickness, but a tortured use of the French language to suggest bad mothering.

Anyway this notion is untrue and unhelpful, its only purpose to generate unjust guilt where none should be. Bonding and emotional care are not just for mothers. Fathers, grandmas, grandpas, uncles, aunts, brothers, sisters and many more also bond and become emotionally involved.

Research on bonding has always had severe limitations. It is hard to measure that human immeasurable – love. If this came in kilowatts like an electric lightbulb, we would know just how powerful it was. In reality, however, love and bonding can only be measured in inaccurate terms, more in keeping with the pop music industry which does not talk of love on the Richter scale but rather in terms of 'how deep is the ocean, how high the moon'.

Researchers can either focus on ducks, sheep and goats or ask parents if they feel bonded or watch how they handle their young ones. Asking parents how they feel about their child is reasonably useful but, in matters emotional, often our mouths can be out of tune with our hearts. You can observe how a mum relates to her child, but there is more to bonding than making faces and talking nonsense in a silly high-pitched voice. The standard of physical care is really easy to measure, but again there is more to love than polished nappy pins and a food-free face. Academics certainly should look at these components but let's not get carried away, they have their limitations.

I believe in bonding, but I don't believe in its elevation to a position of compulsory religion. I resent mums being told how they should feel by someone who thinks they know it all because they read some academic textbook. I also object to the view that there is a critical period of bonding. This idea states that if you mess it up in the early days, a lifetime of emotional hardship is guaranteed. This is definitely not true. If bonding doesn't happen at birth this does not mean it won't happen at all. It just requires patience and the right environment to let Nature take its course.

Bonding – what's usual

For most mums bonding starts early, to become ever stronger and more mature with close contact and the passage of time. One recent study[1] showed that 41 per cent of mothers said that they first felt for their babies before birth, 24 per cent at the time of birth, 27 per cent in the first week, and the remaining 8 per cent some time later. These, of course, were the first feelings, not the full works. It should be noted that over one-third of the mothers in this study claimed they had no great feelings at birth. For them this was a time of numb indifference. Please don't sit around wondering if you feel as well-bonded as some expert says you should. Feelings are to be felt, not analysed. The harder you try the more anxious you become and then this ceases to be a natural process and gets utterly stiff and constipated.

For some, bonding may come with the flash of a thunderbolt, for others it descends unnoticed like the evening dew. Just relax, let Nature take its course – give it time.

How do babies win you over?

Little babies are remarkably responsive at birth when you consider what they have just been through. In the space of a few hours they have been squeezed, their blood circulation has undergone a major rearrangement, their brains now run on twice the richness of prebirth blood oxygen, they lived in warm water for nine months and are now air-cooled like a Volkswagen Beetle. To cap it all their first view of life is being held upside-down with a plastic catheter stuck up a nostril. Yet despite all this the majority of babies enter the world in a state of responsive alertness.

Babies may not be able to talk, but they can win over the hardest adult with their gurgles and seductive use of their eyes. Our eyes are great communicators. Gaze into the eyes of a loved one and you will see warmth, love and trust, whilst the eyes of a used-car salesman may not indicate he is shy, sensitive and always to be believed. Quite probably his eyes flit around like a spectator watching at Wimbledon. The eyes of your baby tell you more than any words could communicate.

Body language is big in babies, but most parents who talk to their little ones have no idea just how much communication is bounding back. Researchers who have taken video recordings of mothers as they talk to their babies have been surprised at the extent of the two-way process. When you play these tapes back slowly, the baby is often seen to be moving in time with the speech. This response is like me nodding my head to let my patients know I am interested and listening and haven't fallen asleep.

The period just after birth is an important one. The baby is unexpectedly alert, almost as though the grand design allowed this as a time for quiet introductions to get life off to a good start. For an hour or so the eyes are open, faces are pulled and the baby stays very awake. Whether part of the grand design or just a matter of chance, this is a time for both parents to be with their new child. It is a time to be savoured.

The baby to mother bond

With all this talk of mothers bonding to their babies we often forget that love has to be a two-way process. Babies must also bond with their mothers. This is one area of injustice and imbalance which most thoroughly bonded mothers prefer not to think about. The truth is that although mums usually bond to their babies near birth, the baby will take almost another six months to fully return the compliment.

In the first months our little ones are blissfully happy in the hands of any warm, loving care-giver. This is usually the mother, although more and more fathers are becoming involved. Between four and six months babies begin to recognise their main caretaker and will tend to settle more quickly for them. It is generally not until the seventh month that strong attachment comes into the relationship. Suddenly the epoxy sets as hard as nails. The baby, who before then was happy to be handled by just about anyone from milkman to maiden aunt, now only wants Mum and no-one else will do. Bonding has now been reciprocated. This attachment is usually given to Mum first with Dad and other close carers being included soon afterwards.

So don't despair, mums, you may have to wait a bit but eventually bonding becomes a two-way process.

Animal and human research

Falling in love isn't just for humans. Ducks, sheep, goats and other assorted livestock also give it a go in their own way. Goats and sheep are interesting to study. If you remove a kid or a lamb at birth and then return it after three days, rejection is more than likely. If, on the other hand, you slip an older foster lamb in with the newborns at the time of birth there is a good chance it will be accepted. These animals therefore do seem to have a sensitive bonding period. If these sheep–goat experiments can be carried over to human kids, then all babies would have to be close to mother in the early days or be rejected. This of course would have major implications in the separation of sick and premature babies in special nurseries. Luckily this is not the case. It is fortunate that most of our fellow humans do not behave like sheep and goats. Those who do can take comfort that even a lamb which is returned to its mother after three weeks, although initially rejected, will with time, closeness and perseverance form an attachment eventually.

There is a strong lobby group which promotes the idea of a critical period for human bonding. They believe that immediate closeness and skin contact are imperative and imply that all manner of psychological disasters may befall those who have failed to do it right in the early days. I doubt their claims. For a start, if early contact is so essential then all adoptions would fail. They don't because adoptive parents have a really strong commitment to their child to make it work. This determination and love more than makes up for anything missed in the early days.

Klaus and Kennell are well-respected researchers who have done much to make hospital care for mothers and babies a more gentle, human affair. In a study they compared one group of mothers who had a small amount of contact with their babies at birth with another group who had unlimited time together. When they followed up the two groups they demonstrated some small improvement in mother–child communication in the maximum contact group, even two years down the track. Impressive as this is, other researchers are not so sure of the relevance of these small differences.

So what are we to believe? For my part the notion that there is a critical period where the whole of life's game is either won or lost is against the teachings of the present. Certainly we must do all in our power to promote good early contact, but let's not go overboard in the process. Extreme views generate unreasonable expectations and anxieties. Lack of early contact may not cause permanent upset to bonding, but the feelings of guilt that come from trying too hard most certainly will.

Other factors which influence bonding

It is easy for those with heads full of theories and feet off the ground to expect every mother and child to behave and bond in the same way. But each of us is an individual with a unique temperament and way of doing things. Whilst most babies are cute and easy to fall for, there are those who quite definitely are not. They are the ones who are irritable, push you away, seem to cry most of the day or gaze at you with a bored expression as you positively ooze love from every pore in your body. Saints may love all equally, humans are more selective.

Other upsets may also take the gloss off your feelings. The conception may have been unwelcome or the pregnancy really difficult. Labour may have been a harrowing experience and this got you off on the wrong foot. There may be the baby blues or postnatal depression, and of course it's hard to bond when your brain is numb, sad and on automatic pilot. Then there are the hassles of unsupportive partners, financial worries, interfering relatives and inadequate accommodation. All these will play their part in the bonding or non-bonding process. Bonding is not solely to do with close contact and the magic of the moment. Environment, individual differences and family circumstances are also important.

Special problems – special bonds

Adoption

With adoption there is no nine-month preparation, no skin contact, no breast-feeding. One moment you are a childless couple, the next an unannounced stranger has arrived in your midst.

Despite all the theoretical difficulties, adoption usually works very well. It works well because the adopting couple dearly want the child and pull out all stops to make it a success. Of course there is always the chance of some hereditary temperamental characteristics which may cause friction, but for most couples this closeness and commitment overcomes anything they may have missed in the early days.

Sick and premature babies

Bonding difficulties have been so overstated by various psychological gurus that the parents of the premature may see nothing but emotional doom and gloom ahead. It may seem almost inevitable that rejection, child abuse or at the very least an inability to love will flow on from such a beginning. This is utter nonsense.

I realise that the start was difficult. Birth came as a surprise and anxiety levels were high. The baby was taken away leaving parents confused and empty handed.

If the baby was extremely sick your subconscious may block the bonding process. There the brain automatically keeps its distance, after all it's always easier to lose something you have never loved than one to whom you are closely attached.

While in hospital a large emotionally charged cloud hangs over the scene, but thank goodness for the recent enlightened attitude. Premature nurseries are now places for parents. They are encouraged to visit and are made to feel welcome and at ease.

All the electronic gadgetry is explained and de-mystified. They touch, hold, cuddle and help care, and when the babe gets stronger have time to become acquainted in a quiet parents' room.

Modern-day nurseries are not just oases of high technology. They are springs of high humanity and quality emotional care. Having a sick or premature baby gets things off to a shaky start, but once the dust has settled the long-term emotional future is excellent. (See Chapter 22.)

Caesarian section

Caesarian mums may not be awake to enjoy those first moments of contact but not to worry, it's just a minor hiccough at the start. They will bond and become as glued together as firmly as any other. Some mothers who know that a caesar is on the cards ask their obstetrician that it be done under local anaesthetic (an epidural). There the lower part of the body is pain free but they still have the full sensation of arms, eyes and brain to hold and cuddle at birth.

Handicapped children

Those of us who have children who are not handicapped should be truly thankful. We are extremely privileged people and must never forget it. It is hard for us to imagine how it would have been if we had been told our new baby had a major handicap. Unfortunately this is all too common, yet life has to go on.

Initially when told the news parents may feel shocked, numb and disbelieving. They feel let down, they grieve and can't see what lies ahead in the future.

This all makes bonding hard and it becomes even more difficult if the baby has been whisked off at birth for investigation or special treatment. Now the parents are left with an empty cot and an overactive mind which conjures up all manner of inappropriate visions. These can block bonding and make the eventual coming together all the more difficult.

It is hard to get any accurate information on bonding with special children but it seems that despite all these difficulties most bond early and well. Your child may have some problems, but when all's said and done he is still yours and love is not selective. Sometimes I feel that the parents have almost over-bonded. They become amazingly over-protective and it's almost impossible to separate them at all from their special one even for a single night of respite care.

For those of us who are not emotionally involved we may find it hard to feel close to children with major disabilities, but that is our handicap, not theirs. Most parents bond early and securely.

Bonding – what should you do?

Birth is a time to be shared by mothers and fathers. Remember that those first couple of hours of life are a time of quiet responsiveness, just right for introductions, so try to be there and be close.

In hospital it is best to spend as much time as you can with your newborn, but don't be brainwashed by those who threaten all manner of life-long problems if you don't play the game their way.

If you feel blue, you are not weak-spined and not going mad. You have the baby blues. Tell someone how you feel, it's all so common, those around you will understand and can help. (See page 50 on postnatal depression.)

If your little one is sick or premature try to visit him as much as you can. Don't be put off by the medical gadgetry of the special nurseries, not only are you welcome, you are encouraged to be there.

Don't get too scientific. Don't psychoanalyse yourself and don't sit around waiting for bonding to drop like a brick from heaven. You can't force feelings. They happen quicker in their own good time. Instant and undying love is only the stuff of cheap comics and fairy tales, lasting relationships come with time, closeness and commitment.

Turn a deaf ear to those out-of-touch teachers who believe that one slip at the start leads to a lifetime of emotional problems. This simply is not so. You may miss the bonding bus at its first stop, but you can always bond later on down the line. Of course it may take a bit longer, but you will still get where you want in the end.

7

Brothers and Sisters – Adjusting to the New Arrival

Yᴏᴜ don't have to be Sigmund Freud to work out that when a newborn barges in on the private kingdom of a resident toddler, the toddler's nose is bound to be put out of joint. Toddlers are interesting little people who generally hit their peak of difficult behaviour between eighteen months and two and a half years of age. If you look at the average spacing between a family's first and second child you'll find that it's just about that length of time.

Toddlers tend to be negative, stubborn and demanding. At the best of times, they seek constant attention, wishing to be on centre stage at all times. They are not renowned for deep humanitarian thoughts and actions such as sharing and, what's more, sense is rarely their strong suit.

If you see it from a junior point of view, it must seem like this. Here am I, the most important person in the house with all Mum's attention to myself. Then she gets enormous, leaves home without taking me, to return with a noisy bundle that everyone fusses over. Now she is tired and snaps at me when I go near the little home-wrecker. It's not fair!

However, before you rush out and sign up for sterilisation, be reassured that a second or third baby does not have to disturb the sitting tenant. All you need is some forward planning, some consideration of the child's point of view and a lot of cunning. So let's see how we can get things off to a good start.

Before the birth (telling the toddler)

It's never that easy to be a laid-back supermum when in the throes and throw-ups of early pregnancy. It's at tiring times like this that many people wonder if one child is not the ideal family size! Forty weeks seems like light years in a toddler's time frame, so it's pointless doing any serious talking about babies until towards the end. Once your size has blown out to the point where even an unobservant toddler can spot the difference, then it's certainly time to talk. Don't get too deep and meaningful in your discussions. They don't need to know all the finer points of human reproduction, just simple bits about tummies, brothers and sisters and a few days in hospital will suffice.

Let them feel the kicking baby and possibly mention a few names you're considering. Talk of dirty nappies and poohing infants is always riveting to toddlers. At this age they see themselves as world experts on such bodily functions. Always emphasise that you are going to need a special little helper if you are ever going to manage.

Sharing love

It's sensible to tell the toddler that of course you will always love him just as much once little brother or sister arrives. Though it's very easy to say, most parents expecting their second child find it hard to believe that they could

ever love another as much as the first. Give it a week after the birth and you'll be surprised to find just how easy it is.

Care when in hospital

Don't leave the arrangements for childcare while you are to be in hospital until the last moment. Plan this well in advance. Grandmas are usually your best bet, but any close friend or relative that the child is happy to be with will do. If Dad can get off work that's, of course, ideal.

It's not a bad idea to have a short trial run with the care-giver before the event. This helps acclimatise the child and lets you see that it will all work when you actually have to go to hospital.

Tidying toddler behaviour

The middle months of pregnancy are a good time to tidy up a few toddler management issues. If, for example, they are still sleeping in your bed, now is a good time to serve an eviction order. If you are holding off toilet training until the summer comes, cut the nonsense and get on with it now. If preschool is about to start it's best to have it established before, rather than at the time of birth. I'm not suggesting that you engage in some sort of behavioural blitz, but now is a good time to tidy up a few loose ends.

Going to hospital

If all your arrangements for care at home have been well planned you should be able to slip off without a lot of fuss and panic. If it's 3 am and the caretaker is in residence, don't stir Junior – let sleeping toddlers lie. A kiss, a hug, a word or two of love spoken over the slumbering form and then hop it quick. For daylight departures, explain once more what is about to happen, say your goodbyes and make a clean, decisive exit. Don't drag it out, as this winds up everyone and you leave upset and feeling guilty.

The hospital

It's good for toddlers to visit Mum in hospital and be introduced to the source of all the tiredness and turmoil of the last nine months. Most hospitals welcome brothers and sisters as long as they don't stampede up and down the corridor, shout noisily, swing on the curtains or turn off ventilators.

Visiting hospital should be a fun family affair and a way of getting things off to a good start. Make sure that the new baby doesn't steal all the thunder. Reserve a large portion of the fuss for your toddler. He's also an important little person and would be the first to admit it. Little ones are sure to want to climb all over Mum in bed and although Florence Nightingale definitely would not have approved of this, her successors will usually turn a blind eye.

The homecoming

The return home is the time when everything should get off to a good start, but often it is handled badly. Mum is tired, clingy and supersensitive to the slightest hint of a toddler terrorist raid on the infant. At the same time toddlers are keen to take up where they left off, and while they are not so greedy as to expect 100 per cent of Mum's attention, they reckon that 95 per cent is a pretty fair division.

When you arrive back home let 'the driver' take care of the baggage and the new arrival, which leaves your hands free to greet Junior properly at the door.

A little present from the hospital shop might be sound psychology. Your friends and relatives should know (or have been primed) not to walk past the sitting tenant in their haste to drool over the new arrival. If they ride in on their camels bearing gifts and greetings from afar at least one present should have a toddler's name on it.

Settling in

The experts tell us that all care and attention should be divided equally between our children (at all times). Now that's all very well to say from the relaxed depths of some academic office, not quite so simple however when you're up there in the front line. All children do not demand the same care and attention and so the division will never be equal however hard you try. I think it's best to keep toddlers riding high on a wave of positive attention. Elevate the toddler to the special status of friend, confidante and mother's little helper. Give lots of indirect attention to the toddler as you go about your care of the baby. This side-stream attention may not be ideal, but it will leave most toddlers happy.

For example, when changing nappies, get your helper to bring the tissues, hold the pins or just keep you entertained with the latest fund of stories from the playgroup. When it comes to feeding, this is a good time to read, play, talk and listen. If you don't plan ahead and set things up to involve the toddler, he will be obliged to gain your attention by less desirable means. When breast-feeding he might demand to latch on to the unoccupied side or create such a scene that you are forced to stop. When everything is delicately balanced in mid-nappy change, he will engage in what sounds like vivisection with the cat and at once he has you hooked. It's best to anticipate these problems and with a bit of cunning steer round them.

Toddler regression

It is quite common for toddler behaviour to regress when a new baby arrives. They may want a bottle, or to be spoon-fed. They may slip back into baby talk and often toilet training will take a nose dive. Don't get too analytical about this. Love, time and sensibly shared attention will soon iron out these wrinkles.

Divided care

Try to divide the care wherever possible. At the weekend, for example, while Mum nurses the newborn, Dad can be off having adventures with Junior, whether it is shopping, playing in the park or helping Dad in the garden. All this helps to spread the load, gives some individual attention to Junior and lets him feel very important.

Behaviour blow-out

Young children are always at their most difficult when stressed by changes in the equilibrium of their lives. Be more accepting of behaviour irritations at this time. Before you blow your top, be sure that it is the tiresome behaviour which is irritating and not just the low tolerance of your own tired brain. Use the old standbys of diversion, pretending to ignore, keeping positive and time apart as the safety valve when you are losing your cool.

Clingy overpossessive mums

I realise that it is hard for the clingy new mum to sit back while prams get tipped over like the *Titanic*, dirty digits get poked into orifices and toddlers mountaineer over the sleeping baby. Now is the time to establish that delicate balance between protection and over-protection. The former is of course necessary for survival, but if overdone, leads to rivalry, resentment and cries of favouritism.

Try not to pounce on Junior every time he comes within a toy's throw of the baby, but rather aim to divert his attention elsewhere. Try to remain as laid-back and philosophical as your sensitivity and commonsense will allow. Remember little ones are a good deal tougher than you think.

The six-month sting

There is another outcome that may sneak up on you unawares. You arrive home with your new baby to find utter peace. Then at about six months, just as you thought it was safe to relax, guerilla warfare hits you with a bang.

Don't panic, this is an extremely common scenario yet one which will still have a happy ending. You see, when Baby first appeared he lay around doing nothing like a big doll who posed no particular threat to Junior. Then suddenly at six months the doll sits up, starts to gurgle and attracts all the attention. Faced with this unfortunate turn of events the toddler reacts against his change in status and becomes a pest.

All you can do is divert him. Keep him busy and ignore as much of the anti-social behaviour as is reasonable. Divided care, visits to Grandma's, playgroups and lots of positive attention are the best ways to cope.

Bickering, fighting and sibling rivalry are all part of the joys of being a parent and will go on throughout childhood. As adults we are just as competitive and jealous of those who seem to have more possessions and get greater attention than we do, so why should we be surprised when our junior versions reaction in a similar way?

Conclusion

A new baby will fascinate most toddlers, but many resent the change it brings to their lifestyle. Toddlers tend to be negative, stubborn, attention-seeking little people who are not keen to share. So when a new baby arrives, they're not always going to be overjoyed.

Try and give toddlers as much attention as you can and enthuse them to help you look after the new member of the family. Plan ahead, try to be as relaxed as possible and not to over-protect the newborn. Keeping Junior permanently happy will not be possible, but you're more likely to keep the peace if you make him feel important.

Spacing of children

There is no ideal gap to have between children. The success of any spacing is going to depend mostly on the temperament of the child you have been allotted and how well your energy reserves hold out.

- If you have your children close together, they are usually great mates who gain a lot of fun from each other's company. However, be warned, close children can bicker and fight endlessly. Two children together leading each other on get into three times the mischief that any child alone could have ever thought up.

- With wide spacing much of the close company is lost, but there are advantages. Mothers enter this later pregnancy better prepared and well rested. An older child is also able to be of some help in looking after his younger brother or sister.

- Personally I like to see a gap of between eighteen months and three years. If less than eighteen months, it is usually too tough on a mother's physical and emotional strength and if over three the close companionship which I see as valuable is lost.

- I get irritated with those who set out to plan their families to almost the exact date of delivery. We can practise birth control with some reliability but conceiving on demand, for many couples, is not quite so predictable. Let's not get too precise, the most important goal for all of us is to have normal healthy children, whenever they choose to appear.

8

The Gear for the Job

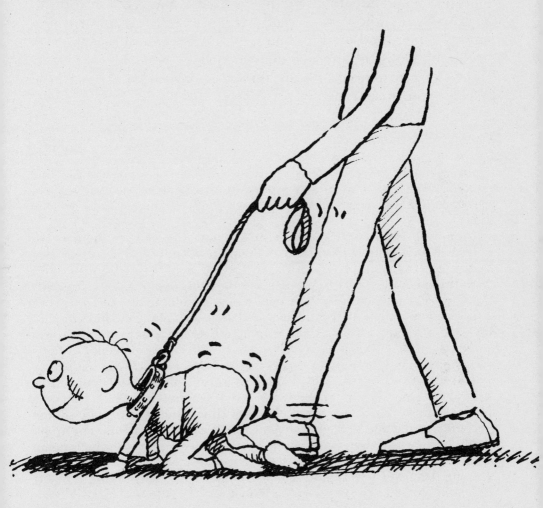

WHEN it comes to preparing for the new arrival, parents can generally be divided into two sorts – the wait-and-see variety and the nesters.

The wait-and-see parents refuse to think of even a name or nappy pin until they have seen the healthy whites of those little eyes. The nesters go through pregnancy like a mother hen getting ready for her chicks. By the ninth month, they seem to have amassed enough gear to stock a baby boutique of their own.

When it comes to choosing equipment for your baby, there are a few absolute necessities, some things you might do without but which make life an awful lot easier, and then all those very nice but very extravagant luxuries. What you buy depends on the size of your budget. The upmarket perfectionist may go for the all-sparkling new, whereas the realist will gratefully accept anything battered, borrowed or sixth hand. My advice is to forget the way something looks, as long as it does the job.

Let's look at some very basic aspects of day-to-day care and the tools for your new trade.

The baby's room

In old-fashioned childcare books we are told that the baby's room should be light, airy and have a favourable aspect. In real life your baby will be very privileged to have a room of his or her own at all – let alone of a favourable aspect.

When choosing a room, ideally it should not be so close to the parents' room that every grunt and sniff wakes them up, yet not so far away that they cannot hear the crying baby. In the real world most will share with other children, some will sleep in a passage way or sitting-room and as for aspect, it will probably be over the railway line or near a building site. In one corner of the room you should erect the nappy change area along the lines that we discussed in Chapter 4. Fitted out with all the lotions and potions, this will become a sort of pit stop area in the racetrack of life where efficient Le Mans-type nappy changes can occur during the day and night. If you happen to have a toddler in the house with a toddler's uncontrollable fiddly fingers, it's best to keep solutions that squeeze out of tubes and ooze out of bottles on a shelf well above his or her reach. The last thing you want is to be sliding gracefully round the linoleum at 3 am like Torvill and Dean. The room should have two kinds of lights, a bright one for seeing clearly what is going on and a dim one near the bed for night-time feeding and checking on Sleeping Beauty. There should also be a comfortable chair to support your tired bones to make the night shift a little less of a hassle.

Sleep and cots

For the first weeks most babies will sleep in a carry cot beside their parents' bed. This makes it easy for night-time feeding to occur with the minimum of disruption. It also allows a bit of supervision until the parents feel confident enough to be separated from their newborn.

If you want to keep the baby close to you for the first year, that's fine if you feel happy about it. The trouble is that many parents find it hard to sleep soundly when their baby is close by. Every little change in breathing rings alarm bells in your slumbering brain, like the sudden change in the sound of a Boeing engine when you're flying 30,000 feet above firm ground. When the breathing sounds laboured you're convinced he is about to breathe his last. When you can't hear any breathing, you're convinced he has!

We are taught that little western babies shouldn't sleep in their mothers' beds, but don't worry if you drift off while cuddling or feeding. Mothers don't roll on or smother their babies – that's just a much-promoted old wives' tale.

Sleepwear should be comfortable and easily washable. At birth most prefer to sleep in some type of restrictive wrap. Swaddling is as old as the hills and most babies like a tied-at-the-bottom sleeping suit or a firm wrap in a baby blanket. Before long they will spend most of the night and day in a stretchsuit. These are unisex, useful, easy care and relatively cheap.

Approved, specially treated sheepskin rugs are popular. These give both comfort and security to most babies. One word of caution, be careful of sheepskins if there is a history of eczema in the family. Wool against the skin can cause great irritation and unhappiness to some eczema sufferers and you can't get anything more woolly than a sheepskin.

If Baby is born during a cold spell and you are afraid that he is going to kick his blankets off and freeze to death in the night, make sure that he is warmly, but not too warmly, dressed before going to bed, then blankets are not so important. When the weather is hot he will need just the lightest sleepwear or even a nappy alone will suffice. With all this skin exposed, beware, if in an area where they abound, of the marauding mosquito, who will probably pay a visit the night before Lord Lichfield is booked in to take the baby's portrait. If mosquitoes are a problem, use a net and elsewhere use a recognised spray. Don't overdo this chemical warfare in your baby's room. We know that it makes little insects pretty unhappy, and though probably perfectly safe for little humans, let's not try to prove the point.

A cot will need to be purchased some months down the track. As you will get at least two years' hard use out of it for each child, you will find that a sound cot is a sound investment. A heavy-duty model is often a wise precaution in case your gentle little newborn turns into a tough, active, little rocker. This kind of child is capable of making the legs of an imperfectly constructed cot do the splits. After a couple of years when it comes to resale all you have is something that resembles driftwood.

Check with cots that have been home-made that the rails on the sides are not too far apart, in case little heads get stuck and injured. Missing rungs are equally hazardous. The lion keeper at the zoo does not tolerate this shoddy set up and neither should you. If you have managed to resurrect some trendy Victorian museum piece ensure that the original paint is not that antique lead-based stuff that can damage a cot-chewer's body and brain. Most cots come with a suitable baby mattress which should be fully wet-proofed. Pillows are not suggested for sleep in the first year, not that anyone is convinced they cause suffocation, but they are not necessary, so why take any chances?

Baby wipes

It's hard to think of bringing up babies without a box of tissues at hand. Their advent has been a God-send for keeping little faces, noses and regurgitating bodies clean.

Now we have moved one step further in convenience cleaning, with those commercially produced packs of ever-wet wipes.

Yes, these are excellent, portable and of great use, but don't forget that good old tap water is still the cheapest and kindest way to wipe.

The ready wet tissues contain some alcohol and soapy additives that can rob delicate skins of their natural oils. They dry and even irritate. If they suit your child and your wallet and your busy lifestyle, then use them. But if not, pure tap water on a cloth or tissue is still the best bet.

Bathing

Despite the fact that each baby spends the first nine months living underwater, once properly dried out a good many are not that keen on any further immersion. It's probably not so much the water that causes the upset but having their warm clothes removed and with them that swaddled sense of security.

The best books suggest a daily bath for every baby, but this is not necessary. If you carefully top and tail them this keeps the upper end and the nappy part hygienic and makes daily bathing unnecessary. Bathing at first should be in a special baby bath or a plastic basin. If set on top of a table make sure it is secure and won't tip. You can use an ordinary wash basin or sink if you want, but guard against bashing baby against the protruding spouts or scalding with an unsuspected drip left hiding in the hot tap. Those babies who resent being washed are probably best cleaned a little at a time rather than in one major splashdown. Those who really object can be wrapped firmly in a baby blanket, gently submerged then unpeeled like a parcel before washing. Some conscientious objectors may be won over if allowed to bath with Mum or Dad in the deep bath. This gives both comfort and cleanliness.

Once a little one is able to sit securely then certainly they can graduate to the big bath, though with care. You can try starting this any time after three months. If you do, put a rubber mat or old towel on the bottom of the bath to prevent a slippery child sliding from your grip, and obviously only fill the bath up a little way, running the cold water last. You can test the temperature with your elbow, which is probably the most sensitive part of your body that is conveniently available.

Most babies do well with a soap-free water wash. After all at this age they don't have quite the same body odours as their sweaty parents and a light sprinkling of water soon has them smelling like a rose. If you do use soap, make sure that it is a mild baby soap and only use it on bottoms and other heavily soiled areas. Baby oil leaves the skin clean and soft, but be careful when your little one is all oiled up like a Bondi lifesaver – one wrong move and he may shoot from your grasp like a cork from a champagne bottle.

A little bath oil can also be added to the bath water which helps to keep the skin soft. Baby oil can also be used but it leaves the bath slippery with an oil slick at the waterline as though a tanker has just sunk.

When it comes to washing the various parts of the body, use cotton wool steeped in clean water for round the eyes, and a bit of surgical spirit for drying up the remnants of the umbilical cord. The scalp can be cleaned with water, mild baby soap or baby shampoo depending on the need. It is best however to leave the ears alone. Many mothers have an irresistible human urge to poke cotton tips into delicate little orifices. Control yourself, it is not necessary and something might get damaged.

Baby clothes

Before birth you have no idea of the size or sex of your baby, let alone the sort of clothing gifts your friends will bring. The sensible thing is to wait and see what you need and when you do start buying, to check the labels to make sure the clothes are the easiest of easy care. It's fine to have a couple of smart show-off outfits that need handwashing and ironing, but all day-to-day clothing should be of the straight into the machine, out, dry and wear sort.

Different fabrics suit different children. Wool and pretend wool fabrics of acrylic can irritate, particularly those with a history of eczema. Cotton is about the most comfortable easy care material when used alone or in a cotton polyester combination. Little cotton singlets can double as T-shirts in the hot months and as warm undervests in the winter. The most useful of all baby clothing is the stretchsuit. This has the advantage of being both comfortable and appropriate to wear day or night. Of course Dad may need lessons on how to fasten the poppers!

Cloth bibs are a must to protect the clothes. Particularly if you have a messy baby who does not always keep milk down where it belongs. Knitted bootees are great for gift givers but are an utter nuisance. They are a fiddle to fasten and endless hours of motherhood will be spent crawling around the floor searching for the lost member of the duo.

In the first year shoes are only for show. Not only are they an awful waste of money, they inhibit walking and are about as much use to a human baby as floaties are to a duckling.

Dummies

Personally, I don't like dummies but if it's between your child being irritable and unsettled, or enjoying a peaceful existence with a dummy inserted, then it's dummies every time.

Dummies are no less hygienic than sucking on fingers, which tend to be poked into various unsavoury places. They are known to be much safer than the highly advertised adult comforter – cigarettes – and considerably more elegant than adult gum-chewing.

If you have an easy, happy infant, then please, no dummy. If you have an unsettled, irritable crier, then pop in a dummy and see what happens. But more of this in Chapter 16.

Carry cots, Moses baskets, slings and backpacks

For the first three months of life a basket or carry cot is all that Baby will need to call home. As well as being his sleeping site, it can also serve as his means of transport. Some models come with a folding base on wheels so that they double as a pram and make for a more portable sleeping platform.

Slings can be used from the earliest weeks and are a method of carrying small babies which is as old as time itself. The simplest sling is in the form of a blanket tied round your neck or waist. The cheapest commercial model is a cloth front pack as sold by your local baby shop. Slings and packs suit most children, especially the ones with a grumbling, active temperament who like to be on the move. They afford closeness while at the same time free up Mum's arms so that she can get on with other things.

After about three months, when head control starts to strengthen, a framed backpack may be the answer, especially for the fell walking family.

Prams and pushchairs

The old-fashioned English pram is now a somewhat outdated mode of transport. It is expensive, heavy and usually doesn't fold up, making it a no-no on just about all fronts. You would need to be planning a big family to get a really worthwhile return from such an investment, though I suppose your little one could always convert it into a go-cart sometime down the track.

There's really no great advantage to a pram over the more versatile carry cot on wheels. They may have a less finely tuned form of suspension, but

they are so much more portable and can be folded to put in the boot of a car. At about three months, it's time to purchase a pushchair. These are a must for every young child. They are light, fold neatly, are easily pushed and let your nosey youngster see where he is going in life. You will usually get at least three years of service out of them which must make them one of the best investments you will make for your baby.

There are also double buggies on the market, which are useful not just for twins, but if you have a toddler in tow as well. Both can be transported together with the toddler walking for a while and then hopping in beside the baby for a bit of a rest. These have a great payload capacity when it comes to carting children and the shopping.

Car seats

Car travel is one of the great hazards of our modern-day lives, with injury affecting both adults and children. You must think about car safety right from the very first trip home from the hospital and never lower your standards from that moment on.

Until recently a carry cot strapped in the back seat with a special safety net over it was the favoured way to transport little ones. Now the accident prevention experts will only accept a car seat.

Specially designed, rear-facing, baby seats can be held in place with a three point safety belt, either in the back or front passenger seat. The latest designs can be safely used from birth and have the advantage that the baby is securely strapped into a seat that is then strapped into the car. Some seats are approved for use from birth to around five years so are well worth the initial investment.

Whatever car safety arrangements you choose to make, the single most important thing is that you use them in every journey you make, however short. The Child Accident Prevention Trust (20 Portland Place, London W1N 4DA. 0171–636 2545) can advise you. They also have a register for car seat loan schemes, both commercial and non-profit making, throughout the U.K.

Make a firm commitment that each time you go out in the car **the journey will not start until all seat belts are fastened. Never let children roam around the car unrestrained and never ever sit a child on your knee in the front seat.**

Car doors should be locked, preferably with child safety locks. Don't leave a child unattended in a car, and certainly never on a hot day.

Baby bouncers and baby walkers

The baby bouncer is relatively cheap and a must for most parents. It consists of a metal frame covered in cloth which props the baby up at an angle of 45 degrees and gives him a little bit of bounce. This lets him get up and see the world from a more interesting level. It is useful for feeding and allowing play with toys. They are light and portable and once the baby is strapped in he can be easily carried from room to room and can watch Mum as she works. Just be careful putting the bouncer on table tops or kitchen workbenches. Children love being up that high as it makes it easier for them to see what is going on, but unless the bouncer is clamped on with 100 per cent security it only takes one bounce too many and down will come bouncer, baby and all, often with major injury. Bouncers are for the floor and not recommended for lifting.

There is no shortage of movement contraptions for babies. They range from the upmarket clockwork cot to the more common baby bouncer. This latter gadget hangs the child from a doorframe like a parachutist suspended on springs. They may be of some benefit to the bored overactive baby but are unnecessary for the average baby.

The baby walker is a mobile seat on wheels which allows little ones to sit upright and skate about the room. They are of most use for active, irritable babies who get extremely bored in the months before walking starts. These babies want to be upright and on the move but do not have the wherewithal to achieve this by themselves.

All child safety organizations strongly oppose the sale and use of baby walkers. However I still see a place for them as a sanity saver, when landed with one of these extremely demanding and irritable infants. If used, the dangers must be addressed, then the infant carefully supervised and restricted to an area far from steps, fire, flexes and danger.

Toys and mobiles

Little babies need few toys. In the early months it is their own bodies that give them the most enjoyment as first they discover their ten fascinating fingers followed by ten equally fascinating toes. These are good for chewing and waving about for hours at a time.

Babies are initially very visually interested. Mobiles hung over cots or change tables are a really cheap source of entertainment. By four months shaking rattles or playing with toys hung from the cot side is fun and at six months they can take hold of toys, change them from hand to hand and generally pop them in the mouth for a good chew.

Cuddly toys may look sweet but probably appeal more to the parents than they do to the very young. Just make sure that whatever you buy is chew-proof and won't come apart into dangerous-sized pieces of stuffing that can be swallowed or inhaled.

Nowadays it seems almost compulsory for every child in the western world to have some sort of shape-insertion game. I don't know if this speeds learning at all, but I do know from painful experience that walking barefoot on the inserts at 3 am brings a parent to full consciousness very quickly.

Don't go overboard with buying toys. What children of this age really need can't be bought. What they need is not toys to play with, but loving parents to play with them.

Conclusion

The tools of your trade will depend very much on what you can afford. If you place safety and usefulness at the top of your list, then you won't go far wrong. Never be ashamed to borrow or use preloved equipment. It makes sound sense.

9
Think Safety

THERE is always a tendency to believe that accidents are something that happen to other people. They couldn't possibly happen to us but of course, as you know, this isn't the case. We live in a hazardous world and no matter how careful we try to be there is always going to be risk.

In this chapter let's look at some of the main areas of danger for babies and see what can be done to lessen these risks.

Household Dangers

For the first five months babies are pretty immobile and any accidents they may suffer are generally adult generated. At about the twentieth week they will start to roll around the floor and this is when child-proofing has to start. The real danger comes when they learn to stand and then nothing that is remotely within their reach is safe. At this age children have no thought as to the consequences of their actions and it is up to we parents to protect them. Trying to educate small babies to such dangers is really an uphill battle.

Some suggestions for home safety:

- When your baby starts to walk, tape and pad dangerously sharp corners of furniture.
- Down-going steps should be fitted with a secure safety gate which should always be kept closed.
- Safety plugs should be fitted into power points.
- All homes should have a life protecting safety switch fitted to the main power board.
- Smoke detectors, with regularly replaced batteries, are essential.
- Dishwasher detergent is especially caustic, yet often within reach of a crawling child.
- Knives, glasses and other sharp objects should all be kept well away.
- All fires should be guarded and dangling flexes kept out of reach.
- Towards the end of the first year, toddler-proof the house. Immobilise some cupboards with locks, or tape and hide temptations.
- Dangerous household substances like drain cleaner, caustic soda, or such-like are best discarded altogether, but if you must keep them then make sure they are kept under high security.
- Never leave medicines within reach or in cupboards that a child can climb up to. Always keep them in a place that can be locked.
- With most household accidents concerning infants it is the changing speed of mobility which usually fools the parents. From five months to ten months an immobile child suddenly becomes a very active and inquisitive one.

Scalds

I mention scalds specifically since these are a major problem with babies. The main causes are either parents spilling hot drinks on the wriggling baby on their knee, or, later on, when cups, jugs and saucepans are pulled down on top of the upright and unthinking explorer.

Some suggestions to avoid scalds:

- Try and avoid cooking and nursing your baby both at the same time.
- Don't drink hot liquids while you have Baby on your knee.
- Don't leave coffee cups or other hot containers on low tables or at the edge of tables or benches once your baby has become mobile.
- Don't leave jug or kettle cords dangling over the edge of kitchen benches.

- Always turn the handles of saucepans inwards when they are on the stove.
- Be careful if microwaving a baby's bottle – it can get an awful lot hotter than you think.
- Turn the bath taps firmly off and always run a little cold water last.
- Turn down the thermostat on the hot water system. You need water to wash, not to sterilise your dishes.

Baths and water

Although it is the inquisitive toddler who is most at risk when it comes to water, babies also need some care. At this age the greatest danger comes from baths and shallow containers.

Some suggestions to avoid water accidents:

- **Never leave a baby unattended in the bath.** If the phone rings bring the baby with you.
- **Never leave a baby in or near a paddling pool unattended.**
- Keep the lid firmly on the nappy bucket or keep it out of reach. Buckets can claim little lives when babies climb up on them and tumble in.
- Don't trust other young children to supervise the bathing of your baby.
- Always be supervigilant when near pools or any water. It can take only seconds to drown and often you don't hear a thing.

The baby bouncer

This cloth-covered frame provides an uplifting experience for most babies who can now get up and look the world straight in the eye.

I find this form of elevation particularly good for irritable, active babies and many parents find they get far more peace if their baby is up in his bouncer on a table or bench beside them while they work. But a word of warning . . . bouncers on these sorts of surfaces can become a real hazard. One bounce too many and they will slide and down they will fall.

These were never designed to be lifted off the floor and if you must raise them only do so if they are 100 per cent securely attached. If you can't fasten them properly to the table or bench top then leave them on the floor.

Bouncers may bounce, but babies who fall don't!

Baby walkers

The baby walker is a frame on wheels into which you strap the pre-walking child so that he can totter round the floor. All childcare experts are now totally opposed to baby walkers.

Personally I believe that the average baby must not have them. But I admit that they have great benefits for the demanding, impossibly irritable baby who is fed up being an immobile infant and wants to start mixing with the world. With mobility and elevation comes some peace for the most difficult of these. Baby walkers are dangerous. Here are some tips if you are going to use one:

- Don't use a baby walker if there are stairs, steps or different levels in the area of use.
- Make sure that all fires are securely guarded.
- Be especially careful of what is now within your baby's reach. Remember that the baby walker has lifted the baby upright and now dangers on benchtops and tables are easily got at.

Change tables

It's nice to be able to change little babies as they lie still at waist level and you don't have to stoop. However as the baby becomes more active and starts to roll and wriggle this elevated situation presents some risks.

A few hints for safety on the change table:

- Makes sure you have all the necessary gear at hand before you change a wriggler.
- Never turn your back on any potential mover.
- Use the floor to change very athletic infants, they can't fall off that!

Safety in Cars

No matter how careful a driver you are, the roads are always a potential danger. You may not make any mistakes, but there is always some other idiot around who might.

All you can do is to think safety. This should start right from the time you take your baby home from the hospital. Having set the trend, never compromise with car safety thereafter. Have proper car restraints fitted and establish a rigid law that they be used at all times and that the car never moves until *all* belts and straps have been securely fastened.

Some suggestions for car safety:

- At birth obtain an approved rear-facing baby seat. These can be bought or hired. For details contact your local maternity hospital, children's hospital or motoring organisation. When possible this is best attached in the centre of the rear seat.

- If you are travelling with your children in a car which has no proper restraints, ask yourself first if the trip is really necessary. If there is no alternative, young babies should be nursed in the rear seat, **never** in the front. Older infants can use the centre lap strap and children should **never** share a seat belt with an adult.
- If you have to leave the car for any reason, try to take your children with you. If they have to be left, make sure that the windows are open to allow a sufficient amount of air into the car, and make sure you are not away for long.
- Don't travel if the driver is drowsy or is liable to get drowsy, and under no circumstances allow any family member to travel in a car with a driver who has had too much to drink. You owe it to your family to be well within the legal alcohol limit when you take the wheel. You may be able to fool the breathaliser, but if you injure your family you'll be fooling no-one.
- Speed is a factor in many accidents. If you have children in the car, travel at sensible speeds. Save lives not seconds!

Sunburn

Babies can easily get too much sun. It is important that right from birth they get shade, sunhats and sunblock creams. Lack of care now will ruin the skin, to leave them looking like a prune by the age of thirty, to say nothing of the danger of skin cancer.

Some rules for your baby outdoors:

- Keep him out of direct sun.
- Cover his shoulders and arms and use a hat.
- Overuse sun creams rather than underuse them
- Never leave a baby in the sun in a car.
- On really hot days try not to travel with your baby.

When Parents Snap

All human beings have their breaking point. For some it's always close at hand, others seem to be able to take far more punishment before it is reached. There would be very few parents with an irritable, whinging baby who have not at some time pulled themselves up, very aware of just how close they have been to doing something they might regret. There's no point being pious about this. Let's be sensible when the going gets tough.

When things get difficult:

- If you feel you're losing control quickly load up the buggy and get out of the house. Crying and whinging never sound quite so bad in the open air and a baby is unlikely to come to any physical harm when in the public gaze.
- If stuck at home and the situation has reached boiling point, put your baby safely into his cot, close the door and go to another room until you have regained control.
- Ring a friend or a counselling service.
- Try to get your partner home to bail you out.
- Go to a friend's home.

First Aid

All parents should have at least a basic knowledge of first aid which should include heart-lung resuscitation, and every home should carry a first aid kit with all the usual tweezers, bandaids, bandages, etc. Another useful addition is a bottle of ipecac to induce vomiting should Baby swallow certain poisons.

If your baby has swallowed a poisonous substance, ring your doctor or take him to your local casualty department immediately. Take the tablets or liquid with you to help identification. Don't induce vomiting unless advised to by a doctor.

As the child safety organisations say – child safety should be no accident.

10

Not Another Nappy!

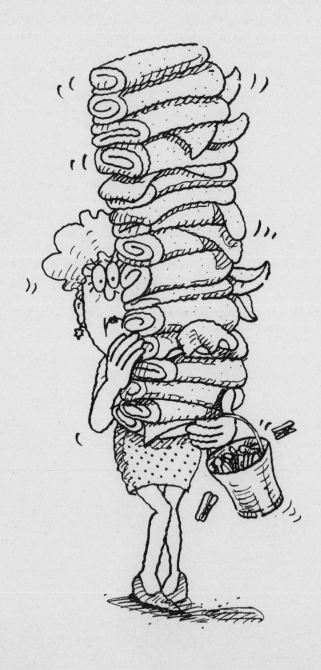

IT is a well-known scientific fact that what you pour in the top end of your baby is sooner or later going to emerge at the other end. Most parents won't be surprised (or pleased) to hear that every baby soils or soaks about ten nappies every twenty-four hours and that this will go on day after day for at least the next two years. A quick bit of adding-up shows that you are now faced with a massive waste disposal project where you will change between 7000 and 8000 nappies before drought conditions finally set in. This is just one of the many joys of parenthood, to be coped with as practically as possible. If you set out to make life easy for yourself you won't regret it. Here are a few tips to start things off:

- Have a waist-high, no-stoop change table.
- Leave wipes, lotions and all gear within easy reach.
- Have nappy buckets with smell-proof lids to catch the discards.
- Have a rubbish bin which can cope with moist waste.
- Leave a few nappies folded ready to use.
- If funds permit, buy some extra nappies to take the pressure off crisis washing.
- Use nappy-soak fluids and try only to wash in batches.
- Use disposable nappies for long journeys.
- If you can afford it, investigate the options of a nappy service or disposable nappies.

If you were a lord or a lady, a little bell would be rung at the first squelch or leak, and Nanny would appear to do the honours. You would never need to get too intimately involved with a dirty bottom. However, if you are like the rest of us, then you'd better get used to doing the job yourself, because no-one else is going to. Let's look at the basics of nappies and see how we can make things as easy as possible.

The traditional towelling square

I think that if I were a baby I would prefer to be snuggled up in a soft towelling nappy (though I can't remember this from personal experience).

The traditional nappy is surely the most comfortable for your baby and the most economical too! In the 'good old days' when you were expected to boil all your dirty nappies to kill off all the germs, nappy washing was hard work. Now, with washing machines a good hot mechanical wash will do all the germ killing for you.

If the nappies have been soaking for a while they should ideally get a quick spin first, followed by a rinse and then a hot wash. Any sort of washing powder will do just as long as the nappy is rinsed out properly. Fabric softeners which make dry nappies feel much fluffier on little bottoms, rarely irritate babies and are probably worth adding. After they have been washed and dried, leave a few folded and ready to put on.

To cope with the average nine to ten changes a day you are going to need at the very least two-dozen towelling nappies. Another dozen would certainly help ease the pressure and keep you in business when wet weather prevents nappies from drying. Don't be too proud to accept a second-hand bundle from a friend whose children have moved on to better things. You can never really have enough.

If you are planning to have a large family, be generous with the number of nappies you allow yourself. At the end of your child-rearing activities they will probably be worn down to their last threads, but will still make excellent towels to clean up after messy toddlers (and you'll certainly need lots of these!).

The tailored nappy

When I mention tailored nappies, I don't mean that you should get on the phone and ask Pierre Cardin round to measure Baby's inside leg. I mean nappies that are cut to size, easy to fasten and which have all the padding situated over the site of the main leak.

Why doesn't everyone use designer nappies? Well, to start with they are rather more expensive than other types, which is always a discouragement. But the main reason is that the thick padded areas make drying very slow. After an hour on the line they are still wet while their towelling counterparts are already as dry as a bone.

These nappies often have cotton ties at the sides rather than the usual safety pin, which seems to me to be amazingly sensible. But still they have never really caught on.

Disposable nappies

These come in a great many varieties, but the basic raw materials in all of them are the same – paper from innumerable trees and plastic made from oil. Since each nappy requires a small branch and a cupful of crude to manufacture, they may be throwaway but the price certainly isn't.

Each manufacturer claims that their brand has superior design characteristics, greater economy, leak-free legs, smarter tying facilities or whatever. Their aim, of course, is to win you away from the traditional towelling squares and to save you from all that washing. Well, if they are all that good, why don't we give the washing machine a rest and go for disposables?

For a start they are considerably more expensive and in some places can prove difficult to dispose of. Garbage bins will quickly get full and smelly and if you are foolish enough to try and flush them down the toilet, you'll soon be calling the plumber to grab his cleaning rods and declog your drains. A few such obstructions and you will have spent almost as much as it costs for a good laundry service.

The paper of which these nappies are made is also rather fragile and needs to be encased in plastic. Though generally not quite as tight as a pair of plastic pants, the lack of ventilation will cause nappy rash in quite a number of children.

However, if your baby is happy enough and you can afford them and your local dustbin men are on side, then it's probably worth your while to find the supermarket or pharmacy that has the cheapest deal. Less than 30 per cent of U.K. mums now use the traditional towelling nappy, and there are more than a dozen brands of disposables to choose from. Many supermarkets and chemist chains have their own brand, as do Mothercare. Prices vary among the brands considerably, although it does seem that you get what you pay for in terms of effectiveness. It is always cheaper to buy in bulk if you can, and both Boots and Mothercare have a free home delivery service for purchases over a certain quantity. At the same time, check out the price of your local nappy service. You may find it is cheaper. (See the comparison of costs on page 93.)

Nappy service

There are obvious attractions to flinging dirty nappies into a sealed container and giving them no further thought until they return the following week all fluffy, clean and smelling fresh as the clear spring air. Most large cities have nappy services and it seems that on average they cost about 30 per cent more than the very cheapest disposable nappies but considerably less than the most expensive throwaway models. If you cannot stand dirty nappies and money is not too tight, then why not check in your phone book or with your local branch of the NCT for your nearest nappy service. You may be surprised to find that it's not as expensive as you thought.

Nappy liners

There are two commonly used sorts of nappy liner, the 'keeps Baby's bottom feeling dry' type and the disposable 'let's not handle the major movements' type.

The dry bottom type is said to pump the wet through into the nappy leaving the child convinced he is dry. This all sounds too good to be true, but it is certainly worth considering in the early months when the nappy situation is pretty fluid. They're not all that expensive, are easily washed and are dry as soon as they hit the clothes line.

The disposable model is just a cheap rectangle of material which lines the nappy and makes cleaning up somewhat less difficult for the delicate. You don't use both together as the disposable square obviously blocks the one-way filter so you will have to opt for one or the other.

In the early months when Baby's skin is delicate and things are generally fluid, it's probably best to start with the one-way liner. Once weaning starts and bowel movements become more solid then the disposables come into their own. Mind you, I doubt whether your child will know or care if you use neither.

Plastic pants

Grandma cuddles tightly to her little angel. Squelch! Drip! It's like squeezing a lemon!

Wet towelling nappies are not much fun when you try to get intimate. They leave you with a wet knee and the baby permanently smells like a hot day at the fish market.

One way to head for hygiene and dryness is to use a pair of plastic pants to cover the wet sponge of a nappy. After all, if plastic pants stop leaks and wet patches, why shouldn't they be used all the time? The only problem with this otherwise sensible suggestion is that they raise the risk of rash. Not only do they protect the clothes but they trap moisture. Soon the inside humidity is approaching that of the Central Congo Basin and before you know it the sensitive baby has a nasty case of nappy rash. Others seem totally immune and must have bottoms as tough as a hippo's hide.

If your baby's skin is in any way delicate then use plain nappies at home and keep the plastic pants for dressing up or going out. You don't need a degree in medicine to know which children have the tough hides and which are the sensitive ones. (See page 91 for more on nappy rash.)

Cloth pants are now available to cover wet nappies. These provide reasonable squelch protection, yet spare little bottoms from nappy rash. They are more expensive than plastic, but generally a better buy.

Nappy soak fluids

Such fluids are by no means a necessity, but they certainly to make life easier. Anything that makes second-hand nappies more pleasant to handle can't be bad and it's nice to think that the cleaning process has started while they're sitting waiting to be washed. If nothing else it helps dispel some of your guilt about that pile glowering at you in the corner of the laundry! The nappies should be left in the solution for at least six hours, but no longer than twenty-four. Replace the solution daily as the cost is not excessive.

Cleaning fluids

The most popular cleaning fluid for a baby's bottom is piped right into your home. It is none other than tap water and should be used with either a very mild soap or, preferably, no soap at all.

Nappy change lotions of the commercial variety are much dearer, but are convenient, portable, smell nice and can give some skin protection. They also have the advantage of keeping your own hands soft. Modern pre-wet tissues are convenient and the majority are gentle to delicate skin.

Nappy buckets

Nappy buckets are a necessity. I mean large buckets with lids that keep the sight and smell of soiled nappies well out of the way. They also make life a good deal simpler.

The wet nappies go straight in without a second thought, while the soiled ones need a quick scrape or removal of the nappy liners, and then splash, in they go too. You can even have one bucket for wet ones, and another for the soiled so that the wet nappies can get a separate light wash and the soiled ones can have a hotter going over. But few of us are that organised.

The buckets should be filled with nappy soak fluid and the nappies should be washed in batches once they have had enough time to soak and you have sufficient numbers to make washing worthwhile. If you haven't got a bucket, a large, securely tied, polythene bag will suffice.

If you have a baby who is starting to get up on his feet, make sure that bucket lids are firmly in place. Little ones have been known to fall forward and become dangerously stuck in these fluid-filled buckets.

Change tables

You can change nappies lying Baby on a towel on the floor if you want to, but this involves an awful lot of kneeling and stooping. After two years your knees will be nearly worn out from going up and down more times each day than the most devout monk at a monastery.

Your options are: a towel on a normal table, a change mat, or one of the custom-built self-supporting jobs. The towel on a table is certainly simple and saves your back, but there is always the danger of an active baby rolling off on to the floor. These rollers may be best changed on the floor as they can't fall any further.

You can put a special change mat on a bed or table. This is relatively cheap, easily washed and has low sides which gives some protection to the young roller. At the top of the range, you can buy a special change table which is designed at just the right height, has a built-in anti-roll device and folds away when you are finished. Whatever you use, it is much easier for you when kept at waist height.

Fancy fold nappies

I don't intend to go into all the twenty-odd ways there are of folding a nappy. I leave that to the origami teachers. Suffice to say that there are a number of different ways and everybody will claim that theirs is the most effective. No one way is really any better than another.

If I were you I would start with the universal kite fold. If you begin to feel adventurous later, there are a few other suggestions at the back of this book (see page 235), or try out your friends' favourite folds.

Wrigglers

Twisters, rollers, wrigglers and kickers are not really a problem in the first six months of nappy change, but after this you can find yourself with your hands full. At one year some are amazingly strong, whilst the eighteen-monthers can be as difficult to hold down as the Incredible Hulk on the mat.

Don't ever let wriggling and kicking be seen as a game. It may seem like great fun at noon, but at 3 am it has lost all spectator appeal. Don't start something now that will later become a rod to your back.

Before you change a wriggler be sure that all the gear you need is prepared and ready to go. Have the new folded nappy out flat and then with speed and single-minded determination, get in and out quickly.

I have heard of some hard to hold babies who are changed tummy down with the nappy arrangement suitably altered. I suppose this enables you to hold the child in something like a half nelson while the necessary adjustments are made, but it must be no easy matter.

The solution to the problems of the athletic wriggler is pre-planning, speed, single-mindedness and never letting it become a game.

Nappy rash

The proper medical term for nappy rash is ammonia dermatitis. This says it all. It's an inflammation of the skin caused by ammonia in the nappy area.

In its mildest form, the skin becomes a bit red. When more severe, the skin thickens, wrinkles, cracks and may become ulcerated. Secondary infection, especially with thrush (monilia) is very common.

Freshly passed urine contains no ammonia but lots of urea which is pretty inert and would not upset even the most delicate of skins. However, once it has sat in the nappy for a while, certain bacteria break it down to ammonia. These busy bacteria are the harmless bugs that live in the normal gut and are always in high supply around the nappy area. There they lurk, just waiting to turn uninteresting inert urea into caustic ammonia.

The whole process is accelerated by warmth and an environment of high humidity. Put a pair of plastic pants over a wet nappy and this raises the humidity and holds in the heat by its blockage of evaporation. Now the bugs whistle away, overjoyed at such an ideal working environment. Change to a dry nappy, rinse the bottom or leave it all exposed to the air and they are out of work. Obviously the longer they have to act, the more of the urea will be broken down. Also, the longer the ammonia is in contact with the skin, the more damage it is likely to do.

Understanding this process explains why a newly wet nappy will smell fresh like the morning dew, but leave it for five hours with the bugs, and it will pong like a sunbathing fish.

Each baby is born with an individual sensitivity to nappy rash. Some become red within an hour, while others are unmarked after a long night of sodden sleep. It is often the 'good' baby who suffers most. He will sleep quietly all night. If he had screamed, a couple of changes would have been necessary before dawn.

Well, what can be done to prevent and treat nappy rash? There are a number of practical things you can do:

- Change wet and soiled nappies as soon as possible.

- Rinse the bottom well with water to remove excess urine and bacteria. Then dry well.

- Make sure that you have enough nappies. Don't be a Scrooge when it comes to changing.

- Avoid plastic pants. Use cloth ones instead.

- Avoid cheap disposable nappies if rash is a problem.

- Use a skin-protective product. Either one of the trade names advised by your chemist or the always reliable zinc and castor oil cream. These protect the skin's own natural oils and create a barrier to keep the ammonia away from where it can cause damage.

- Night-time is when the baby's bottom is most at risk of rash. When preparing for bed, take extra care. Wash and dry carefully then apply a liberal coat of protective cream. A one-way nappy liner may be used and changed as soon as possible in the morning. Where rash is a real problem, changes during the night may be necessary.

- Remember the basic rule. To have a nappy rash, first you need a wet nappy. When a rash is really bad, little bottoms need frequent changes or to be left exposed to air. Where there is no nappy in place it helps healing but is not very practical if you have a fully carpeted home.

- If you have tried all these suggestions but the rash persists or gets worse then it's time to seek help from your health visitor or family doctor. It is probable that a prescription treatment is needed and very likely that there is secondary infection with thrush (monilia).

Thrush

Thrush (monilia) is often a troublesome free-loader on the nappy rash which makes it hard to heal. Often, it is completely unnoticed, though sometimes it will have the appearance of raised round patches all over the nappy area. Sometimes it affects the creases. When in doubt, it's best to treat it anyway.

Treatment involves an antifungal cream e.g. Mycostatin (Nystatin), Canesten (Clotrimazole) or a steroid/canesten mixture e.g. Hydrozole which requires a doctor's prescription. If you're not sure which approach to take, then consult your health visitor or doctor.

Conclusion

If you have a baby, you have to have nappies. Use the type that suits your pocket and lifestyle. Make things as easy as possible for yourself. There are going to be at least 7000 changes before you're finished. Nappy rash is extremely common and often strikes the best babies. Change your baby regularly, keep him dry, clean him well, waterproof the skin and where it becomes a problem, avoid plastic pants. A rash on your baby's bottom is a sign of sensitive skin, not bad parenting.

Disposable nappies
- These come in various sizes, makes and designs.
- There is a price difference between your chemist's discount offer, the supermarket special and the full retail price.
- Large packs are much more economical.
- At the time of writing, the cheapest nappy costs about 7p, but you could pay as much as 12p for something similar.
- Over a year this comes to between £218.40 and £374.40.
- Shop around and always buy the larger packs.
- Check on the cost of a nappy service. It may cost no more and think of the trees you'll save from the pulp mill.

Nappy services
- Look under Nappy Service in the telephone directory.
- Most companies require at least a one-month contract.
- The recommendation is for sixty (girls) and seventy (boys) nappies each week.
- Soiled nappies are scraped, no nappies need to be rinsed.
- Each nappy costs on average 9p but prices vary considerably.
- Over a year this represents £270.

11

Feeding the Natural Way

FEEDING little humans is an operation which has been elevated to the status of a science, way above its rightful place. There was a time when mothers were content doing what felt right and came naturally to them, but now they are bedevilled by doubts as they read the mountains of literature churned out on baby feeding. After all, dogs seem to feed their puppies quite successfully without consulting anyone and most animals thrive without reading a single book.

But when it comes to human babies, for some reason the whole matter takes on a degree of complication which practically requires a university degree to sort out. In these next three chapters let's demystify feeding. Let's separate what's useful information from what's just hot air and return feeding to its rightful position as a simple and natural part of life.

Breast or bottle?

There is no doubt that there are definite advantages to breast-feeding. There is, on the other hand, no doubt that bottle-fed babies will thrive equally well in most aspects of physical and emotional health.

The decision on how you are going to feed your baby is yours and yours alone. Never allow noisy activists to force you into doing something you don't want to do. Reluctant breast-feeding will always be a chore and will do no good to anyone, whilst mothers persuaded to bottle-feed reluctantly will also be unhappy in the long run.

If you are uncertain as to what to do always opt for the breast. You can always stop if it doesn't work out and change to a bottle, but you can rarely do a swap the other way round.

Breast-feeding – the advantages

Safe, clean and transportable

It is in countries with unreliable water supplies, poor hygiene and no refrigeration that babies gain the maximum benefit from breast-feeding. The breast is the most efficiently packaged milk container ever designed. It is safe, clean, transportable and always at the correct temperature.

Enjoyment and satisfaction

It's all pretty subjective, but most mothers who voluntarily breast-feed seem to enjoy the experience. What's more those who feed their first baby this way will rarely have it any other way the next time around.

Convenience

Breast milk is instant self-serve. There is no need to sterilise equipment, make up formulas or warm containers. This is convenient for Mum, who can feed her baby where and when she pleases. I suppose most fathers also find it pretty convenient as they can remain the sleeping partner when it comes to the night shift.

Infection protection

As well as avoiding bottles and water that may not always be clean, breast milk itself contains some substances that endow some protection from infection. These are antibodies that pass to the baby's gut, strengthening it against some gastro bugs. At the same time breast milk itself breaks down in the stomach to form a homely environment which encourages benign bugs to multiply and, as they do, crowd out other dangerous intruders. In third world countries, bottle-fed babies have a very poor chance of survival.

Many researchers claim that breast-feeding also gives some protection against other infections, and is also associated with lessening the risk of cot death (S.I.D.S.).

Natural is best

Presumably after a few million years of evolution cow's milk has been refined to suit little *cows* best, goat's milk to suit little goats, and therefore human's milk to suit little humans. Of course babies can thrive well on other varieties, but it would seem sensible to use the product recommended by the manufacturer.

Body contact and bonding

You don't have to breast-feed to bond with your baby. If this was necessary, fathers and grandparents could never fall in love with the baby and all adoptions would fail. Closeness, however, is important in developing any strong relationship and you can't get much closer than when you're breast feeding.

Cost

It's a popular belief that bottle-feeds are expensive and breasts are free, but don't be fooled, there's not much you get for free these days. Each mother will have to consume 750 extra calories (3100 kilojoules) a day to keep up the flow. That's fine so long as you eat sensibly, but spoil yourself with connoisseur cuts and you might exceed the cost of bottle-feeding!

The baby's view

To be honest no-one has yet managed to get a definite answer from a newborn baby about his preference, but I can make an educated guess. If I were a baby, given the choice between a warm, soft breast attached to a warm soft mum and a cold rubber teat left soaking in liquid which tastes like old swimming-pool water, I know what I'd choose. Babies aren't stupid!

Breast-feeding – the disadvantages

A solitary pursuit

This book is all about families, relationships and shared parenting, but breast-feeding is not really an activity to share. OK, Dad can change the nappies and bring the baby to Mum at 3 am, but it still isn't an equal division of labour. Being unable to let others share the feeding also limits Mum's freedom when it comes to leaving the baby. Some babies will take a bottle from the babysitter without complaint, but others just scream as they tell all in earshot that it's breast or nothing.

Effort and commitment

Successful breast-feeding doesn't just happen, it takes determination and effort to make it work. Anyone can bottle-feed, but breast-feeding needs commitment. This may be very natural, but it's a learned art.

Uncertainty

Anxious mothers who breast-feed have no easy way of seeing how much milk is being consumed. There are indirect methods of assessing this, but none with the visual impact of watching a full bottle becoming an empty one.

Transfer of medicine into milk

This is not some sort of divine intervention, but rather the concern that certain medicines taken by Mum can transfer through the milk to the baby. In fact only a few commonly used drugs are contra-indicated in breast-feeding, but we'll discuss that later.

Greater demand

As the comfort of the breast far exceeds that of a bottle, breast-fed babies may demand more feeds. This is good for the baby, but somewhat tiring for Mum, although the convenience of breast-feeding must compensate to some extent.

Militants

The 'breast is best' bicycle is frequently pedalled by militants who have all the vision of a blinkered horse. There is no doubt that breast-feeding is to be strongly recommended, but one of its greatest disadvantages has to be those people who try to ram it down your throat.

The physiology of feeding

There are three different stages in the process of breast-feeding. First of all, the breast needs to be prepared for the task that lies ahead and this is done by the action of the hormones of pregnancy. Next the glands in the breast need to start production of the milk. This happens after birth when the sucking of the breast sends messages to the mother's pituitary gland which then releases the hormone prolactin which makes milk. Lastly the milk that is made and sits in the glands must be released down to the nipple. This release is called 'the let down' and is brought about by the action of another pituitary hormone, oxytocin. This one is again activated by sucking, but also by emotional cues. It sounds complicated, but it goes like this.

Throughout pregnancy the breast was being primed, ready for action. You knew this was happening as the size changed and there was discomfort. At birth the breasts are larger but making little real milk. When the baby first

sucks he gets a substance called colostrum which is low in nourishment but is jam-packed with anti-infection antibodies. The sucking stimulates the pituitary gland and prolactin is made which sets the breast to make milk. It takes a bit of time for proper production but in three to four days milk will usually be in good supply. The more sucking and the emptier the breasts at the end of the feed, the more prolactin is made. Prolactin is inhibited by worry, tiredness or pain and so milk production may fall when any of these feelings occur.

The let down can feel like a pleasant tingling sensation that comes after about ten to thirty seconds of sucking or when just thinking about a feed. When a mum is really sensitive to this emotional cue the milk can be let down so fast that it can leak everywhere before you have got the baby near the breast. As oxytocin controls the let down and is the same hormone which is produced to make the uterus contract at birth, it's not surprising that afterpains are often felt in the early days of feeding.

Please don't get too bogged down in prolactin, pituitary, oxytocin and let downs. What you must know is that the best results come with ample sucking, good emptying and not too much emotional worry or tiredness.

If you think about it, breast-feeding is not unlike the financial management of any government department. You are given a certain volume of funds to spend. If you make sure you use every last penny and leave nothing to spare, then next time you will be rewarded with a bigger budget. If, however, you are an efficient, careful manager and save on your allowance, your reward is a cut in what's on offer next time. The same goes for breast-feeding. Constant demands and the use of the last drop establishes the best long-term flow.

Breast-feeding – the technique

Start by getting yourself comfortable. Feeding is going to take up a big whack of your time in the next half year so make it as easy and enjoyable as you can. The right posture in a suitable chair is important, for example, an old rocker.

In the early days the hospital staff will be encouraging regular periods of sucking. Remember that this is not a high nutrition nibble, the baby will get a bit of colostrum and minimal milk, but that's all he needs as he is born with quite a reserve of food aboard. What is important is the sucking which gives a major message to signal the start of milk production.

To start feeding you first need to get the baby's mouth to the breast. Touch the baby's cheek or lips gently with the nipple and with this he will automatically turn towards it. This is called the 'rooting reflex' and is one of those amazing bits of prebirth programming which ensures that little ones feed and survive. Now all they need is to be close to a source of food and off they go.

As the hungry baby approaches the breast, the mouth opens. If the mouth stays shut, nothing much is going to happen. With the mouth open and tongue down flat, move the baby on to the breast.

Put the nipple and an amount of the surrounding breast tissue in the mouth. When the baby has had enough he will come off the breast.

Initially there may be a little tenderness but feeding should not hurt. If it is painful, the baby is probably incorrectly attached and you should start again. To move the baby away, insert a little finger gently into the baby's mouth, break the suction and you have release.

When feeding is properly established your plan will be to feed for as long as it takes to empty the first breast, then burp and offer the other breast. Start each feed with the breast that was last used the previous time. This allows maximum stimulation and emptying to alternate. If you are as forgetful as the rest of us, put a safety pin round one bra strap and move it as a marker of where next to start.

With feeding you need a comfortable supporting nursing bra and ease of access clothes. Remember that there is nothing to be ashamed of with breast-feeding – it's very normal and natural. You don't need to feed behind locked doors. Forget your prudish modesty, you can do this discreetly almost anywhere.

Increasing the milk supply

As you try to get the feeding pattern going there are a number of ways to give your milk supply a boost. The mainstay of it all is effective sucking and emptying. When milk supply is low, expressing milk for five minutes manually gives extra stimulation and some to store in the freezer for emergencies.

If milk supply is not abundant when you are still in hospital then you must always feed your baby yourself at night, rather than letting him be given a bottle in the nursery. This does nothing for your tiredness but it keeps up stimulation and production. Try to avoid top-up bottles if you can. The road to failed breast-feeding is littered with complimentary feed bottles. Of course you must never become so militant about breast-feeding that your little one starves as a victim to the cause. If breast-feeding is obviously becoming an uphill struggle, there's nothing too smart about turning a pleasurable, natural process into an uncomfortable, scientific obsession. When uncertain which course to take you will get good guidance from your health visitor, doctor or breast-feeding counsellor.

Worry, tension and tiredness all rob you of milk output. Try not to let the worry about the adequacy of the milk supply become the reason why that supply is inadequate! Give it your best shot, but if it doesn't all come together than it's not the end of the world. Just try and relax, put your feet up, especially in the afternoon when tiredness is greatest, and let Nature take her course.

When feeding really starts to get going, you will be using about a litre (1.8 pints) of additional fluid each day and perhaps 3000 extra kilojoules (750 extra calories). There will be lots of spare kilojoules to turn to milk, but unless the fluids are kept flowing, milk production will drop off.

Is he getting enough?

With breast-feeding there is always one haunting unknown – how much is your baby actually getting? You know that your baby has latched on like a bomber refuelling over Libya but you don't know how much is passing down the tube. At least with bottle-feeding you can count the empties at the end of the day.

There are, however, a few indirect ways of gauging intake. Let's consider them.

Weight gain

You should expect a weight loss in Baby for about the first five days and then ever-improving weight gain. After the fifth day the gain should be about 30 g (1 oz) a day. As weight fluctuates with good and bad days, not too much can be read into one weighing. It's best to take a longer view over a one or two week period. Some very normal babies will gain more than their average 30 g (1 oz), others less. Weight gain is no more than a guide and though helpful you must never be ruled rigidly by the scales. (See weight gain on page 106.)

Contentment

The ideal baby has six feeds a day, sleeps for four hours between each one and is contented. The problem is that few of us seem to have ideal babies.

In the early weeks the normal well-fed baby feeds between six to twelve times a day, sleeps between one and six hours between meals and cries for between one and four hours in each twenty-four. With these figures it's always hard to know how contented a baby needs to be before you call him contented. There is also the problem of when he's irritable, not sleeping well and grizzly. Does this mean lack of food or is he just a grizzly little person? If you have an ideal baby then be reassured about feeding. If he is discontented then look at weight gain, the nappies and the overall appearance of the baby before blaming it all on hunger.

Nappies

What goes in the top must come out the bottom and if the nappies are pretty dry, fluid intake may be low. If there is a daily flood, then it has to be good. You should expect about six to eight good wets each day and if you have these, milk production should be fine.

Test feeding – an outdated technique

One millilitre of breast milk weighs approximately 1 g – or to put it the old-fashioned way, 1 fl oz of milk weighs 1 oz. Armed with this information and an accurate set of scales it is easy to calculate Baby's daily intake. Weigh your baby before the feed and again directly afterwards before changing the nappy. With a bit of simple subtraction, you should now be able to record the weight gain.

In the first few months the average intake should be approximately 150 ml for each kg of ideal body weight per day. (See the conversion chart on page 250.) I say ideal because we feed the overweight baby less and the thin baby more. This sounds really accurate, but it is not. Each breast-feed is of a different volume and you would need to test feed quite a few to get a clear picture. What's more, quantities vary from day to day and also the anxiety generated by test feeding may itself diminish the flow.

Try not to get too academic about breast-feeding. Most breast-feeders around the world seem to manage very well without a set of scales and an over supply of helpful advice. Try to relax, getting too concerned and scientific not only takes away the joy but ultimately the milk supply.

Common concerns

Does your baby need extra vitamins and fluoride?

It appears that the vitamin wheel has turned full circle. In the past it was not thought necessary to give babies extra vitamins. Then the gurus deemed it a good thing. Now we're back to advocating nothing extra again. If Mum has a good balanced diet then Nature can do the rest. If the baby isn't getting any vitamin-containing solids by eight months, then some vitamins are advisable after that age.

Additional fluoride is not given to the totally breast-fed baby, whether the local water is fluoridated or not.

Drugs and noxious substances in milk

In my more cynical moments I wonder whether breast milk is as pure as we like to think. The cow munches through a monotonous diet of grass which by rights is relatively unpolluted, that is, if the local nuclear reactor is in good working order. We humans, on the other hand, eat so much food that has been tarted up and fiddled with before it reaches us.

There are over 2000 legally permitted additives used to tart up our food and on top of them there is an army of pesticides and other pollutants from our high technology farming. Some of this must work its way into breast milk, though it is said to be benign.

When it comes to prescribed drugs, some will get into breast milk, but most stay out and have no effect on babies. While breast-feeding you should do as you did during pregnancy – only take medicines that are necessary and stay off drugs that you do not need, whether safe or not.

The following information is meant only as a rough guide to some commonly used drugs. However the literature changes from month to month and if you are in any doubt then don't hesitate to ask your doctor or pharmacist for an update.

Aspirin, paracetamol, Ventolin-type asthma drugs, iron, penicillin, amoxil-type antibiotics and most vitamins are safe. So if you have a headache, wheeze, sore throat or anaemia go ahead and treat it.

Sulphonamide antibiotics such as Bactrim or Septrin are of slight worry in the first weeks but safe later on.

Valium, Librium and other tranquillisers are generally quite safe in moderate doses but high levels are not recommended as they make a baby sleepy.

Anti-depressant drugs are mostly safe, but your doctor must check the specific brand before prescription.

Most anti-coagulants which stop blood clots such as warfarin and heparin are not a problem.

The anti-convulsants that we use for epilepsy are mostly safe and certainly safer than allowing an untreated mum to have a fit while nursing the baby. These medicines will have been given right through pregnancy and the levels a baby will get through the milk are minute in comparison with what would have been coming through the womb.

Alcohol passes into the milk but seems harmless in small quantities. Chronic alcoholics and binge drinkers are a hazard and should not breast-feed or have children at all.

Smoking reduces milk supply but not much of the pollutant actually enters the milk. I suppose the side-stream smoke from Mum or Dad will last for eighteen years and this is the real health hazard. Anything in the milk is trivial by comparison.

Marijuana and cannabis have so far not been deemed detrimental to babies, but no-one is completely sure of their long-term effects, so please play it safe.

Caffeine from tea or coffee is found in the milk but the amount is so minuscule that there are no hazards if these beverages are drunk in moderation.

Contraception and breast-feeding

As many mothers have learnt to their surprise, breast-feeding is not a reliable form of contraception. The thing is that until Mum's body gets back into shape, most other forms of contraception are equally unsuitable.

The standard combined two-part birth control pill (oestrogen and progesterone) is not a good idea. It disturbs milk flow and can have hormonal effects on the baby. The one-part progesterone only 'Mini Pill' seems to be pretty safe for Mum, Baby and milk supply.

The sensible thing is to let the body settle down for some months before starting to take any contraceptive pill. This is a good time for husbands to take responsibility for contraception.

Engorgement

In the first few days there is a drought of milk, but often when it comes it arrives in a flood. It will take some time to get this whole supply and demand mechanism in tune. In the meantime breasts may get overfull, become tense, lumpy and painful. If this goes on they soon become too tender and distended to allow sucking and then the situation gets really painful. Don't despair, this is only a temporary problem. Some excess pressure can be lost by manual expression of milk and once the edge is off the tension, sucking can resume. A comfortable bra is a necessity. Cold compresses are an old remedy that can provide a bit of pain relief. If a painful area of redness develops, this may suggest an infection (Mastitis). Antibiotics are probably needed, so consult your doctor.

Cracked nipples

In the early days of breast-feeding the nipples are vulnerable to small injuries or cracks in the skin.

The best course for cracked nipples is prevention. Ensure the babe is correctly attached, and don't pull the firmly fastened baby off the breast in mid-suck. Feed in a position which is comfortable for you and does not drag on the breast. Keep the breast area as dry as possible and ask your local health visitor or chemist for their recommended tube of nipple nourishment. Then there is the natural cure. Just rub a little breast milk on the area and let it dry. The milk fats soften the skin in their own gentle way.

Biters

This is obviously more of an eye opener for the mum who feeds long after the teeth are through than for those with little babies. Babies can't bite and suck at the same time, so they can't be too interested in feeding if they bite. Hold the head, insert your little finger and remove the baby from your breast. If he wants something to bite on, get a teething ring. He must realise that mums offer food and are not for nipping.

Afterpains

In the first days after birth the uterus will still be enlarged and pretty responsive to any strong hormones. Oxytocin is the hormone which sets the milk flowing and this is the same one that caused the contractions of the uterus during birth. So don't be surprised when crampy pains occur at feed times. This is only a temporary worry, so there's no need to rush out and get your appendix removed!

When and how to stop

Once feeding is going well it seems a pity to stop before four months and not go on for most of the first year. The important thing is to do your own thing. If you and Baby are happy then get on with it and ignore the brainwashing of others.

Recently I was lecturing in my old home town of Belfast and did a phone-in for a local radio station. One upset mum rang to ask whether she should stop breast-feeding her two-year-old. 'Do you want to stop?' I asked. 'It's all my family and friends who think I should,' she replied. 'Are you enjoying feeding?' I said. 'Oh, yes.' 'Is the toddler also enjoying it?' 'He certainly is.' 'Well as far as I am concerned you can feed him until he goes to high school,' I replied, tongue in cheek. Both mother and interviewer loved the reply, but once off air the BBC were bombarded with calls from listeners who felt that my suggestion was obscene.

Whether obscene or not, it is true. It's entirely up to you. You must feed for as long as you wish, the only limits are to introduce some extra iron and vitamin-containing food as well as the milk by eight months and give something with texture to accustom your child to chew and swallow by nine months. When it does come to stopping, however, you have the choice of gradual withdrawal or going cold turkey and stopping with a bang.

The gentle way is more comfortable, natural and to be advised. You start introducing solids between four and six months. At first the amounts will be so small that it will take over a month before you get enough in each feed to knock the edge off your baby's appetite. Then, if you want to stop breast-feeding you should increase other fluids, leaving the breast as the comfort at the end of a fine meal, rather like a glass of brandy for the adult gourmet. Soon the only breast-feed will be given to soothe Baby to sleep. This provides more comfort than kilojoules, and before long you should be able to stop altogether. If you want to be even more gentle, then introduce solids and when other fluids are needed you can wean your baby straight on to a cup. It's up to you.

The tough method involves determination, discomfort and is only necessary if feeding has to stop quickly for some medical or other reason. If you stop all sucking and emptying, within a week milk supply will cease. The first few days will be extremely uncomfortable. To see this through, both Mum and her breasts will all need good support.

Infant feeding

Demand feeding is the rule today. Whether breast- or bottle-fed, 'they get it when they want it'.

Approximate volumes of milk taken

Birth to one week: A small intake initially (e.g. 60 ml per kg body weight per day), increasing to full quantity by day five to seven.

One week to four months: Average intake 150 ml per kg body weight per day. (Usual range 120–180 ml per kg.)

Four months to one year: Reduces gradually from 150 ml per kg at four months to about 100 ml per kg body weight at one year.

Average number of feeds each day

Six feeds per day in first two months.

Four to five feeds per day thereafter.

Remember it is demand feeding and the demand may be four to eight per day.

Average weight gain

Birth to one week: In the first two to three days up to 10% of the birth weight is lost but regained again by one week.

One week to four months: Gains 25 g per day (average). Usual range 150–200 g per week.

Four months to eight months: Gains 16 g per day (average). Usual range 90–150 g per week.

Eight months to one year: Gains about 10 g per day. Usual range 60–90 g per week.

Note: The rate of weight gain lessens as the months pass. Don't brood on daily weighings. It's much better to weigh your baby weekly or fortnightly, always at the same time of day. That way you'll have a more accurate record.

Feeding and the figure

If you are worried about your figure it's too late! The stable door was left ajar nine months ago and the horse has long since bolted. It's not breast-feeding that stretches and deflates breasts, but nine months of pregnancy. Luckily most women can give birth and breast-feed without any long-term alteration to their figure. (See page 226.)

Weaning – a sad time for mothers

When breast-feeding stops this is a time of very confused emotions for many mums. It is the end of an era, a closeness that will never return.

Parenthood is punctuated by many of these milestones. Often we would love to keep our children at that stage for ever like little Peter Pans, but that's not what life is about. The sadness can be stressful for a while but it soon passes.

Conclusion

The choice of whether you breast-feed and when you wean is yours and yours alone. In the end it comes down to what feels right for you. Don't be pressured by experts who think they know it all. Breast-feeding should be enjoyable and undertaken in a relaxed way. You should continue it for as long as you and your baby wish.

12

Bottle-Feeding

Iᴀ you have decided for one reason or another that you are going to bottle-feed your baby, don't get brainwashed into believing that you are selling your loved one short. The formulas available on the market these days are almost equivalent in nourishment to breast milk, and when it comes to comfort it's the warmth and care of the feeder that counts, not the breast or the bottle.

This chapter deals with bottle-feeding. It looks at the types of milks and formulas to use, the equipment you'll need and the various ways of doing it.

The Milks

With the wide range of milks available today, you might well be excused for becoming confused and wondering which type of milk you should be pouring into that bottle.

Milk formulas

Most formulas come as dried powder in a tin, though some of the more upmarket brands come in the ready-to-drink form. All those on the market are safe, with lowered salt, balanced nutrients and added vitamins.

As you look at the rows of tins on the chemist's shelves, it's easy to become totally confused. One brand will claim to have added iron, extra vitamins or unsaturated fats, whilst another will claim to be the most convenient or the most economical. Yet another will claim to be so perfect that it's almost better than breast milk itself. I see all these milks as being pretty much the same. If your baby is going to thrive he will thrive well on any of them.

When you leave hospital your bottle-fed baby will already be established on one brand of formula. If this suits you, then continue it, but you mustn't feel compelled to use it if you don't wish to. Much in the same way as hotels tend to sell a certain brand of beer, or garages only one type of petrol, so too hospitals are encouraged to stock certain brands of baby formula. It will of course be an excellent formula, but it has been chosen by the hospital for its bulk contract price and not for its economy to you when bought in small amounts from a local supplier. So don't be concerned about changing your brand, when you get home, to one that better suits your wallet. One plea however, please don't embark on a milk swapping spree. One change at the start is fine, but continual chopping and changing leads to confusion and does nothing for the baby.

It's worth remembering that the milk you put in your child is much the same as the petrol you put in your car. Despite what the commercials tell you, the well-tuned car will run just as well on Esso, BP or Shell. The badly tuned car will run badly on all of these, but that's not the fault of the fuel. So too with babies. They run just as well on any good formula when in a well-tuned condition. Like petrol they give similar performance, the only difference being in the constitution of the exhaust gases! It is advisable to shop around before choosing a formula. Often you will find that the brands stocked by the large supermarket chains are significantly cheaper than those from the corner chemist. (See page 115 for the comparison costs.)

Doorstep cow's milk

For many years the most popular form of milk was the cow's milk delivered to your doorstep by your friendly milkman. It wasn't given straight, but was boiled and sterilised, then diluted with water and sweetened with a little sugar to balance up the nutritional load. This modified bottled milk suited 99 per cent of babies and provided the cheapest of artificial feeds. Unfortunately it received bad press about fifteen years ago when it was discovered to be responsible for a rare, but dangerous form of salt-overload dehydration.

The problem was that cow's milk has a very high salt level which is almost five times that of breast milk. This can be partly lowered by the addition of water, but never enough to completely remove the risk of dehydration. A healthy baby with healthy kidneys can cope with this. The trouble comes if a baby has a fever or gastro-enteritis. With this the body fluids may be lowered and the salt level rises. When this happens, the high-salt cow's milk will produce much the same effect as if you were to drink seawater while dying of thirst on a life raft. The fluid is there all right, but the resulting salt overload makes you more thirsty and can do terrible things to your body and brain.

Cow's milk actually contains more protein than breast milk but some of it is not very easy to digest so the end result works out about the same. The undigested portion scoots through the intestines as curds, which explains the difference in nappy products in breast- and bottle-fed babies.

I know that 99 per cent of babies will thrive on ordinary bottled cow's milk, but for the sake of the other 1 per cent I think you should play it safe, at least until twelve months of age. The safest milks until that age are either from the breast or from a recognised formula. You can, of course, use cow's milk for all custards and cooking without any worry, and most mums use it for making up cereals. After the twelfth month, then it's open season on cow's milk used without modification or restriction.

Goat's milk is again in fashion. It is used by parents who believe that their babies are allergic to cow's milk and rarely helps allergies. It must not be drunk unboiled, it needs added vitamins when used in the young and is best reserved for little goats.

Special milks

Just as all that glitters is not gold, so all that is white and flows from a teat is not milk. You can obtain white non-dairy fluids which are made from a vegetable base, usually the soya bean.

I must be old-fashioned, but I still think of milk as something that comes from a mammal, not a vegetable processing plant. At present there is a great push in the advertising industry to have us believe that non-dairy products are healthier. Personally, I believe that low fat milk products that come from a cow can help you and your family stay just as healthy as pretend milk, although low fat milks should not be used until two years of age. What's more, with all the talk of milk allergy, it is seldom realised that soya allergy is almost as common as cow's milk allergy.

Having said that, soya milk does have a very useful role for those occasional babies who have a true cow's milk allergy. These babies have major skin rashes and become ill when they drink cow's milk and for them the vegetable-based milk is the best alternative.

However, when it comes to colic, crying, snuffly noses, wheezing and other vague symptoms, milk, whether from the cow or vegetables, rarely has any part to play. Using special milks to try and cure noses and chests achieves very little, except adding greatly to the wealth of your local chemist.

Most people who work in the field of gastro-enterology or dietetics in the leading children's hospitals support these views. Even so, the 'take them off cow's milk' lobby is still amazingly strong, so please be very cautious.

Feeding

This is where the one great drawback of bottle versus breast comes in. With breast-feeding all you have to do is undo a few buttons and hey presto it's all there, warmed, sterilised and ready to go. Not so with bottle-feeding. Before your baby is able to feed you need to assemble the basic equipment, mix it up, warm it and make sure you've got the volumes right. Here's what you'll need and how it's done.

The equipment

You'll need bottles, teats, a bottle brush, sterilising fluid and a container for soaking the empties or a steam steriliser.

The bottles can be made of glass, which is easier to clean but makes them heavier, or of plastic, which is harder to clean but makes them lighter and able to bounce when dropped. The easiest way to make up formula feeds is to have a jug and to make up the whole day's feed in one go, storing the rest in the fridge with a cover over it. One jug and two bottles should be sufficient for this. Some mothers prefer to prepare the whole day's feed at one go in bottles ready for warming. The only problem with this otherwise good idea is that you will need at least six bottles to cover the twenty-four hour period.

You should use a standard teat which should release the milk at about two drops per second when the bottle is held upside-down. You can buy teats of silicone or rubber and of all shapes and sizes ranging from the trickle feeder to the Niagara model. You may have to experiment a bit at first to see which teat suits your baby best, but don't chop and change as this confuses little feeders.

Cleaning and sterilising

Milk left sitting for hours in an unclean bottle is a health hazard. It is an excellent culture medium in which bacteria thrive and multiply like rabbits. During your baby's first year cleanliness and sterility are of the utmost importance.

After feeding the bottle should be immediately washed in warm, soapy water, rinsed and immersed in a container of sterilising fluid. There it should stay for at least an hour or until the next feed. When it is needed again, just shake off the excess fluid and use it without rinsing. The small amount of fluid that remains is safe and will be so diluted that your baby won't notice it. It tastes a bit like the chlorinated water in public swimming pools. You wouldn't choose to drink a glass of it with your dinner, but in small amounts it's perfectly harmless.

Teats should be washed both inside and outside with a detergent. It used to be said that greasy discoloration could be removed by rubbing it with dry salt used as an abrasive, but this is considered out of date now. Like bottles, teats also need a good hour immersed in sterilising fluid and shouldn't be rinsed on removal, but stored in a clean container in the fridge. Don't leave them immersed all the time. Hygienic as this may be, the rubber will soon perish and burst; or alternatively take on the texture of a water-logged toffee.

Though the soaking method is undoubtedly the commonest way of sterilising, it is by no means the only way. It is just as effective to use a steam steriliser or to boil them for ten minutes on the stove.

All milk formulas must be made up with boiled water and should then be stored in the fridge ready for use. It is best to use the main body of the fridge as the temperature of a shelf in a frequently opened door will vary. Don't keep unused bottles for more than twenty-four hours and never store half-used feeds. If a quarter of an hour has passed and there is no sign of a second sitting then dump the remaining feed at once.

Little breeding nasties thrive in milk during those long, lazy days in warm temperatures. When travelling in summer use warm bottles quickly and store others in a cold, insulated box to increase their safe life. Another method is to fill the bottles with boiled water and not add the milk powder until feedtime. This helps prevent infection and, as most modern formulas mix so easily, it can be done in the bottle.

Making up feeds

Cleanliness, accuracy and a minimum of effort are the three main ingredients of making up formula feeds. Although you have to sterilise bottles and teats and boil the water you use, scoops, spoons and measures are safe with just a simple wash under the hot tap. Before you start, read the instructions on the formula tin and do exactly what they say. **Don't compress the powder in the scoop**, fill it gently and shave it off level with a knife. **Don't be tempted to add a few extra kilojoules** or another scoop 'for the pot'. Making up overstrong feeds not only causes obesity but can also be dangerous due to salt and solute overload.

The volumes

The expected food intake is calculated by a simple formula. The volume required each day is 150 ml of milk per kg of the ideal bodyweight for the age of your baby. Ideal bodyweight is usually just the actual weight of your baby, but I mention it because the very fat baby obviously should be given less and the very thin baby more. (See usual ranges of intake, page 106.)

Most babies will demand six feeds a day, some dropping the night-time feed around the sixth week, leaving them with just five a day. Unfortunately none of the little vultures have read this book, so don't be surprised when you find them demanding between 120 and 200 ml per kg of milk a day or between four and ten feeds. The secret is **not to get over scientific about all this**. Leave your slide rule in the drawer and use rule of thumb instead. **If your baby is happy, thriving and gaining weight, then you must be doing it right**. Babies are like adults, they each take different volumes at mealtimes. While you are trying to decipher your baby's feeding pattern just put an extra 25 per cent in each bottle and discard what's left. You'll soon learn exactly how much to make up each time.

Warm or cold?

Everyone knows that you have to warm a baby's bottle . . . but hang on a moment. Could it be that, in fact, everyone is wrong? Studies done with hot and cold milks have shown that there is in fact no strong preference between them. The temperature is largely a question of habit, rather like Australian cold beer as against the warm British variety.

The habit in our country is for warm milk, so if it's not too inconvenient keep up the habit and use a jug of warm water to warm up the bottle. Don't forget the ritual of shaking a few drops of milk on to the back of your hand to test the temperature before the teat goes anywhere near the baby.

The microwave is not a recommended way of heating bottles, though many parents use this because of its convenience. It's far too easy to overdo it and have the bottle spurt steam like an early steam engine. If you do use the microwave, heat the bottle without the cap or a teat in place. Remember, different ovens heat at different rates. The final temperature varies by how warm or cold the milk was at the start. Most bottles take about forty seconds in the microwave. **Always check the temperature carefully before use**.

Added vitamins, iron and fluoride

All formulas are fortified these days with the necessary vitamins to keep the average baby for at least the first eight months. This includes vitamin C, so there's no need to start squeezing rosehips, blackcurrants or oranges into tiny mouths. In those areas where the water is fluoridated there is no need to add any extra fluoride. If you live in areas where there is no fluoridation don't worry for the first 6 months of life, then get fluoride tablets from your local chemist. Your dentist will advise how much to give each day. (Usually 1 tablet dissolved in a litre/1¾ pints of water and used over four days.)

Most babies should be getting at least a sniff of solid foods by eight months and these will give an even wider variety of vitamins and iron. If bottle-feeding continues past this age as the only method of feeding, it's best to ask advice about what extra may be needed.

Although vitamin C-enriched drinks aren't necessary, a word of warning to those who use them anyway. It is best to dilute 100 per cent orange juice to avoid what in many babies may be an explosive bowel-emptying. Some blackcurrant products are appallingly sweet and can start the child off on bad dietary habits as well as being bad for teeth when they come through. We know that a little vitamin C is necessary for us all, but despite what some claim there is no evidence that large quantities improve health in any way.

Conclusion

Bottle-feeding can provide your baby with balanced nutrition, but it is important to remember a few main points. Here's a checklist:

- Choose the formula that suits your pocket. This may not be the one introduced by your hospital.
- Shop around when purchasing. Supermarket lines are often cheaper than the standard chemist's stock.
- Stick to one brand of formula, don't chop and change. It will not alter behaviour or health.
- Straight cow's milk can be used for cooking and making up cereals, but not for drinking in the first twelve months.
- Non-dairy milks are only of benefit to rare cases of true milk allergy.
- Make up feeds cleanly and accurately.
- Sterilise all bottles and boil all water for the first year.
- Don't compress extra powder into the scoop. Overstrength formula can be dangerous.
- Don't pollute the bottles with custard or cereals. Drink is drink and solids should be taken as solids.
- No added vitamins or iron are needed for the average milk-fed baby for at least the first eight months.
- Fluoride should be added only if there is none in the water supply.
- Don't become obsessed by accurate intervals between feeds and exact volumes consumed. Demand feeding is what we practise and that's a laid-back approach. Feed them when they want it.
- If your baby is happy, thriving and gaining weight, you must be doing it right.

For more information on weight gain see page 250. For the comparative cost of formulas, see below.

Sterility in food preparation
- Wash hands before preparing.
- Use boiled water to make up milk for one year.
- Soak bottles and teats for at least one hour in sterilising fluid or boil them for at least ten minutes.
- Spoons, measures, plates etc. can be washed without special precautions.

Infant feeds in the U.K.
The main milks available are:

- Premium, Step-up, Plus   Cow & Gate
- First, Second, Follow-on   Farleys (Heinz)
- Milumil, Aptamil   Milupa
- White, Gold, Progress   SMA

These are available from your local chemist or from supermarkets.

Shop around and don't get too bogged down with the promotional literature. Healthy little children will thrive well on any of these approved formulas.

Prices vary a little depending on whether you buy your chosen formula and in what quantity. If a supermarket or chemist own-brand is available, this is usually cheaper.

13

Feeding – From Slushes to Solids

THERE is no more controversial a subject than the art of weaning your baby off milk. In mediaeval times mums were told to rub goat's dung on their breasts to give Junior the not-so-subtle hint that the store was about to close. These days many people get wound up with more complicated ways of doing it, although the truth of the matter is, that weaning is a simple, natural part of life and not one to be approached with some sort of ritualistic fervour.

Weaning is a gradual process. It's not a question of the breast on Monday and a well-done steak on Tuesday, but rather a spoonful of cereal here and some squashed banana there until Baby starts to understand that not all food is liquid.

The best way to accustom your baby to this gastronomic upheaval in his life is by gentle trial and error. First see what happens when the chosen food is put in his mouth. If it is sucked up with the whoosh of a vacuum cleaner then you're probably on the right track. If it pops back out again like a yo-yo then try something else. If nothing seems to be working, leave it a couple of weeks and then try again.

When to wean

The time to wean your baby lengthens and shortens like the hemline fashions. At one time doctors said that nine months was the best time, then that was reduced to three, and then it went back up to six months. It seems to me that where such variations of view exist the actual starting time cannot be all that critical. Somewhere between three and nine months seems to be the time with a preference for about **four to six months**. Like most things to do with your baby, a lot will be up to him in the end, though there are some good reasons for not starting solids too early and others for not leaving it too late.

Early solids

It is well accepted that milk is the best fuel for young babies. It's easily digested and provides all the nutrition a baby needs. Bearing in mind just how remarkable the rest of the design is, it's probably wisest to use the maker's approved fuel. In theory you could feed some solids to a newborn baby and after a month it would be reasonably successful, but there are some good reasons why you should not do this. First, solids will be incompletely digested in the early months. Then there is the worry that early introduction of solids can increase the risk of allergies in later life. Personally I'm not convinced of this. I don't believe that extra allergies are caused by the early introduction of solids, although any that are lying dormant may be brought to a head at a much earlier age. Another concern is that feeding solids too early can produce weight problems. Certainly high kilojoule spoon-feeds coupled with high kilojoule milk are more likely to produce a blubber baby.

Late solids

Starting solids too late on the other hand also has a couple of disadvantages. First you run the risk of nutritional deficiency. After eight months iron and some vitamins will start to run low. Of course this can be overcome by adding artificial vitamins and iron, but since Baby's gut is by now revving up for a bit of real food you might as well start to go the natural way. After nine months of nothing but milk some babies become milkaholics and are quick to tell you what you can do with anything else. It's best therefore to introduce some texture into the repertoire at around six months with some lumps and little chewy pieces at nine months. This can save a lot of problems later on.

The foods

At birth your baby is taking nothing but milk. By the age of one he is enjoying a cut-up selection of the family dinner. What happens during the intervening months is a gradual introduction and increase in textured food.

There is no one correct way to introduce solids. Having said this, most parents will start with a rice baby cereal. It's not that wheat based cereals are inferior, it's just that very occasionally they precipitate what's known as coeliac disease, a chronic malabsorption-wasting condition. It must be emphasised that this rare complication would probably have occurred at a later age anyway when wheat was introduced, and that by starting later it is easier to diagnose and treat if it appears.

After rice, most babies will move on to fine purées of fruit or vegetables, with lean meats and thicker purées coming in about one to two months later. When you start at four months you first use sieved or blended foods or else you can make up your own in the blender. Most fruits and some vegetables melt to a textureless pulp after a long spin in the blender, but you'd better leave meat off the menu for a few months as it can tend to remain a bit stringy and it's harder for Baby to digest. Don't forget delicacies like liver. It may make the parents feel ill but most babies like it and it's pretty nourishing.

At six months 'chewing' starts, or to be rather more precise, Baby starts to gum his food. At this stage food of rather greater texture can be tried. Baby tins can make way for junior tins, chicken can become scraggier, meat and vegetables no longer need to be a textureless pulp. By eight months a slice of bread can be chewed and a biscuit sogged and sucked. Mashed vegetables can be added and yoghurt can accompany mashed fruits.

At nine months you need hardly depress the blender button at all and finger food like biscuits, cheese, toast or fruit can be put on offer. Soon mince, rice and pasta can be added to the menu and little cubes of food will be chewed. By his first birthday your little gourmet should be able to cope with cut-up food from the family table.

Please don't approach the introduction of solids as some scientific ritual. Just relax and find the sequence that suits you best.

The technique

Try to introduce one new food at a time. In this way you can easily see what's popular and what's not or if there is an allergic reaction. Aim to rotate food so as to give a variety of different tastes and textures. Give the food straight, don't add sugar, salt or seasoning just to make it palatable to you. Baby food is for babies and would never be a big taste sensation at the Ritz. If you pollute it to coincide with your palate you may run up against a mouth shut as tight as a Scotsman's wallet.

At the start don't expect to see vast quantities of food disappearing as the swallowing mechanism at this stage is pretty immature and it will take some time for your baby to get the hang of it. It's best to begin by offering him one spoonful during half-time in a bottle-feed and see what happens. If he enjoys it offer him a couple more and then more the next day. Be prepared to experiment and be flexible. There is no magic to starting solids. All you require is a spoon, a bib, some slushy food and a ton of patience. If your baby won't take the food this week, don't worry. Try again next week.

The bowels

It is said that 'what goes up must come down'. With baby feeding, it is 'what goes in must come out'. It's only logical that the gut, having been used to an all-milk diet for so long, will show some changes when faced with solids. The result of course will be much more solid bowel motions and dirtier nappies. Different foods produce different results. Some fruits and juices scoot through as if by jet propulsion while some vegetables can appear to pass right through the baby without any hint of digestion. Sometimes they re-emerge so untouched that there is not even a change in the tone of their colour. Not to worry, that's not malabsorption, it's perfectly usual, especially with carrots and corn. Now's a good time to start using disposable nappy liners. These make waste disposal a bit easier and much less intimate.

Tins or home brand?

Pre-prepared food in tins or jars is certainly convenient and provides all Baby's nutritional needs. Much of it is a blend of various substances and can be of a rather monotonous texture and taste. It can also become rather expensive. Home cooking, on the other hand, leaves you in no doubt as to the contents. It also gives you greater control over the consistency of the food and allows you greater scope for experimentation.

Your baby is going to get all the nutrition he needs whether he is fed on tins or home brand. I am all for home cooking but this must be done with an eye towards cost and convenience.

Convenience cooking

Good nutrition for babies means a proper balance of protein, fats, carbohydrates, vitamins and minerals. The truth of the matter is that once that food hits the stomach it doesn't matter at all whether the protein was steak or lamb, the vitamin C orange, rosehip or from a tablet. When time is short don't provide the sort of widely varied menu you expect to find at the Hilton, opt for convenience.

Armed with a blender, a few ice cube trays and some freezer space it becomes very easy to store meals. Set aside a little food from the normal family meal, blend it, and store it in the ice trays. In no time you'll have enough little frozen squares to provide an à la carte section. Now mealtimes can be as easy as watching an ice cube melt.

Good nutrition habits start early

Good nutrition is a family affair. There's no point complaining about your flabby unfit offspring if all the while you are equally flabby and eat a diet of utter junk. If you want to have healthy children then parents have got to create a healthy lifestyle and example for their children.

There are four main aims both adults and children need to adopt when it comes to improving nutrition:

1 To increase the complex carbohydrate level.
2 To reduce all fats (particularly saturated fats).
3 To cut down on highly sweet and refined foods.
4 To cut down on salt intake.

To modify the complex carbohydrate level we need more unrefined energy foods like bread, rice, pasta, potatoes, vegetables and fruit. These are fine in themselves and shouldn't be greatly polluted with fat, salt or sugar. If the bread has some extra grain or fibre in it, better still, but its benefits are soon lost if it is heavily greased with butter or margarine and heavily loaded with jam, honey or salty spreads. Potatoes and vegetables are excellent nutrition. They have lots of fibre and few kilojoules so long as they're not fried or buried in a ton of butter.

After the age of 5 years it's important to reduce fats by less frying, less fatty meats, fewer fatty spreads and generally watching fat intake. As for salt, it should be taken off the dinner table altogether and less used in cooking.

Now this is all very smart for adults, but how does it affect babies I hear you ask?

Taste starts from day one and it's best to introduce your baby to a wide variety of foods as early as possible, without allowing him to get hooked on a sweet or a salty diet. By the age of one your child will be eating the same meals as you, so if your diet is a healthy one so will his be. There's no need to go completely overboard about it on the other hand. Your baby isn't going to collapse if he doesn't get stone-crushed wheatgerm bread and sticks of celery a foot long. Less refined carbohydrates, less fat, less salt and you're in business.

Weaning the milkaholic

Most babies take to solids like a duck to Peking. There are a few unfortunately who will refuse point blank, as they are now hardened milkaholics. For them spoon-feeds become a miserable failure and they leave you in no doubt whatsoever as to what you can do with your spoon. In this case you have two options, the *gentle, charitable* approach or the *take it or leave it* method.

I would go for gentleness if I were you. Start by reducing Baby's milk intake by a third, offering extra non-milk fluids as a substitute and try to give him a little solid food early in each feed. If this doesn't work, next reduce the milk by half and see what happens. It usually brings a cure within one week.

The tough way is to stop all milk, administer juice fluids only and set in for a siege. This does no-one's nerves any good, though it can be fairly effective if you have the determination.

If you suspect that your baby has a problem with either chewing or swallowing, then have this checked out. But if there appears to be no problem, then you'll have to be firm and keep up the regime.

The hooked-on-baby-food baby

Rather in the same way as some teenagers are hooked on no-taste TV dinners, some babies get hooked on no-texture baby foods. Nothing will they allow past their lips unless it has been mashed to minutiae or passed several times through a sieve. You can prevent this unfortunate habit by ensuring that a bit of texture and variety are offered by seven months and a few lumps by nine months of age. Here you will find that home food preparation will give you the most flexibility.

If your baby is used to taking only food of some bland, highly filtered variety, don't disappoint him. Continue with this, but gradually readjust the contents. You can start by adding a speck of home cooking, and increase the amount until after a few weeks, unknown to him, it's all coming from your blender. You can hurry this along by reducing the milk volume which will tone up the appetite.

Beware and prepare for the toddler backlash

Once weaned most babies enjoy their solids which they attack like lions at the kill. They will accept an extensive range of meats, fish, fruit, cereals and vegetables – and even smile as the last trace of spinach slips out of sight! Oh, that this would continue, but regrettably for some it falls apart around the first birthday.

It is as though someone has turned off the mains switch and the eating mechanism refused to function. It's nothing to get unduly worried about. This is all due to an interesting stage of life called toddlerhood. The toddler may only reach up to your kneecap, but as anyone who has met a leprechaun will tell you, this doesn't stop him telling you exactly what he will and will not do. The toddler has a lot more determination and stubbornness than sense, which makes food fights a monumental waste of time.

Another factor is temperament. I believe God made two types of feeders, those who take food very seriously and those who think of it as some sort of joke. The serious won't lift their eyes until they have practically scraped off the pattern of the plate, whereas the joker will play with his food, doing just about anything he can with it except eat it.

The first rule is never to fight about food, as it will get you absolutely nowhere. Forget all dreams of introducing your child to the entire contents of your Delia Smith cookbook and narrow it down to a few palatable formal meals altogether and resort to eating on the hoof. Grazing is good for millions of sheep and it must be good for toddlers too. Now it's cheese and crackers, cold meats, a cold sausage, fruit and lots of nutritious sandwiches all washed down with a good vintage white (from the milkman).

In summary then

- Weaning means trial and error with gradual introduction.
- If the food you offer reappears, try something else. If it disappears you're probably on the right track.
- Don't start too early or too late. Four to six months seems ideal.
- Rice cereals are best before six months. Start wheat cereals later.
- Baby rice, vegetables and fruit are the favourite starters.
- Little kilojoule intake from solids is achieved in the first month of weaning so don't take it too seriously.
- Baby tastes and adult tastes are different. Don't season Baby's food to your palate.
- Honey can carry infection. Avoid it until the first birthday.
- Egg yolks are out until six months, and egg whites until one year due to allergy.
- A healthy diet is a family affair. Aim for more complex carbohydrates, less fat, less over refined sweet food and less salt. Healthy parents teach by example to their healthy children.

Foods that may cause loose bowel motions
- Most 100 per cent fruit juices, especially apple and orange

Foods that may reappear undigested
- Carrots
- Corn
- Sometimes peas

Foods that may alter the colour of the bowel motion
- Iron tonics and medicines (black)
- The artificial sweetener sorbitol (pink diarrhoea)

Food that may change the colour of urine
- Beetroot (red)
- Some food dyes
- Vitamin B supplements (yellow)

Foods best avoided
- Egg yolk – first six months (allergy)
- Egg white – first year (allergy)
- Wheat based cereals – first six months (possible coeleac diseases)
- Bottled cow's milk to drink – first twelve months
- Honey – first year (botulism)

14

Colic – What it is

Colic is an imprecise term used to describe a pattern of unsettled behaviour and crying common in the first months of life. It usually occurs in the late afternoon or early evening and comes on shortly after feeding. The baby is distressed, seems in pain and is extremely hard to console.

The definition of colic is vague and it means different things to different people. Most view it with very loose limits. For them it describes any fussing or unsettled behaviour which occurs after feeds, especially in the late afternoon and evening. Others try to adhere tightly to a definition such as crying in the first four months of life in a healthy well-nourished baby, who cries at full force for a total of at least four hours in one day, this occurring at least four days each week.

Although it has been around for centuries, no-one knows for certain what causes colic. It makes children cry and almost impossible to comfort. It can turn happy, confident parents into defeated and demoralised ones. Though an anxious mother may make it worse, it is the colic which causes the anxiety in the first place, definitely not the reverse.

Many academic doctors find the whole concept of colic beyond them. The descriptions are too vague, there is no pathological explanation, and it can't be measured by blood test, biopsy or any medical medicine. Whether or not you can measure it, colic is a very real condition and one which causes considerable stress for both Baby and parents.

The picture

Your baby has been a model of good behaviour in hospital and you go home full of the joys of life. Parenthood seems a breeze and your thoughts turn to having another child next year. Then after a few days the crying starts. You have just fed Baby that afternoon or evening and your first impulse is to give him more. But after the first few sucks the screaming returns, louder than ever. You burp, bounce, pat, change the nappy, give yet more food and start to feel thoroughly incompetent. Nothing appears to help.

His face is red, his knees are drawn up and the cry is now like one who is in great pain. This goes on for between one and six hours day after day. With this you gradually disintegrate, and while this is going on your baby is thriving, gaining weight and generally looking a picture of rude good health. Confusing isn't it?

Colic occurs somewhere between a few minutes to the full hour after feeding and is usually made worse, not stopped, by food. The most usual time for it to happen is between 5 and 10 pm, but it can occur at any time of the day or night. It usually starts when the baby is about ten days old, though it has been known to commence right from birth. It usually eases up by two months of age and stops altogether by three months, though again in some cases it can continue until six months.

It is estimated that 5 per cent of all babies born will have severe colic and probably around 25 per cent have a mild degree at some stage in their early lives. These figures of course depend on the definition you use.

The cause

When the first hot air balloon was invented the great problem was finding a way to generate enough hot air to keep it afloat. Had they known some of the worthy experts who have expounded their theories on the causes of colic they would have had no trouble at all!

The most plausible theories focus on some immaturity of either the gut, nervous system or balance of the body's hormones. The gut at birth is a poorly exercised bit of tubing that has never before received anything that resembles food. It is possible that it hasn't quite got its act together by birth and resents having food run through it. Maybe, on the other hand, the nervous system that controls everything is not quite up to it. There is also the possibility that the baby is suffering from a withdrawal of Mum's hormones, which he shared before birth. Some of these hormones have a muscle-relaxant property which allowed Mum to stretch enough to permit the baby to be born. Possibly removing these relaxing hormones causes spasms.

All this is unproven speculation; however, there are some popular theories.

Wind

Being a keen sailor I know a lot about wind. I can tell an ill wind when I see one, be it in boats or babies. Each day all around the civilised world billions of babies are bounced and burped in the ritualistic pursuit of expelling the last knot of wind from either end.

These wind watchers will tell you confidently that this is the cause of colic as they lift their baby up from the horizontal position of the cot, and lo and behold exhibit a small gas explosion. There is, however, one major flaw in this argument. Gravity affects colicky and normal babies alike. Any baby lifted from the horizontal to the vertical will tend to burp.

Many health workers I greatly respect are still convinced that careful feeding and winding will help some colicky babies. For me I am still not sure and believe that no amount of wind-free feeding, patting or burping is going to relieve colic.

Anxious parents

For years it has been fashionable to see colic as a symptom of anxious, inexperienced parenting. You know the syndrome – tense mother generates tension in her baby and causes crying. Once again there is absolutely nothing to support this theory.

It is a fact that first babies seem to cry more than later editions. This has nothing to do with anxiety. The first-time mum is just more aware of crying and less skilful in stopping it. There is probably no more colic among first babies, it's just more obvious when you are unused to parenthood.

Colic is a great cause of maternal anxiety and feelings of incompetence. These feelings are not however the cause of colic. Having said that, I do believe there is a vicious circle in which crying babies make mothers anxious and anxious mothers then make their babies cry more. I also believe that postnatal depression may contribute to colic in many more families than we realise.

Incorrect feeding

Hunger pains and colic are definitely not the same. A hungry baby will cry before food and stop when fed. Lack of milk may certainly cause hunger, but it won't cause colic. Another myth is that it is the quality of the breast milk which causes colic. This is utter nonsense. The quality of all breast milk is always grade A, you either have top quality milk or none at all. It is also true that colic is about as common in bottle-fed babies as it is in the breast-fed.

There are those who are sure that colic is due to feeding too fast and still others who believe it is caused by feeding too slow. Some quite unnatural feeding positions have been devised to act on these theories, and while these may help a few, I have to say that I am unconvinced.

Substances in mother's milk

It is true that certain substances eaten by the mother can pass into her milk. Some babies find that second-hand garlic, spices and broccoli are not to their liking, while others find their mothers pleasantly soothing after a well-lubricated party.

Dairy products cause the most interest and dispute. Some mothers have found that relief comes when they stop all dairy products in their own diet. Though I am not really a believer in this, it's so simple to do, that if you're in doubt, why not cut them out for a week and see for yourself.

Cow's milk allergy

There is a very strong anti-cow's milk lobby who claim that cow's milk may be fine for little cows but that it is no good for little humans. Colic, they believe, can be improved by removing cow's milk from all bottle-feeds.

Most studies, however, have not been able to support these claims, though there are occasional babies who certainly seem to get relief. Once again I am not convinced that there is a connection between cow's milk and colic, but as it will certainly do no harm, why not try removal of cow's milk as a short trial when all else has failed?

Oesophageal reflux

It was recently discovered that many colicky babies have a leaky valve at the top of their stomach. 'Eureka!' cried the scientists, 'At last we know the cause of colic'. The theory was simple. Acid leaks up from the stomach to the sensitive oesophagus to cause pain and crying.

Unfortunately this has now gone the way of most theories – out the door. Certainly some colicky babies have this leaky valve, but so also do many normal, happy babies.

Those who have specifically studied the oesophagus of colicky babies have found that there is not much sign of any inflammation or irritation in these children. This must make the theory of regurgitation causing pain unlikely. Another group of scientists who placed an acid-sensitive recorder in the oesophagus of babies who had colic and reflux found that the acid leak bore no consistent relationship to the time of crying. One would have thought that if colic was due to the irritation of acid, the leak and the crying would always come together.

There must be some colicky babies who have pain from reflux and it must be worth keeping in mind but, from my experience, it is not common.

Temperament

Temperament cannot be said to cause colic, but certainly there is a type of baby who is more prone to this affliction. The active, awake, busy, tense baby is more likely to have colic than the more placid ones. It is possible, I suppose, that babies with a tense temperament also have a tense brain and tense gut. Possibly they also have taken their genes from tense parents!

In later life it is often found that those who display active, inflexible and tense tendencies have frequently suffered from colic as a baby. Colic does not come from one clear cause. Unknown physiological factors, the child's individual temperament, factors in the environment and the parents' tolerance to crying, all play a part.

Treatment

Many professionals and parents can see one, and only one, possible treatment for colic and this they pursue with all the fervour of a revolutionary fanatic. The trouble is that they will not believe that any other treatment can have merit.

It is easy to make great claims for your chosen treatment of colic, particularly if you persist long enough, as all babies always get better in the end.

God matures and cures, but we experts are quick to claim all the glory. There is no lack of remedies for colic and crying, the trouble is that few work really well. If you are prepared to be flexible, to experiment and to work for a percentage improvement, not a 'bolt of lightning' type miracle, then I guarantee that things are about to take a change for the better.

When you seek treatment, I believe you can't go past a professional who is practical, understanding and knows what it means to support. I believe that spirits lift and the situation improves significantly once you realise that you are not alone and that there will be light at the end of this relatively short tunnel.

For treating your baby, Chapter 16 is cram packed with ideas. It's best to start with finding the most soothing posture, then introducing certain gentle movements. Patting, rhythms, soothing sounds, sucking and medicines may also help.

Use not one, but *a package of ideas* together. *Experiment* and keep adding new ones until you get some relief.

If all else fails you may be driving round the block at 3 am to try and soothe Baby, but let's hope you don't get that far. Before you do, have a look at the suggestions for treatment in Chapter 16.

15
Crying – What Does it Mean?

Most new parents find their little ones cry considerably more than they ever expected. Often they feel overwhelmed and exhausted as this crying will usually come on for no apparent reason and, what's worse, will be devilishly difficult to stop.

We are told that the average young baby cries two to three hours each day, but the reality is that there are few average babies. There are some angels who are almost too good to be true and some who cry so much that their parents are reduced to quivering blobs of jelly.

Parents are further confused by all the unrealistic folklore that clouds childcare. We are told that the properly fed baby sleeps peacefully for four hours, wakes, smiles, cries gently, is fed, burps and goes off to sleep once more. Some children certainly behave like this but it will be unusual and you will be privileged if your child does. Other unfounded myths tell of the dangers of letting a baby cry. Belly buttons blown out, children have convulsions and hernias drop down. Then there is the fable which gives a stern warning not to spoil your baby. It implies that the little baby who is comforted when he cries becomes spoilt silly and will be demanding for years. This is not a true tale and in fact there is some evidence that the babies who receive the most comfort become the most secure and least demanding.

So, I hear you ask, why do little humans need to cry? Unfortunately, no-one really knows. Only a few other animals have tears. Cormorants and albatrosses cry, but this is for another reason. Unlike us they use their tear ducts as a second set of kidneys to wash out a bit of extra salt. I suppose that if we drank seawater and had a diet of anchovies it might bring tears to our eyes too!

Let's look at what the different types of cries mean, their effect on temperament and finally what crying does to us poor parents.

Types of Cries

The newborn nursery in the hospital is filled with a chorus of cries indistinguishable to the untrained ear, but most mothers can identify the chirp of their own chick after about three days of age. At first all sorts of crying sound identical, but as the weeks pass different patterns emerge indicating different needs. There will be a cry of pain, another of hunger, while a lesser cry may simply signify boredom or grumbling. Often you just won't know what it means.

Please don't get too scientific about this as it's often very difficult to distinguish crying accurately.

The cry of pain

When it comes to the cry of pain there is generally a gasp and then a loud bloodcurdling screech which is followed by a short pause while baby winds up to start all over again. The knees draw up, the face goes red and the child is inconsolable.

Though we know that this is a cry of pain the cause of it is often obscure. Many will have colic. Others will wake from a deep sleep with a jump and then scream, and some just scream for the hell of it. By all means check for nappy pins sticking into little bottoms, wet nappies and assorted illnesses, but by and large painful crying usually occurs for some reason known only to God and the baby.

The cry of hunger

The hungry baby communicates with a more regular cry which lacks the pitch, knee drawing and intensity of the pained cry. It occurs some time after the last square meal and, though it can be stopped briefly by comfort, it is really only a large dose of kilojoules which is going to provide proper relief.

Grumblers

Bored, lonely, tired, cold or uncomfortable babies are likely to grumble. Others, who have none of these problems, will grumble anyway because, rather like some adults we all know, it's just in their nature. This sort of crying is of a lower pitch, coming and going before winding up to a real cry. Alternatively they may just grumble themselves off to sleep. Generally

132

speaking with a bit of comfort and instant entertainment matters can be relieved. Grumbling seems to become an art form after about the first four months. Before then most babies seem either to cry properly or not at all.

Temperament and Tears

As everyone knows all babies are not born the same. Each baby from his first cry will show an individual temperament. Some are quite content to lie gazing at the ceiling for hours, whilst others want to be up and about observing the world at its business. Some will sleep for long periods, while others will wake every two hours whether well-fed or not. Some are fussy, some are jumpy and others just don't want to be disturbed. Some are comforted by the slightest touch, while others will remain inconsolable despite feeding, bounding, driving round the block, the tuneless drone of the vacuum cleaner, Willie Nelson records or other such sounds. Of course, it's the hard to comfort, tense and active babies who cause the most anguish.

Tense babies

Some babies are tense and jumpy from birth. They will jump as the nursery door closes, hate any changes, prefer not to be handled too much, and take great exception to being stripped and put in a bath. They respond best to quiet, firm holding, gentle movement, dim lights, swaddling, sucking, gentle massage, soothing talk and music. Noise, tension, bouncing and any frantic movement is best avoided because it will stir them up.

Active babies

These bright-eyed little humans want action. They have neither the time nor the inclination just to lie on their back being a baby. No lying flat in a pram for these babies thank you very much, they want to be upright and on the move. They like to be strapped to your back or sitting in a pushchair where they can see everything going on around them.

Though entertained by activity and movement, these little people are easily bored when the merry-go-round stops. They are happiest when the house is full of action and noise with lots of dogs, children and adults romping around.

Active babies tend to be more irritable in their first year and demand a lot of individual attention. They improve dramatically once they are upright on their own feet and independent. This improvement can be accelerated by careful use of a baby walker.

The most important time when active babies need to be soothed and calmed is when they are tired and it's near bedtime. At this time activity will wind them up and make sleep difficult, so soothing care is necessary if you are going to cool down their fast-moving brain enough to permit sleep. This is the time for quiet holding or just putting them down to settle in the same way as you would with a tense baby.

What about the parents?

Easy babies produce relaxed, confident, competent parents. Inconsolable, irritable children inflict immeasurable psychological pain on their unsuspecting parents. Sometimes it is hard to understand why your baby responds with nothing more than continuous crying and apparent unhappiness when you are heaping love, care and attention on him. Where are you going wrong? Why can't you cope when all those other mothers out there seem to be doing so well? Crying is a real confidence crusher.

The answer of course is that you are doing nothing wrong at all. You are every bit as good a parent as the next one, it's just that you are unlucky to have been dealt a difficult baby.

I believe there are no saints in this world. We do what we do because we get our own particular rewards. Mothers who give their all to their babies need a return on their investment and inconsolable crying gives none of this. Soothing the unsoothable is one of life's most soul destroying experiences and is guaranteed to reduce the competent to a feeling of utter impotence. Excessive crying, especially when coupled with a lack of sleep, can easily lead to parents with numb, befuddled brains. This in turn leads to tension and irritability which is in turn communicated to the baby who then behaves even worse, and so the vicious circle spins round even faster like a catherine wheel.

There are, I'm afraid, no miracle cures for such babies, but hopefully some of the ideas in the next chapter will ease the burden a little.

16

How to Comfort a Crying Baby

WHEN it comes to comforting crying babies I'm afraid there are no hard and fast rules. The whole thing falls into the category of 'seat of your pants' science.

In this chapter I'll be discussing a wide selection of comfort ideas. Some are effective for the majority of children, some for a select few, and I must admit some may not work at all. Comfort is a peculiarly personal affair and certain techniques which may be good for one type of child may not work on another. What is good for the active baby may not work on the tense, and what is good for the grumbler may not necessarily help with colic.

For most first-time parents, the right type of comfort is discovered by trial and error. By consulting the lists in this chapter, hopefully you will have more ideas for trial and less room for error.

Top tries for different cries

Before you get totally bogged down in what follows, let's steer you towards the best strategies for the main types of crying. As you scan the lists you may wonder what happened to milk allergy, gastric antacids and tapes of pretend heart beats. I have to confess that I have moved heavily towards all the old-fashioned, well-tried remedies. I am sure that they leave what's new and trendy for dead. Soothing by gentle movement, postures, swaddling and sound is as old as civilisation itself. These forms of soothing have stood the test of time and are still streets ahead of anything new today.

The list that follows is beautifully black and white, but don't let this fool you for a minute. Nothing in your life or mine is as cut and dried as this. Use these suggestions as a guide from which to choose your next move. Use a package of three or four ideas at the one time. There's no guarantee of success first off but some guidance beforehand has to save a bit of emotional energy in the long run.

Colic

Posture – over knee, arm or bed
Apply gentle pressure to abdomen
Movement – firm, one step per second
Patting and rhythm
Sucking
Swaddling
Medicines

The active baby

Slings, frontpacks and pushchairs
Baby bouncers, baby walkers
Allowing baby to sit up and look around
(He'll be more content when he starts walking alone)

The grumbler

Patting
Dummies
Music
Changing nappy
Leaving alone

The tense baby

Swaddling
Firm holding
Firm stroking of the back
Gentle rhythmic movement
Leaving in peace

When all else fails

Get out of the house with Baby
Visit friends, playgroups, baby health clinic
Ask for help
Ask friends or family to mind Baby for a while
When you can take no more, put Baby in the safety of his cot and move away

Posture

For every crying, unhappy baby there is a particular position of maximum comfort. The trouble is it takes a lot of experimenting before you find it.

Most babies just like to be close to their parents, probably held up against the chest, where they can snuggle in, hear a heart beat and possibly peep over the shoulder (Diagram 1). A simple sling made from an old sheet or a commercially made frontpack will give comfort to both the holder and 'holdee' and frees up Mum's hands to continue with her work (Diagram 2).

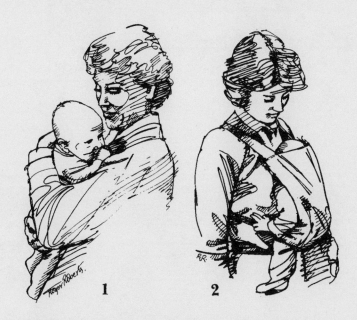

The tense baby will accept most positions so long as he is held firmly and not fussed over. The active ones prefer to be upright, on the move and able to see what's going on. With them slings, pushchairs and baby bouncers are the answer.

The colicky baby is usually happiest when held in a position which puts some gentle pressure on his tummy. This can be achieved either by lying his tummy down over an arm (Diagrams 3 and 4), knee or pillow (Diagram 5) or folding him gently in the middle which enables a little squeeze to be given to his troubled tummy. By folding I mean letting him sit in the crook of your left arm with his knees drawn up and his body flexed forward (Diagram 6). Another favourite hold is with your baby's back against your chest, facing out in front with his legs held up against his abdomen or moved gently in a bicycling movement (Diagram 7).

Try a number of positions until you find the one that suits you and Baby best. Some, such as carrying him over an arm, give portability whilst soothing over a knee or pillow ties you down.

These illustrations were compiled with the help of the staff from Torrens House – CAFHS, Adelaide.

The correct posture will help most criers but there may come a point when whatever you do does no good. When that happens, it's probably best to put your baby down in the safety of his cot. Being glued to an inconsolable child can create more tension and frustration than is good for you or your baby. There is a time when it's best to separate, in the name of safety, before something snaps.

Movement

Movement has always been recognised as the great baby soother, but be careful not to overdo it. Gentle rhythms give good comfort, but wild gyrations do nothing but stir up and unsettle young ones, so take it easy.

Most babies like to rock gently with Mum on a rocking chair or to walk slowly round the room with her. The operative word here is walk. Don't prance from foot to foot as if you're walking on hot coals. One small step per second will give the right rhythm.

Quiet babies enjoy long periods of horizontal meditation in a pram. Active babies, on the other hand, seem to be allergic to this. Being compulsive nosey-parkers, they like to be propped up on pillows so that they can see what's going on.

The pushchair is a device which is ideal for the active baby. He can then face the oncoming world at eye level (well, at knee level, perhaps). The only problem is when the pushchair stops. You will find that long chats in the street are out if you want to keep a busy baby happy.

Movement in a car often soothes the active or colicky baby, but he won't cope well with traffic jams and red lights. On the other hand, many an exasperated parent has had welcome relief from a trip around the block at 3 am.

Soothing sounds

Since the Dark Ages lullabies have been used to soothe babies. The words are irrelevant, but the rhythm and tones are low-pitched with long, drawn-out syllables and have special meaning.

If you can sing then let your baby have the full works. If you can't, then forget the words and just hum along – the effect will be the same. If, however, you are tone deaf you can always buy the latest tape of womb sounds. These may not feature in the Top 40 but the gushes, wooshes and gut rumblings are said to soothe some babies as surely as the choir of heavenly angels.

Babies are not quite as discerning as their parents when it comes to soothing sounds. Some babies will relax to the roar of the vacuum cleaner, while others positively purr to the strains of the washing machine, and even the white noise of an untuned radio station is another popular soother.

The important thing here is experimentation. You never know what's going to be best until you try it. Keep it simple and don't get too scientific.

Swaddling

Back in biblical times swaddling was very popular, and it's still good value today. Remember that the newborn has been effectively swaddled for nine months inside Mum's tummy and it's not surprising that he likes returning to the pretend womb of a tightly wrapped blanket.

In the first weeks most babies prefer to be wrapped firmly. They are ill at ease when stripped off and left lying free in space. Swaddling is particularly good for tense babies who gain great comfort from being bundled up. Wrap them tightly, leave them alone and they are at their happiest.

Active babies, on the other hand, object to being restricted. You may swaddle them as much as you like but they jack up and will kick their way to freedom.

Sucking and dummies

A great many criers are helped by sucking. It's not the kilojoules that they're after but the soothing sensation of a breast, bottle, hand or dummy.

Colicky babies don't want food, but they do like to suck. They get this by snuggling up to a breast, a dummy or bottle. I must admit that I have often put a little soothing solution of some anti-colic medicine in the bottle to suck. I don't really believe this will make a lot of difference but it's a nice idea to offer two soothing treatments at the same time.

Whatever you do, as you hold them in the approved position, walk them at the correct speed, or pat them with perfect rhythm, try a bit of sucking at the same time.

When it comes to grumbling babies, a dummy will be most useful. They can lie in their cots, sucking a bit and grumbling a bit at the same time. For them this little bit of oral entertainment keeps their minds off the woes of the world.

Don't be frightened to introduce a dummy for fear that you will not be able to break the habit later. If it helps keep the peace now, then that's most important. (See Chapter 8 – Dummies.)

Try to keep dummies reasonably clean. They can be scrubbed, soaked in bottle-sterilising solution or boiled clean in a saucepan but don't dip them in sugar solutions as this is bad for teeth when they come through.

Hot water bottles and hot baths

Just as young girls suffering from period pains are often told to go to bed with a hot water bottle, so can babies be soothed, who have what is believed to be a crampy abdomen.

Fill the bottle with hot, but never scalding, water then wrap it in a soft towel. Hold the warm towel against the baby's abdomen and lay him down on the bottle. As the warmth makes contact, start to massage and gently pat him to produce a super soothe.

Upset babies won't thank you for being stripped off and put in a baby bath, but an adult bath may be a different matter. Get the temperament just right and then slip in with your baby. This allows togetherness, body contact and for some is as therapeutic as a plunge in healing hot springs.

Massage

As you will know if you are a pet owner, all dogs and cats have their favourite stroking spots which leave them drooling in a state of blissful euphoria. Human babies too can be soothed by a gentle touch.

The back of the neck, down the back (beside the spine) and the abdomen seem generally to be the prime spots, but only trial and error will let you know where your baby prefers. It is best to sprinkle him with baby powder to allow your hands to glide smoothly over his little chassis, though you could always douse him with oil for that real GTX-low-friction massage.

Massage works best when it is unrushed. A warm, dimly-lit room with your favourite tape playing softly in the background is the ideal location. You should first experiment with your baby in times of peace and wakefulness. Once you have found the best technique for him, then you can give it a try when he is tense and crying.

Wind and gas

While wind certainly upsets the stomachs of sea-sick sailors, I fear that it is greatly overrated as a cause for crying babies. However, experiment for yourself and if you find that releasing the last gurgle of gas brings relief then by all means go ahead. I'm certainly convinced though that the rock-pat-burp routine gives closeness, rhythm and movement and that must be good for any upset baby.

Changing the formula

If my car starts to smoke and backfire I know that there is something wrong with the motor. This needs a mechanic, not a change from one brand of petrol to another. Likewise if your baby is crying and colicky on one formula, changing his fuel to another brand isn't going to do much more than perhaps change the colour of the exhaust products.

Please don't go off on a formula shuffling spree. If your baby is breast-feeding and thriving, don't stop. It may occasionally help if you cut out dairy products from your own diet for a while, but even that's uncertain.

It is true that occasionally babies do have a real allergy to cow's milk and become extremely sick, blotchy, pale and wheezy. Lesser allergies are also said to cause a multitude of minor symptoms from a runny nose to colic.

Although many do not share my view, I have rarely been impressed with claims that crying has been cured by a switch from cow's milk to a pretend brand, but if in doubt, give it a short trial.

Extra kilojoules and solids

Some people may argue that since donkeys have four legs, then everything that has four legs must be a donkey. However, this logic does not work with starving babies. Starving babies cry, but most crying babies are not starving. If your baby is unsettled, is thriving poorly and homes in on food like a famished vulture, then it is time to investigate his intake. If, on the other hand, he is robust, healthy and cries regardless of his nourishment, then the answer does not lie in food. If you're in doubt about the adequacy of your baby's food intake then talk to your health visitor.

Wet and dirty nappies

New mums are always told to check for wet nappies and sharp pins, when their youngsters cry. I don't believe that most babies are that sensitive to damp. After all, they are submerged for the first nine months and then dribble, spill and wet for most of the next two years, without too much upset.

As for being impaled on a pin, it must be pretty rare if proper nappy pins are used and if the parent who uses them pokes them through with hands that are being guided by a functioning brain.

I admit that the grumbling baby may fuss less when dry, but I am afraid that the screamer is usually as vocal whether there is a flood or drought down there in the bottom paddock. If you are in doubt then change the nappy, but don't be surprised if it doesn't stop the crying.

Medicines

Most parents with a consistent crier will eventually experiment with a few medicines. These range from homeopathic drops to camomile tea, or from gripe water to sedation. While there's nothing wrong with using any safe medical or alternative preparations, my own experience shows that they rarely seem to work.

Last century gin was the standby of the professional baby minder. A couple of glasses for them, a teaspoonful for Baby, and by the end of the evening no more crying was heard. I know some people still swear by a little brandy diluted with warm water, and sucked off a spoon, but alcohol is probably best left as an interesting relic of the past. Gripe water has been popular for generations of mums with criers. It has its devoted followers, but once again there is not a lot of convincing evidence that it works.

Other medicines are said to break up gas bubbles in the gut and guide them gently towards an opening. This sounds more commendable, but I don't really believe that gas is the cause of continuous crying either.

The drug Merbentyl was, until recently, the most specific and effective colic medicine. Though it is still on the market, it is not recommended for babies under six months of age now, due to reports of some significant, though admittedly rare, side effects.

Some doctors will prescribe sedatives when crying is constant and inconsolable and the parents are close to breaking point. I don't see them as a great evil and, when the chips are down, if they are going to help keep the family intact, then they probably should be used.

However, before you decide to use medicines I think you should try the simple, soothing ideas mentioned above first. Then have a chat with your local chemist. He'll be able to tell you what sort of snake oil or jungle juice is rating well with babies in your area.

Although it's not easy to remember when the tears are flooding and your befuddled brain has zero confidence, colic and crying are very short-term problems. Time is an amazing healer, and it should be of some consolation to know that your baby will soon move on from this distressing stage.

Time to oneself

It's not hard to imagine what happens to a parent's self-confidence when Baby has been crying long and hard and all efforts to comfort him have collapsed. All optimism is replaced by a focus on failure. Now this is the time to down tools and get out.

Load up the pram or pushchair and head for the wide open spaces. Crying is often soothed by movement and, if not, it is always less upsetting out of doors.

Isolation is the curse of many families. Now's the time you need Grandma, Aunty or support from any kind, caring friend. You need time to get out, to unwind from tension, to clear the brain and to regain an identity other than that of a failed mother.

Isolation can be deepened by fathers who see baby care as a soft option. They refuse to release funds for child minding and without this much-needed sanity saver some mothers get more and more isolated. As depression, demoralisation and tiredness take over, many mothers find it easier to stay in the rut than muster the energy needed to get up and go. Others are so delicate and paranoid that anyone else coping where they have failed is seen as the ultimate insult.

Time to oneself is for all mothers, not just for those in strife. Time to recharge the batteries helps both you, the baby and everyone around you. If you can get some time to go out, grab it with both hands and don't let anyone make you feel guilty. Mix with other adults, do some exercise or just involve yourself in something quite different from the daily grind of nappy-washing, house-polishing and husband-feeding.

When all else fails

When all comfort fails, there is no help, you can't get out and you can't take any more, then you and your baby must separate. Take the inconsolable baby, put him in the security of his cot, close the door and move outside or to the most distant part of the house. *This is time out for Mum and is much better to take than be driven over the brink.*

Accepting advice

One thing is absolutely certain in this world. There is no shortage of free advice from well-wishers telling you how to manage your children. Theoretical advice from highly trained academics is all very well, but when you are shattered and hanging on by a whisker, only good, sound, practical advice will do.

When the going gets tough, advice should only be accepted from friends and family who offer to roll up their sleeves and help. The others can keep their theories to themselves. Criticising relatives are best dealt with on a fair-trade basis. You'll accept their criticism if they're prepared in return to help you with some regular day-to-day care. In my experience a few difficult days and noisy nights soon separate the hot air merchants from the genuine helpers.

It is important to choose your helping professionals with care. What you need is an expert who will give help with the minimum of professional pontification. You need a whiz-kid doctor who can quote all the latest research papers like an Eskimo needs a lawn mower. Whether it be health visitor, psychologist or doctor, you need a listener, a communicator and someone who understands how you feel. They must be able to boost your confidence and send you off with a list of practical ideas that work for real people.

Conclusion

All babies cry with different duration, style, intensity and ease of comfort. Those parents with easy babies have no idea just what their friends are going through.

Continuous, inconsolable crying transforms the confident, optimistic parent into a demoralised defeatist. There are no sure-fire cures for crying. You must experiment and pick a package of ideas which will give some relief, while time does its healing work. Don't give up. Crying always improves as the months go by.

Parents matter too. When the crying is getting to you, seek help and don't feel guilty about taking time out to cool off by yourself. Helpful friends and family are to be blessed, empty air-filled critics should be ignored, though they deserve something much nastier.

17

Sleep Problems – How to Solve them

How much does a new baby sleep? Probably a darn sight less than most parents ever expected. Though sleep is a big part of our lives, we are still uncertain how it revives tired brains and bodies. What is certain, is that without sleep we would soon fall apart.

Sleep deprivation is not just unpleasant, it is a form of torture. Secret police use it to soften up those they bring in for a chat. Come to think of it, after a week of disturbed sleep the average parent is about ready to confess to anything.

Most babies in the first three months are going to wake once or more each night. You may become resigned to this fact and when it happens view it as normal. If by some great fortune you score a super sleeper, then that's a bonus and a pleasant surprise. By six months about three-quarters of all babies sleep through to sunrise but this still leaves one-quarter who continue to wake, many of whom keep up the antics right through toddlerhood.

The sleep-deprived mum can be spotted at a distance of one hundred paces. She has bags under her eyes and the defeated stoop of someone who has run (and lost) a marathon. Such is her exhaustion and despair that anyone who could cure the problem would probably be left money in her will.

All children are not born with an equal capacity to sleep. A few will sleep perfectly, right from birth, many will wake a bit and others will be total disaster areas. The most difficult sleep problem I ever cured was a boy who, at eight months, had never slept for more than one single hour at a time and never for more than four hours total in a day. When I say cure, he eventually slept for six hours each night and none by day. This may be unimpressive to the average mum but for this one she felt it was a miracle.

Of course, we can't cure the incurable, but if you have sensible expectations, introduce a good sleep routine and use my controlled crying technique (see page 153), all should gain improvement and most will find a cure.

The Science of Sleep

It is impossible to make any adult or child sleep deeply and continuously all night, this is just not how sleep works. Sleep is not one unbroken, dead to the world state, but a glide through a standard sequence of levels of consciousness. Deep sleep – light sleep – a period of dreams – a brief awakening and roll over – then down into the depths once more and so the cycle goes on all night.

If you attach electrodes of a brain wave test (electroencephalogram – EEG) to a sleeping human, the tracing tells us much about the states of sleep. This shows if they are deeply asleep, dreaming or floating on a lighter plane. It measures the length of the cycle and tells us how much time is spent in each state along the way.

From this we discover that adults sleep a ninety-minute cycle from start to finish. This means that every ninety minutes we wake briefly, open our eyes, stretch, grunt, roll over, register that it is still dark and then go back to sleep again. When we wake we keep it to ourselves and don't wake our partner to share the moment.

New babies ride a cycle with a shorter frame, one which measures only sixty minutes. Being shorter it increases the potential number of wakes possible each night, leaving the daunting possibility of a wake every hour on the hour if you are really unfortunate.

As parents, we can recognise some of these light periods of sleep. Sometimes the baby will stretch, grunt, yawn, open a sleepy eye and drop off again. Sometimes they start to cry in a half-hearted way, uncertain if they want attention or whether it is better just to grumble themselves back to sleep. It is also at these times that they move around the cot, kick off the blankets and of course may well wake and shout for attention.

It is nigh on impossible to make little children stay deeply unconscious all night, they will always wake. What we as parents can do is to teach them to wake quietly, get themselves back to sleep without help and not to disturb their parents.

The brain wave tests also show that little children fall asleep much faster than adults. While we glide through every level down to the deep sleep, they drop like a brick in a bucket. Splash! – right to the bottom. It seems that little babies are either very awake or very asleep, and don't spend much time in between.

This explains why your baby can be all smiles and activity one minute and the next so deeply asleep he would sleep through a heavy metal rock concert – and have missed nothing. When very asleep, you can take them to restaurants, parties and generally be as noisy as you like at home. Babies usually sleep deep.

147

Other EEG findings show how much we dream. Adults spend about one-quarter of sleep time in dream sleep, whilst newborns show an unexpected pattern of dreaming 50 per cent of the time. Now we don't know if this is dreaming as in adults, but if it is, one wonders what they know that we don't!

As parents, we can often spot these times of dreaming. The mouth may move, the eyelids flutter and beneath them the eyes are probably racing around like grand prix cars.

All this talk of the science of deep sleep has probably left you yawning but it explains much of what we see.

- Sleep is in a series of cycles.
- We all have the potential to wake in the night, little children more so.
- Adults drift to sleep, babies plummet.
- Babies sleep deep and are relatively immune to noise.
- Adults when they wake have learnt to put themselves back to sleep. Little children must be taught this social skill.

How Much Sleep is Enough?

It is pointless me dictating exactly how many hours your baby will sleep. Each child is an individual with his own sleep needs and patterns, and will go his own way whatever I say. We do however have some idea of the range of sleep habits you can expect at different ages.

The newborn

In the first weeks of life, most babies will sleep between fourteen and twenty hours each day. They take this as a series of snoozes, each lasting between one and six hours, with an average length of three to four hours.

At birth, the sleep periods are spread out evenly throughout the twenty-four hours, with no preference for night or day. It is interesting that before birth the setting of the sleep clock is actually loaded against night sleep. Little British babies seem tuned to Australian time, being more quiet by day and practising the high kicks of the cancan when it's dark and Mum is trying to sleep.

At three months

By now the average baby will sleep fifteen hours each day, with two-thirds of this at night. About half will be sleeping right through with the other half still keen to call for room service at least once before dawn.

At six months

By six months the sleep pattern has become much more predictable and there is sufficient maturity to start moulding the poor sleeper towards a more sociable habit. Now about three-quarters will be sleeping right through the night.

At one year

Now the usual pattern is of thirteen to fourteen hours each day with two day-time naps, the longest after lunch and a shorter mid-morning one which will soon drop off.

At two years

About one-fifth will still be waking most nights and many more will be very reluctant to go to bed. There's now only one nap, this usually being in the afternoon. At this stage some of the busier little bees will be all for losing this and will go to their cots with a fair amount of protest. If they show no fatigue, it might be best to forgo this sleep and maybe read to them instead. Some sleep well in the afternoon but at the cost of making them hard to settle at night. So a choice has to be made. The day-time nap usually disappears before the age of three, though a few would gladly snooze up to and even while at infants school.

Older children

After this, sleep patterns are all very individual. For example, most ten-year-olds sleep for about ten hours, whilst late teenagers often come down to just seven or eight. Whether that is due to bad habits or is simply all the sleep they need is unclear. Even adults have completely different needs. Some declare that they cannot function with less than ten hours, whilst the Churchills and Thatchers of this world, in common with many other driving individuals, seem to thrive on as little as four hours a night.

So what is the message out of all of this?

- Each baby is born with a very individual sleep profile.
- In the first three months expect most babies to wake once or more each night.
- From three to six months expect about half to wake.
- After six months the sleepless reduce to about one-quarter, but you now have the ability to change the situation.

To be (or not to be) tough

A non-sleeping baby can enfeeble the most robust of parents, yet there is not too much you can do about it in the first three months. From three months until six months is a time to concentrate on *good routines*. Where sleep is a problem after six months of age you have the power to change things, and now you must decide whether *to be or not to be tough*.

Basically you have three options. You can smile like a saint and accept this as a minor hassle and all part of the joys of parenting. You can throw up your hands in despair, do nothing, and proceed through life like a member of the walking dead. Alternatively, you can become utterly bloody minded, determined to stop the problem, and finish it right here and now.

Forty years ago there wouldn't have been any question about what you should do. In those days babies were treated very firmly right from their earliest days and mollycoddling them was to be avoided at all costs. Those were the days of fixed feeding times, not rushing to cuddle a distressed child and being very strict with them at night-time. Babies of that generation were quickly taught that bed was a place for sleep and not some stage upon which to perform a late night show.

Then we entered the present 'give 'em all you've got' era. Now we feed on demand, comfort them whenever asked, whatever time of day or night it is, and are told that we cannot spoil a baby. But remember, childcare fashions come and go like the passing seasons and I believe the winds of change are starting to blow down the corridors of baby care once more. Ten years from now I am sure the teaching will be for much tougher limits on our babies. If your baby has a sleep problem, but it isn't causing you too much upset then you can grin and bear it. If it is making everyone's life an utter misery, then treat it. Not next week, or next month, but tonight!

Let's look at this in two ways. First, prevention by starting out with *good habits* and then, *the cure* for when prevention fails.

Setting Good Habits from the Start

Some babies are built to sleep soundly no matter what you do. Others are lousy sleepers and will wake up at the drop of a pin, making the night shift a long and difficult one. A great many of these, however, have the potential to sleep really well but somehow have lost their way and got off on the wrong footing. Here are some ways to encourage a better sleep pattern.

A consistent routine

Just like adults, children thrive best on a consistent sleep routine. The time of going to bed and getting up should, as far as possible, be constant and late nights should be avoided whenever you can. Children of all ages like routine and quickly come to accept it, and although such a sleep routine may not make an enormous difference in the first months, it should bring its rewards later on.

Cues and rituals

As adults we tend to lead much of our lives with our brains in neutral and our bodies locked into automatic pilot. We go about the day's routine firmly guided by previous programming and cues from our environment. For example, we know it's time to get up because it's daylight, we eat lunch at a certain time because the clock says midday, we prepare for bed with a ritual of teeth-brushing, undressing and reading a book to help us unwind. All in all we function like factory robots, taking our cues from our environment and being creatures of habit.

These cues and rituals which get us so comfortably through the day are also important for our children. Try to develop a standard sequence of cues and rituals to prepare Baby for sleep. Don't make them too complex or it will take all night to get ready for bed. But once you've worked them out, stick to them each night and always maintain this good pattern. First there can be a bath followed by a nice warm rub-down and then get Baby dressed in his sleep attire. Take him into his bedroom, dim the lights and give him his goodnight bottle or breast. From here on consistent cues should be given such as gentle patting, talking quietly or even singing (if your voice is up to it). Then, before he has fallen asleep, you should just walk out saying 'Goodnight'. Go through this ritual every night and your baby should very soon catch on to what is expected of him.

The put-down

If you are graced with the kind of baby who drops like an autumn leaf from a twig every night, then whatever it is you're doing must be right so keep on doing it. If, on the other hand, his night-time antics are more akin to a bedroom farce, then it's time to look at how you're dealing with Baby at bedtime.

As we have already seen, babies, like adults, come close to consciousness at regular intervals through the night, but whereas we adults can open our eyes, see that it is still dark and crash back to sleep again, some babies may find this difficult without you coming in to comfort them. This difficulty is often caused by never being allowed to fall asleep without your comfort. If your baby is put to sleep every night by being rocked, bounced and cuddled tight, caring and charitable though this may be, it could well lead to big trouble when it comes to the 3 am eye-opener. At this ungodly hour your baby may well refuse to go back to sleep unless you turn on the full show again, and understandably you will be less than enthusiastic about it.

Though most parents are going to cuddle their little babies to sleep, there is more chance of establishing a good habit if you let them fall asleep in the comfort of their own cot without too much parental prancing about. If they manage to fall asleep without your close contact at bedtime, they are more likely to drop off again without it later on. Just pop Baby in the cot, pat him gently, talk soothingly and be in the room but don't lift, rock or cuddle him. Your presence alone will suffice, and if he drops off to sleep this way then the chances are he will do the same when he wakes in the wee small hours of the morning.

Sleep – The Cure

There is a noisy lobby group who believe that it is every parent's duty to be up all night every night, ready to rush in the moment their child makes the slightest squeak. This is one of those wonderful childcare theories which looks fine in books, but when you are faced with the constant crier it's not so wonderful. Multiple nocturnal disturbances may suit some parental masochists who feel you must suffer to be a good person, but for most of us it's a one-way ticket to collapse.

There is another group who believe that all babies should be handled firmly from their earliest days. If they wish to cry at night then that's their problem and they should be left to get on with it. The theory is, that if left, they will soon get the message. The problem is that babies often become hysterical, get themselves into a lather and sometimes vomit all over their cot if left like that. The answer, I believe, has to be somewhere in the middle, with a bit of firmness but never fear or hysterical crying.

Since 1974 I have been promoting my controlled crying technique for helping young children to sleep and with considerable success. The aim is to

let them cry for a short period of time, but not long enough for them to get upset or hysterical. You come in and give them some basic comfort, but the moment the crying abates and turns to sobs, you leave at once. They will protest immediately but this time you extend the time by several minutes before going back in to comfort them. Then you go in, comfort them and again put them down the moment they stop crying and leave at once. This will build up by small amounts each time until eventually the little one realises that the parents will always come if he needs them, but that it's really not worth all the hassle. Then he sleeps without disturbance.

When I first started this technique I didn't try it on any child under the age of eighteen months, but by 1980 I found that ten-month-old babies could be treated just as effectively. I now find success right down to the age of six months.

The controlled crying technique

If sleep disturbance has become a major problem after six months of age follow this technique firmly and do not give up until you see considerable relief. As every child and every parent is different, you have to adjust the method to suit your stamina and style. If in doubt start gently but never back off and, hard as it may be in the early days, don't give up.

1 When the baby first starts to cry resist running in to give instant comfort.

2 Wait five minutes if you are feeling tough, three minutes on average, one if you are a bit fragile, and go straight in the first time if you're really delicate or worried about the baby.

3 Go in to Baby and make your presence felt. You may lift, cuddle and comfort him if you wish but it is preferable just to pat and soothe him where he lies.

4 When the crying has ebbed to a series of soft sobs and sniffles, that's the sign to cut the comfort and clear out. Once you hear that sniff the infant Einstein is saying to himself 'Aha, now I've got them!'. But this is where the young Albert has it all wrong. If you leave him, the little sobber will say to himself 'Hey! What's going on here? My audience has walked out'. Nevertheless you must be firm and go, even though the crying will start again with gusto.

5 This time allow the crying to go on for a slightly longer period before returning to comfort him. If, for example, it was three minutes last time, then this time leave him for five.

6 Each time you go back remember just to comfort Baby until the cry stops and the sniff starts then put him down and scram! Don't feed or cuddle him off to sleep. That's not part of the deal.

7 Eventually the message will get through that Mum or Dad will always come when he cries, but is it really worth all the effort?

8 Keep this routine going tonight, tomorrow and for as long as it takes to work. Don't give an inch whatever you do. The cry periods should rise to a maximum of ten minutes (fifteen minutes at absolute most) and plateau then.

9 With babies over six months of age you should get about an 80 per cent cure within one to three weeks, while many of the remaining 20 per cent should show a significant improvement. Most cures are actually secured well within the first week. I find those who have been terrible sleepers from birth are usually more difficult, they take a little longer and have a lower complete cure rate. Those who have slept well and have wandered off-course along the way are generally easier to cure.

10 If you are feeling particularly fragile or the crying is going on too long then, with medical guidance, you can introduce a little sedation (see page 158). After half an hour of being awake and using the controlled crying method, the child can be sedated. This will guarantee a good night's sleep but gives the child a major message while the sedation is working. Sedation takes half an hour to act and you keep the technique going until they finally drop.

Some Practical Points

Night feeds and the milkaholic

When babies are very young they feed to gain nutrition, but by the age of three months the night-time nibble is moving more towards comfort than kilojoules. By six months it is certainly only a soothing suck they are after and so now's the time you can discard it safe in the knowledge that you won't be the cause of night starvation!

Feeding a baby until he drops off to sleep is a bit like rocking him off to sleep. It might all be very cosy and comforting, but you run the danger of making a rod for your own back. In time you may set up a dependence that creates a no-suck–no-sleep situation.

If your baby has a reasonable sleep pattern and the night feeds suit you, please feed. It's only when you are becoming exhausted that the firm approach is needed.

Breast comfort and the night-time curfew

Little babies may not yet have the refined tastebuds to tell Pepsi from Coke, but they can sure tell the difference between the bottle and the breast. At night-time it's comfort not content that matters to Baby and, let's face it, even at that age they aren't stupid. Given the choice between a nice warm breast and a cold rubber teat soaked in some smelly sterilising fluid, which would you prefer?

I believe it's best to feed and comfort your baby in the first six months. After that you can keep the night shift going if you are happy with it, but if it has become an exhausting experience then it's time to call for a curfew.

You do this by giving the child his last breast-feed on going to bed and refusing to offer it again until morning. If the baby wakes up in the meantime then by all means give him comfort, but don't feed him. The most effective way of ensuring this works is getting Dad to sign on for the night shift. After all he doesn't have the equipment to feed so the only thing he can give is comfort.

Dummies and sleep

Some babies love to suck a dummy to soothe them to sleep. Unfortunately there is one great drawback to this. The dummy eventually dislodges and all hell breaks loose. Trying to play 'hunt the dummy' in the dark at one in the morning is not much fun. Some parents go to inordinate lengths to ensure that child and dummy stay attached. Safety pins and tape are common additives but it would be a brilliant baby indeed who could work out how to haul in a catch like that in the middle of the night.

Some parents have been known to hang dummies along the side of the cot like balloons at a carnival on the basis that at least one has to be within range of the baby's mouth when the grizzling commences. Unfortunately they never seem to make contact.

Dummies at night are generally more trouble than they are worth and unless they are bringing big benefits it is best never to start using them in the first place. As for keeping them in place, I have no answers. Your options are either to ban them from the cot and put up with protest, or refuse to replace them in the early hours in the hope that they will be forgotten.

Sometimes it is much easier to go in and insert a dummy than to fight over sleep. If this approach suits your style and brings night-time peace, then do it.

The light sleeper

On going to bed most babies will drop quickly into the deepest sleep becoming dead to the world. One minute they're all smiles and gurgles, the next nothing short of a 10 megaton blast will make them blink. These young babies are oblivious to such things as whether the lights are on or off, and can sleep happily through the noisiest party. There are, however, a small group of children who seem to have their senses turned to a supersensitive level and who will wake at the slightest disturbance. This can become an utter pain for parents who then have to tiptoe around the house avoiding squeaky floorboards, keeping the TV turned down and leaving the toilet unflushed.

If the situation becomes quite unbearable, there are ways of desensitising Baby. First, introduce a little noise into his life and then build it up gradually until he becomes immune. You can do this with the help of a simple transistor radio. On the first night leave the set on zero volume. Next night turn it up a little, and then night by night thereafter turn the volume up little by little until eventually the bedroom resembles a Michael Jackson concert. Actually, gentle music from an all-night radio station is probably the best choice, but sometimes the very sensitive children may even wake with the gaps in the records. If this is the case tune the radio to an FM station and then shift the knob a fraction so that you get the static instead of the station. Start this as a gentle hiss on night one and increase it to the sound of the Niagara Falls, it will have the same effect.

Other children sharing a bedroom with Baby

If your baby is over six months old with disturbed sleep patterns and your poor, tired brain cannot cope any longer, then you need a cure. The controlled crying technique should sort things out for you, but if the baby is sharing a bedroom with a brother or sister who is a sensitive sleeper then you have a problem. Once the controlled crying starts you end up with two non-sleepers instead of one!

Don't despair. The treatment is easy, though somewhat unjust. Put the better of the two sleepers into another room and if another bedroom isn't available, then use the sitting room, kitchen or a passage way for a bit. Since this is only a temporary measure nobody need feel he is being got at. Now that the coast is clear set up the controlled crying technique and when peace returns you can reunite the sleeping beauties.

Whose bedroom?

For the first couple of months most babies will sleep in a carry cot before moving on to a cot. These are so portable that at this early stage Baby can be left to sleep in almost any location. The question is whether to have him sleeping next to you or in a nearby room?

It really doesn't matter where he sleeps. The important thing is that all parties get as much unbroken sleep as possible. Having Baby next to the parents' bed is certainly convenient for the night-time feed, but parents being only human usually cannot sleep sufficiently soundly this way, tending to keep one ear open to monitor all the grunts and chokes of their newborn.

Although it doesn't really matter where Baby sleeps during the first couple of months, I do feel that once he moves into a cot it should be in a room separate from the parents'. This is not always possible, but if space in your home allows, separation is best.

Deaf dads

I've never actually seen it published in a scientific journal, but there is good evidence to support the theory that many husbands go stone deaf once the lights go out.

'Did you hear the baby crying at 3 am?' – 'No, never heard a thing!' I bet if he were expecting a phone call to confirm he had won the lottery he would bolt out of bed on the first ring. Of course what we are talking about here is not a permanent problem, but a well-known male affliction called selective deafness. Luckily this is not incurable. A sharp kick in the shins at 3 am seems to help tune in the male hearing once again, most effectively.

When to start curing sleep problems

Things will usually get worse before they start to get better. Once you commence the controlled crying technique you can expect at least two difficult nights before the benefits start to show. With the very young it can sometimes take a couple of weeks before you get relief.

Unfortunately many parents do not have sufficient spare emotional energy to cope with this initial disruption. They are exhausted and go from day to day hanging by the thinnest of emotional threads. It is often easier to continue in this chronic state of suffering than to stir things up, which might snap the thread and lose what little stability there is.

Don't start a sleep programme unless you feel you are together enough to see it through. Start when you are in your strongest frame of mind, there is some chance of support and you have time to catch up on some lost sleep. If you enter this programme with a wishy-washy, fail-before-you-start attitude then you are wasting your time. If you are going to embark on the technique, try starting it on a Friday night. Most people don't have to go to work on Saturday so there's some chance of support and time to catch up on lost sleep. Don't start when the baby is sick or when you are about to go on holiday or there is some family disruption.

Is it sickness?

It is almost impossible to be firm if you suspect that your child may be sick. Certainly if the baby has dull eyes, fever, is off his food and is unwell both day and night then this is genuine enough and you are going to have to expect to be up all night every night until it passes. This, I am afraid, is one of the responsibilities of parenthood which we all experience.

Chronic illness as the cause of sleep problems is however greatly overrated, I believe, and extremely rare. In my work with toddlers, many children sent to me have had sleep problems blamed on conditions ranging from glue-ear to constipation and everything in between. I don't believe a child will wake up two or three times each night for months or years on end due to these sorts of problems. To my mind these children either have a non-sleep temperament or, more likely, they have just got into a bad habit. If you have any doubts about your baby's health, get your doctor to check him out, but once given a clean bill of health, get on with your own treatment.

One word of warning about acute illness however. Many long-term sleep problems start following an acute illness. Your child is no fool. He enjoyed the attention and fuss he got when he was sick and will try to keep this going once he is better if you will oblige. So once the sickness has settled, be firm. It will save you a lot of trauma in the future.

Sedation

I don't believe children should be sedated unless there is a very good reason for doing this. There are a number of occasions when it is called for.

When a family is hanging on by a thread due to chronic sleep starvation, then sedation can provide a valuable safety valve. When the going gets really tough and you feel you are being pushed over the edge, then short-term sedation may save the situation. If you have a disabled child who is irritable most of the day and cries much of the night, then use sedation. This may only be a bandaid but sometimes a bandaid applied at the right time can be a lifesaver.

When the controlled crying technique is failing due to a resistant infant or fragile parents, then giving sedation, along with the programme, can provide the catalyst that 'saves the night'. Sedation given alone, however, without the technique, will have no long-term benefits, as once you stop it the problem returns. Sedation given after half an hour of controlled crying on the other hand has ensured that the message has been given loud and clear before the sleep sets in.

Until recent times, parents could buy children's sedatives without a prescription. Now however most can only be obtained with a doctor's script. These prescription drugs are quite safe as long as they are administered in the proper doses and for the correct reasons.

It is important to realise that all children respond to sedatives in different ways. Some drop into the deepest sleep with little more than a sniff of the uncorked bottle. Others are more resistant and the trick with them is not to give the sedation at bedtime but to wait until they first wake up during the night. It is always more effective at this time and usually guarantees sleep in those important hours from midnight till dawn.

Sedatives don't suit some little children at all. They can turn them, like Jekyll and Hyde, from an awake child into an obnoxious little drunk who will tumble around walking into furniture or, if not at the walking stage, become noisy and restless. Be particularly careful with this group and if you are planning an overseas trip, whatever you do, don't try your first sedative on a long air flight. Travelling for hours at 33,000 feet with a little drunk is no fun for anyone. Try out the medicine at ground level first and test the effect!

In conclusion, yes, I do agree with sedatives, but only when prescribed sensibly, and sensibly means for short periods, in times of crisis or as the catalyst to make a faltering sleep programme work. There is a sedative and dose to suit every child, but it often takes careful adjustment by your doctor to get it right. (See the list of sedatives in the Appendix on page 234.)

Daylight saving

'A thousand curses on the man who invented daylight saving!', I hear you cry. I'm sure it had to be a man, as no mum would have been so keen to reshuffle their children's sleeping patterns.

Changing to British Summertime is of greatest pain at the beginning because you lose an hour. You have just got yourself organised with a 5 am start to the day when that certain Sunday rolls around and bang! You have a 4 am start instead. Give it a week to realign. It's all done by gradually readjusting the whole routine, bedtime, feeds and cues. It's not all bad. When summer ends the clocks will go back again and you'll get a boost in the other direction.

Sleep programmes – do they damage children?

When I first started to work with sleep problems, I was harangued with questions like, 'How do you know that setting limits at night won't cause long-term psychological scars?'. The answer is frankly that I don't know.

I cannot say with any certainty that giving Baby an injection to prevent the measles, removing a perforated appendix or going to the dentist isn't going to cause psychological upset either. What I do know however is that the proven benefits of these actions far outweigh any theoretical concerns, and so it is with sleep programmes.

Of course if we lived in an ideal world where every mum was Wonderwoman and every dad Superman, then we could give comfort all night every night. But in the real world, sleepless children make for tired, irritable parents who give very poor care to their children by day. Sleep problems certainly put enormous stresses on some marriages. It is as though the sleepless child fires a bullet which wounds his parents and then ricochets back to harm him as well. Children must never be allowed to become the instrument of their own destruction or yours! Treat sleep problems seriously.

18

Common Baby Illnesses

ALL babies fall ill from time to time and often parents worry because they're not sure how serious the illnesses are. In this chapter we're taking a quick look at the six most common problems I encounter in my practice. If you are still uncertain or worried about any condition your baby may appear to have, you should not hesitate to seek a medical opinion. It is always better to be safe than sorry.

The common cold

Common this may be, but when your perfect little newborn baby catches his first cold bug, what a drama! The main problem with colds and babies is that little ones of this age don't like living with a blocked nose. It makes them uncomfortable and upsets feeding as they attempt the impossible and try to suck milk and breathe through their mouths at the same time.

Colds can cause poor food intake, fever, irritability, disturbed sleep and even vomiting, but often there is nothing more than a snuffly nose.

The common cold is caused by a number of viruses, none of which unfortunately produces any sort of long-term immunity. It's not like measles or mumps which you catch once and that's it for life. With colds you can be infected this week, catch another variety next month and then be smitten again by the original some time later.

Little babies generally lead relatively isolated lives and are therefore not quite as prone to outside infection as are toddlers and school children. Nevertheless it is still possible for Baby to catch a cold. As the cold virus is not helped by antibiotics, your doctor won't prescribe these. He is not being incompetent, just practising good sensible medicine. Occasionally a secondary bacterial chest or ear infection can come along following a cold and of course these need treatment, but that is a different matter.

Despite what your granny may have told you, you cannot catch a cold from being cold, and getting wet or chilled will not move a cold to your chest. Also, despite forty years of claims that vitamin C prevents and cures colds, there is still no conclusive evidence to support this.

Treatment

The best treatment for a cold is no treatment at all. Of course if there is a fever or some irritability, a little paracetamol may help, and if the nose is blocked and making feeding really difficult, a decongestant could be prescribed, but reluctantly.

Don't poke cotton tips up your baby's nose either as this will do nothing for a cold and may harm the nose.

Vomiting and diarrhoea

All little babies will have some vomits and diarrhoea. If they vomit once or twice or have occasional loose bowel motions, this is generally nothing to worry about. You start to worry when it is persistent and the child obviously looks sick.

Gastro-enteritis is uncommon in young babies and exceptionally rare in those who are totally breast-fed. The very little baby who vomits, more often than not has a benign problem of regurgitation due to his immature stomach. Slightly loose bowels are usually caused by such things as fruit juices, certain solids and often for no very apparent reason.

161

When infection is the cause of vomiting or diarrhoea, it's more likely to be the result of a cold, flu or a sore ear rather than due to a primary gut infection. Where there is a genuine gut infection (gastro-enteritis), its danger has little to do with the number of times the baby vomits or the number of dirty nappies, but rather by its effect on the baby's body fluids and salts. If these get low the urine output reduces, the skin gets dry and the baby looks withdrawn, dull-eyed and unresponsive. This is dangerous and your baby should be seen by your doctor immediately.

Treatment

With gastro-enteritis the aim is to prevent dehydration and its dangers. So please forget the kilojoules and concentrate on getting the fluids in. Never mind any weight loss, this is irrelevant at this time.

If the problem is very mild, just ease back and be selective with the solids and give the milk as small, more frequent feeds. If there is a significant problem, however, then stop all solids immediately to give the baby's gut a rest. If the baby is being breast-fed, carry on with this but with greater frequency and added clear fluids. On the other hand, if your baby is being bottle-fed, then stop the milk for half a day or so and replace it entirely with clear fluids. These will be much easier for Baby to digest and a whole lot easier to clean up if returned.

These days the recommended fluid is a commercially prepared electrolyte-sugar rehydration solution bought from your chemist, e.g. Dioralyte. Of course, you will rarely have these on hand when you want them, but lemonade, Cola (not diet), or unsweetened pure fruit juice will do, if diluted one part to four parts water.

Whatever you use it must be given only in **small amounts** and **offered frequently**. Don't be impatient to reintroduce solids as this can unnecessarily delay the cure. Go easy when you restart the first few bottles of milk. It might even be an idea to dilute these to half-strength for the first day.

Antibiotics have no place in the treatment of gastro-enteritis and often can make it worse. Medicines to stop vomiting are not recommended for small children as they can have undesirable side effects and do little good.

Vomiting and diarrhoea by themselves do not harm a child, it is the dehydration they may cause that is very dangerous. If your baby becomes dull-eyed, unresponsive, passes little urine and clearly looks sick, get medical help immediately. Babies under 6 months of age can deteriorate particularly quickly and must be seen by a doctor early on.

Fevers and high temperatures

Fever is the body's signal to tell us that there is an infection in the house. Maybe as the body heats up it helps kill off the unwanted visitors and certainly in moderation raised temperatures are harmless. Strangely the level of fever is usually out of proportion to the severity of the illness. For example, the fever associated with severe meningitis is often lower than that of measles, and an acute perforating appendix may produce a lower fever than say a kidney infection.

Most childcare books suggest that you keep a thermometer at hand and check out your child's temperature the minute you have any concern. Personally I have never taken my children's temperatures and I tend not to place much emphasis on what a child's temperature is. I believe that sick children look sick, well children look well and I reserve my thermometer for telling if the water is warm enough to go for a swim!

The main concern with high fevers in the young is the risk of fever fits (febrile convulsions). The immature brain of little children can be sensitive to raised temperatures and it is possible for a fit to occur. This may affect up to 5 per cent of all children, but is extremely rare under six months of age and unlikely before nine months. In older babies and toddlers there is a case for keeping fevers under some control.

Treatment

- Leave the child dressed only in a nappy and vest or covered by a sheet depending on the room temperature. Don't put on extra clothing or blankets.
- Don't give the child icy cold baths or point a fan at him.
- If there is a chance of fever fits, a gentle sponge down with tepid water or a lukewarm bath water will help to cool him.
- Keep fluid intake up (small amounts frequently).
- Paracetamol and aspirin both help to lower temperatures, but aspirin is not recommended for children.

Rashes and spots

Babies, as we've already seen, get lots of different sorts of rashes and very often even the cleverest doctor is at a loss to diagnose the exact cause of some of them. (See Chapter 3.)

There is a school of thought which says that all spots which are accompanied by a fever must be measles. Rubbish! For a start measles is almost unheard of in the first year. Rubella (German measles) could possibly occur but it is likely to be so mild that it is doubtful if it would even be diagnosed.

Chicken pox is usually a very mild illness in a baby. All you're likely to see are one or two little spots like flea bites and nothing else.

The message here really is: don't get unduly wound up over every little spot and rash that appears. Most of them are due to Baby's delicate skin getting accustomed to the real world, minor viral illnesses and allergies of uncertain origin.

If in doubt, by all means see your doctor, but I suspect that most of the time he is likely to turn a Nelsonian blind eye towards the skin and say he sees nothing to worry about.

Ears and throats

Tonsillitis is not a baby illness, but rather more a problem for the preschooler. When a baby has a cold, the back of the throat may become a bit red, but this is part of the cold, not tonsillitis. Frankly, it's hard enough even spotting the tiny tonsils in a baby, let alone calling them infected.

Ear infections, on the other hand, are much more common. They develop in the inner part of the ear called the middle ear which lies hidden behind the ear drum. When this gets infected it is called otitis media and can often follow a head cold.

The infection can cause great pain but unfortunately the baby cannot tell you where it hurts. He will tend to become irritable, sleep poorly, feed badly and will be miserable and restless all the time. If your doctor looks into the ear he will see the eardrum red and bulging and this will alert him to the fact that there is an infection trapped inside.

Treatment for otitis media is usually through antibiotics given by mouth coupled with paracetamol for the pain and fever. Sometimes the first you ever know about this condition is when you find a speck of blood on Baby's pillow which shows that the eardrum has burst. This is undesirable, though not a major problem as most heal again completely without any residual problems.

When to Seek Help

It is difficult for a new parent to look at his or her sick baby and know when to sit tight and when to shout for help. Since little babies are in no position to tell us anything about how they feel, you must **always play it safe** and seek help when in doubt.

Here are a few pointers which may help:

- If your baby is bright-eyed and bushy-tailed, alert and responsive, then generally speaking there is unlikely to be any serious problem.
- If your baby starts to look withdrawn, distant and sickly then call for help immediately.
- Watch out for the frightened-looking baby who is pale and has a cold sweat. He is certainly sick and needs urgent help.
- Watch for rapid or laboured breathing which continues for some time.
- Watch out for any severe pain which comes on unexpectedly and cannot be eased.

- Watch out for any strange postures, odd eye movements or periods when your baby stops breathing.

To sum up in one sentence, well children usually look well and sick children look sick, but if you're ever in any doubt, seek help. Little children are too valuable to put at risk.

Getting the best out of your doctor
I believe that it is every person's right to be made to feel at ease, be given a listening ear and have communication in a clear day-to-day language. Getting the best out of your doctor is not difficult. Here are a few suggestions:

- Know what you want to ask before you even get to the doctor's surgery.
- If you get flustered, write a list and don't leave until you get your answers.
- If you don't understand what has been said, ask again and again if necessary.
- Request to be told in everyday English, not medical mumbo-jumbo.
- Don't bury the doctor in an overwhelming fog of vague complaints. 'Well, what's wrong?' – 'Everything!' – Bring the important problems to the top.
- Don't use diversionary tactics. Don't introduce new complications and problems all the time. This prevents your doctor from gaining a clear picture of how to help.
- Although I believe that it is every person's right to seek a second opinion and that no doctor has the right to obstruct this, beware of multiple opinions (shopping around). If you're not careful no one person will feel a direct responsibility for your care and when a crisis hits you will be left totally unsupported.
- Don't put too much pressure on your doctor when it's obvious that there is really nothing more to be done. When pushed past a certain point, he will feel obliged to do something useless and irrelevant, just to clear you off his back. Be careful!
- A good doctor is prepared to tell you that he doesn't know what is going on with your child. This is called honesty and must be respected.
- A good doctor will not always do what his patients request. If he believes you have a viral cold and refuses to give you the antibiotic you demand, this is called good medicine and should be applauded.

- Often there are several drugs which will cure the same ailment. Don't be afraid to ask for the one with the best taste and the least doses needed each day.

- Don't get carried away with the advocates of the no sugar, no colourings, no flavourings brands. These may greatly impress the academic diet freaks, but if they smell and taste awful, they will certainly not impress your child.

Unnecessary investigations in medicine waste a large percentage of the national budget each year. This is where tests are done not to help the patient but to help the doctor keep a step ahead of the malpractice lawyers who stalk him. Personally I hate this wasteful approach and believe that it is harmful to our children.

Every decision we make in life has a calculated risk and when it comes to investigations, I believe unless we're pretty certain the test will help, it should not be taken.

Holding down little children and inflicting pain to do unnecessary investigations is a cruel part of our litigation-conscious society. If parents are prepared to be 99.9 per cent certain, not the full 100 per cent, they have the right to ask for only those investigations really needed.

Doctors have feelings. They get frustrated and upset when unable to help those they care for. We all have good and bad days and doctors are just like anyone else. At times there is just not enough emotional energy to provide as much support as one would like.

You don't need a scientist, you need a human doctor, but remember humans are only human.

19
Temperament and Behaviour – The Great Debate

DESPITE the writings of various leftists and religious gurus, all humans are not born equal. At birth each of us possesses a unique predestined package of heredity which will influence physical growth, academic achievement, behaviour and temperament.

It is no longer believed that each little baby is born an amorphous blob ready to be moulded into any shape his parents wish. Those of us with a number of children have discovered to our cost that once we started to mould, we found that the concrete had already set and all we could do was to round off a few rough edges. All children are born unique individuals and we must then give of our best to ensure they realise their full potential. As parents we can gild the lily, but we cannot change a lily into a rose.

In the last century many people believed that achievement, intelligence, misconduct and one's place in society were exclusive products of heredity. But, as with many theories, these ideas changed with time, eventually to be replaced with the exact opposite view.

By the mid 1950s most childcare experts were teaching that child behaviour and temperament differences were produced directly by the parents – Mum in particular! If you had a child with a simple behaviour problem, you were made to feel guilty, inadequate and incompetent. These experts believed that parenting and the child's environment were all-important and every little environment imbalance was thought to leave its scar and had to be put right. Commonsense, instinctive parenting was no longer good enough.

Fortunately, in the midst of all this there remained some professionals who continued to view life with their eyes partly open. They saw the different qualities and temperaments present in each newborn baby. They looked at their own children and noted that, though equal care was given, each was endowed with very different behaviour and temperament. The gurus of the time were quick to explain these differences in terms of one child bonding closer and getting better care than the other. When parents objected, as they knew that their children were loved equally, some were then told that obviously one child was nurtured on the good breast and one on the bad!

Others who found the dogma of the day hard to swallow were the staff of the special care nurseries. They saw each baby as having a very different temperament long before his mother had even touched him.

Studies in Temperament

In the mid 1950s a group of over 140 newborn American babies were thoroughly assessed to see if patterns of individual temperament could be measured. Those 140 babies, now adults, were followed and observed and from this study we have objective evidence to show how temperament differs right from birth. As the group was observed, it seemed that there were nine dimensions of temperament. Some of these were clear cut but others overlapped greatly. Some were to be of great influence when it came to whether a child was to be easy or difficult to manage, whilst others were interesting but pretty irrelevant. These dimensions outlined below are not black and white, and may come in many combinations and shades of grey. Sometimes I feel that such is the overlap between some that maybe only six clear groups exist. At any rate, don't get bogged down with the detail and grey edges – just look at the overall concept which is fascinating.

Activity

All babies enter life programmed to function at a certain level of activity. Some are destined to sit quiet and content, to smile placidly and do little else. Others hit the world like a tiny tornado and, as babies, need to be bounced, carried, wheeled up and down in the pushchair and whizzed round the block in the car. They hate lying flat, they wriggle during nappy changes and seem able to move about the floor long before they can actually crawl.

These are usually the early walkers, climbers and specialist cupboard rearrangers. As toddlers they are active, sleep restlessly and have forever fiddly fingers. Later they fidget during homework, find it hard to sit still through mealtimes and on wet days they pace around the house like caged animals.

Activity is usually a life-long characteristic, only partly influenced by the activity of those around you. There is a large hereditary component where active parents tend to produce active children. This is most clearly demonstrated when an active, driving father produces an active, driving son.

Rhythmicity

The rhythmicity of a child refers to the regularity and predictability of how he functions. Some babies are really predictable. They sleep at a fixed time, get up at a fixed time, eat a certain amount of food at a regular hour, even their bowels have set opening hours. Other babies function in a totally haphazard way, their exhausted parents never knowing what is going to happen when.

A child who is programmed to an easy rhythm tends to continue along that path. The irregular ones may change a little, but they will never run like clockwork.

Approach/withdrawal

This describes a child's initial response to meeting new people or situations. Some will approach the unknown with adventurous ease, whilst others withdraw, hide and cry.

The approach-type baby accepts new foods and enjoys his first bath. As a toddler, he will greet strangers openly and when he starts school, it is well accepted. When he is away from home, he will sleep well, even in a strange bed.

Withdrawing children initially resist new situations and are a bore when it comes to trying out any new food. They often cry when they see strangers and it takes time for them to fit in with other children. When school starts there are separation problems and lots of difficulties before they settle in. Such children are not adventurous in approaching new activities.

To some extent all these characteristics continue throughout life making children either easy, or not so easy, to cope with.

Adaptability

This is the quality of adapting to the demands put on us by new situations, our parents and life in general. The adaptable baby accepts and complies without fuss. The unadaptable baby is unaccepting, digs in his heels and life will be far from peaceful. There are some obvious overlaps between this and the approach/withdrawal type of behaviours mentioned above.

The adaptable smiles his way through nappy changes, baths and dressing. As a toddler he learns quickly what is acceptable and what is not and tends to be compliant.

The unadaptable may resist nappy changes, bath and dressing. Haircuts may be a hassle and new foods resisted. He often disobeys and does not seem to learn easily from experience. He will be more difficult no matter how he is handled, and parents may find that discipline is about as effective as whistling to a duck.

The parents of the adaptable generally breeze through life oblivious to the great difficulties experienced by those of the unadaptable.

Intensity

This refers to the intensity of the reaction to a given situation. Some greet life's joys, griefs and frustrations with the laid-back acceptance of a Buddhist monk. Others always react at full throttle with the intensity of an Italian taxi driver.

The quiet reactors are not too fussed by a wet nappy and put out a low-key grumble when hungry. When, as a toddler, their favourite toy is snatched by another child, they look startled but never think to retaliate. When hobbies or homework are not going well, they whisper 'oh bother', and plod on.

The intense react in a way that makes a drama out of everything. When food is not wanted, they spit it out, arch their backs and the dogs of hell are unleashed. Childhood is always sparky with no-one left in any doubt about whether they are pleased or displeased.

High intensity children tend to feature more strongly in politics and other behaviour problem groups. They are generally more fun to look after, but like old gelignite they are pretty unstable, highly explosive and need to be handled with extreme care.

Threshold of responsiveness

This refers to the amount of stimulus needed to engage or distract a child. Some will ignore all but the most major events. Others will be distracted by the slightest trivia.

The low threshold child may for instance stop eating when the dog barks and cannot achieve academically in a noisy classroom. When it comes to hardship and discomfort, it only takes a little upset and he is soon shouting.

The high threshold child gets on with the serious business of living and reacts only to the most major stimuli. As a baby he will tolerate wet nappies and will eat just about any food put in front of him. Later he fusses much less about change, noise and what is going on around him. Most probably, when he learns to read, he will become hypnotised by print and oblivious to all sorts of commotion going on around.

Mood

Here we have the friendly, happy child versus the one who is grumpy and dissatisfied.

Some babies are sunny and full of smiles from dawn to dusk. They are a joy to be with and nothing seems to be a bother. Others, however, wake up grizzly and may continue to grizzle. Nothing ever seems right and the air seems tense with negative vibrations.

Distractability/soothability

This is the ability to pacify a baby and divert him to a different course. Some babies are soothed and diverted quite simply, whilst others need volumes of enthusiastic input to achieve anything near the same result.

The soothable baby stops crying when lifted and takes little effort to comfort even when hungry. As a toddler, he is easily diverted away from

171

unwanted behaviour and quick to steer in the approved direction.

The hard to divert, unsoothable baby cries a lot no matter how much comfort he is given. As a toddler he is hard to console. When a favoured toy is removed, all hell breaks loose and no possible substitute will ever bring peace.

Attention span and persistence

These refer to the ability to stick to a task and see things through to the bitter end. It is hard to score these in an infant as concentration and stickability are not too prominent at this age. By six months the attentive, persistent baby will probably watch the mobile above his cot intently. At a year he will play happily in a playpen, and listen to stories with pleasure. The toddler will enjoy sitting still and doing puzzles, which he will perform with great care. He listens intently when shown how to do something. As a school child, homework is done carefully and reading is usually a pleasure.

The inattentive and impersistent baby sucks the dummy for a few seconds and spits it out. He will be bored with the playpen and will lose interest in toys quite quickly. When learning new tasks he is quick to give up a puzzle when it proves a bit difficult. At school he fidgets and fails to get things finished, whilst with homework he is up and down like a yo-yo.

Obviously attention and persistence must have a strong bearing on the quality of a child's academic work in the school years.

Clusters of features

When these nine dimensions were analysed, there appeared some clusters which were usually associated with problems and others that seemed to assure peace.

Five adverse features kept coming up in the most difficult children – irregularity of rhythm, poor adaptability to change, high intensity of reaction, initial withdrawal and a negative mood.

The opposite five features seemed to make up the easy child.

This analysis of behaviour was then taken one step further to find out how common the various groups were. About 10 per cent of babies fall into the difficult category with about 40 per cent falling into the easy group. Looking again at the figures, it seemed that another 15 per cent have many of the difficult characteristics but with very close supervision and high quality care, parents could keep them on the straight and narrow reasonably reliably. As this group took some time and effort to get going they were referred to as the 'slow-to-warm-up' group. That then left 35 per cent who were called the 'intermediate', who had the middle-ground, non-extreme patterns of behaviour. These are the children we call average.

What Does this All Mean?

If these figures are correct, it follows that about 40 per cent of all parents will have an easy baby, who will tend to graduate to be an easy toddler and school child. Little ones like this endow their parents with a great feeling of competence, and even superiority. From this position it is all too easy to criticise those less fortunate or to even believe that superparenting alone has brought about such a perfect child.

Ten per cent of parents will not be in such a happy position and a further 15 per cent will suffer less but still considerable worry. When your babies are far from easy it doesn't take long for your confidence to be shattered. Friends who have been fortunate enough to have one or two easy children presume you are just an inexperienced and incompetent parent.

You will get no criticism from me – parenting is quite hard enough without the interference of meddling outsiders. If you are being criticised by parents who believe they have moulded their God-given perfect child, all you can do is ignore them, secretly hoping that next time they conceive a really obnoxious little terrorist.

I don't mention these figures to strike despair into the hearts of good parents, but I want to show that life is by no means the same for all of us. What works for the mother next door with her particular child may be quite out of place in your household. Just as children have individual temperaments, parents and childcare styles also need a certain amount of individuality.

Finally I have to admit that nothing is quite as black and white as this. Some very difficult babies move on to become angels and sometimes the opposite will happen. **Temperament is important and interesting but fixed typecasting at birth is unwise and counter-productive.**

Conclusion

Temperament certainly has a constitutional basis but can be greatly modified by a child's environment and is further helped by the maturation that takes place with age. We can't send back our little ones for some genetic engineer to adjust their temperament with his silver screwdriver, but with good handling by confident parents we can get the absolute best out of what we have been given.

20

Discipline – How Much Does a Baby Need?

WHEREAS toddlers and adults can most certainly behave very badly, when it comes to babies there is no such thing as a true behaviour problem. Your little one may be irritable, sleep poorly, cling to you like a leech, or repeatedly turn your cupboards inside-out, but he will not have acted with premeditation. His behaviour will not be bad, but rather the usual antics of a baby who doesn't think too deeply about what he does.

These acts cannot possibly be seen to be in the same class as the Oscar-winning performances of toddlers who perfectly stage-manage tantrums, selectively refuse food and perform all other sorts of attention-seeking antics.

We have looked at the behavioural concerns of crying, colic, sleep and general irritability. In this chapter, however, I want to focus on two areas of confusion which generally arise in the minds of new parents. How much discipline does a baby need and what makes all easy-going babies suddenly become clingy?

Discipline

The word discipline often conjures up terrifying images of angry parents towering over their offspring, wooden spoon in hand; but in reality it doesn't have to imply something nasty.

Discipline has its origins in the Latin word, 'to learn'. Go one step further and, from a biblical viewpoint, a disciple was someone who learned through love and example. Now if that's what discipline is really all about, then I think we could all do with a lot more of it. If, as parents, we're happy and in control of our lives, then love and our own good example should be all that a baby requires in the way of discipline.

There is another definition of the word, however, as in leading a disciplined lifestyle. This means a life of structure, healthy habits and sensible routines which can't be bad for anyone, Baby included.

So do babies need discipline? Yes and no. Yes, they need love, example, routine and good healthy habits right from the start. No, they don't need rigidity, frigidity, smacks and shouts.

Can you spoil a baby?

The professional opinion on this swings like a pendulum. At the moment the general consensus seems to be that babies cannot be spoiled, though give it a few years and I suspect we will come back to a rather more conservative middle-ground position.

In the 1940s parents were taught to be firm with their offspring. They fed them with a strict regime and if they woke at night they were left to cry. It was thought that babies who were lifted too often became spoilt and difficult. The teaching of the present day has swung to quite the opposite extreme. Now babies don't need any discipline at all and we are told that you can never spoil a baby. If they cry, then you comfort them. If they are hungry, you feed them. If they are bored, then you entertain them. All this is said to cement a superbond between baby and parent that gives the soundest of foundations for emotional growth. There are those who now believe that the babies who get the most comfort in fact become more confident, independent and will cry less. So, that's the position at present, but who knows what it will be in a few years' time!

Do all babies need equal discipline?

No, of course not! Each baby has his own individual make-up and some need minimal guidance to keep them on the straight and narrow, whereas others need the reins held ever so tightly. You should judge for yourself what is best, always remembering that what is needed for the child next door may be totally different to what is appropriate for your own child.

Can a ten-month-old be disciplined not to touch?

I get depressed when I hear boasting parents tell me how they are teaching their ten-monthers not to touch things. Every time the child's natural curiosity gets the better of him and he comes near one of his parents' precious ornaments, his hand is smacked and he is told he is sinning. Their view seems to be that they lived in the house first and Baby will just have to smarten up his act and keep to the rules, behave on their terms and so it goes on, 'Don't' – slap – 'Stop it' – whack – 'Don't'.

Throughout this strange and painful ritual, the child smiles benignly or cries noisily, utterly incapable of understanding what's going on. It would have been so much easier just to lift temptation out of reach!

Of course, if you persist long enough, you can teach any young animal to perform tricks. All you need is enough punishment and conditioning. But let's face it, this sort of parenting is about as sensible as smacking the dog because he barks.

Sensible parents keep valuables and breakables shut in a cupboard or up on a high shelf out of harm's way. If Baby then turns to dropping teaspoons down the toilet, then tie, jam or otherwise immobilise the cutlery drawer. Batten down all cupboards with a catch, length of sticky tape or elasticated baggage straps. These allow the adult instant entry but totally defeat even the young Houdini! Safety plugs should be put in all but most used power sockets and dangerous items should be kept under lock and key. All drugs, medicines, caustic cleaning fluids and such-like should be securely locked away from ever-prying little hands.

This just leaves the big things which you cannot easily lift out of the way like the television. With such a small repertoire to protect it's relatively easy to divert their attention and train them to stay away. It's not a bad idea to allow a couple of your cupboards for them to play in. They can't do much harm to the saucepans or the vegetables but it gives them hours of fun juggling onions or rattling saucepans.

The message here is simple. You can eventually teach your baby not to touch things, and by taking the bait off your hook you are unlikely to catch so many inquisitive little fish!

Strict or permissive?

I believe that we adults are much happier in life if we know exactly where we stand at any given time. We may complain about rules and regulations, but from them we get a kind of mental security. Children too thrive on this sort of consistent limit setting and like to know just how far they can go. The question is just how strict or lax should those limits be?

To be honest I don't think it really matters at this age. We should be guided by what feels comfortable to our own particular style of parenting. I doubt whether you could see any great difference between a child who has been brought up strictly and one who has had a rather more relaxed upbringing by the time they both reach the age of twenty. The real difference will come out when they themselves become parents, because inevitably they will mirror the behaviour of *their* parents.

I think the secret really is just to be positive, enthusiastic, and above all consistent, ensuring that your little one always knows just what you will accept and what you won't tolerate. Do that in an atmosphere of love and behave in a way which feels comfortable to you and you can't go far wrong.

Discipline – the recommendations

- Start to introduce routines and good habits from an early age.
- Punishment is not for babies.
- Don't expect a ten-month-old to behave like a mature adult.
- Feed the hungry, comfort the crier, lift the grumbler – that's the teaching of today.
- Start to mould the behaviour from the end of the first year. Praise and reward the good behaviour, deliver a low-key response to the undesired.
- If sleep problems are shattering your sanity and grizzling has you tearing your hair out forget all this philosophy and be as firm as is needed to keep the peace.
- Children thrive equally well on both strict and permissive discipline. What they can't take is inconsistency, parental conflict and not knowing where they stand.
- In short, the best way to bring up children is first to get your own act together, then teach through love and example. If what you are doing feels right and works for you, do it!

Separation Anxiety – Why do Babies Become Clingy?

This may come as a bit of a blow to some of you, but it is a fact of life that babies are not totally attached to their parents in their early months of life. Of course they love the warm, caring home environment you give them, but rather like cats, they might be just as happy and contented in an equally good environment somewhere else. However this state of affairs changes rapidly at about seven months. Parents will be very aware of this change as after this age they become strongly attached to one person, usually Mum, with other close care-givers gradually being allowed into the select inner circle.

Separation anxiety and its attendant clinginess start to intensify at this age, reaching a peak soon after the child's first birthday. At this stage some mums are so clung-to that it begins to seem as though life is being led with a little child permanently attached to her skirt hem. Even a short visit to the toilet can become a conducted tour!

At the age of two the child likes to play close to his mother. He may pop outside briefly, but he'll be back every couple of minutes just to check that she's still there.

By preschool entry most children are ready to be separated from their mums, though a few are still far from ready for this big step. By school age however this urge to cling has diluted to such an extent that they can go off to school quite happily, but come 3 pm and they are still mighty pleased to see you.

Well that's all very fine, but what bearing does it have on the practical management of our children?

For a start it means that up to the age of seven months the child can be left quite happily with a babysitter and handled by strangers without any protest. After this age they gradually become more and more clingy and they suffer from separation anxiety. Don't let anyone tell you that this is a pathological state. It's a perfectly normal part of childhood. It just means that they love you so much they don't want to let you out of their sight.

As a doctor I am made very aware of this sensitive stage of development. When I examine a tiny baby I whisk him up on to the couch, where he lies gurgling without a worry in the world. Try the same at ten months and the chances are I will be quickly told to get lost. That's why we tend to examine older babies and toddlers with them sitting securely on their mother's knee.

When hospitalisation is necessary, I believe that the very young baby suffers little from the traumas of separation, but the same cannot be said for Mum. She is devastated.

When separation is a major problem, we aim to keep little children out of hospital as much as possible. Out patient investigations and day-stay surgery are a help, and when babies have to be admitted, there is twenty-four hour visiting and parents are encouraged to live in.

When it comes to babysitters, obviously you have fewer problems if you are lucky enough to have grandparents, or other emotionally close people to call on. With other sitters some babies will object noisily when left, this protest making you feel a heel for deserting them. What's worse they often start up again when you return, to punish you and let you believe they cried non-stop all the time. Don't feel concerned or guilty. As long as they were happy and settled between times, that's OK.

The life of a parent is subjected to such extremes of behaviour and emotion. At one year many mums are so clung-to that they would give anything for a life lived without an infant permanently clamped to their leg. By primary school age they have become so independent, you look back longingly at that long lost time of closeness and total trust. Childhood passes so quickly we must always try to savour the current stage. Once gone it won't come back.

21

Normal Development – Bringing Out the Best in Your Child

ALL of us would like to have clever children who achieve well in life. Some parents pursue this goal to extreme lengths with their young placed firmly in the academic rat race almost the moment the umbilical cord is cut. Others appear to do equally well by adopting a much more laid-back style. Though I favour the gentler approach there is certainly room for both philosophies.

In this chapter we will look at the normal patterns of development, see their value to predict intelligence and then see how we can bring out the best in our children.

What makes children clever?

How much of our children's intelligence comes from the genes and how much is the product of pushy parents? It is a combination of both. Our children are born with a certain potential to succeed which is then modified by the environment in which they live. Einsteins are not made by the academic cramming of parents. They are born brilliant and then brought to full potential by the love and efforts of their parents.

We can bring about great changes to our children's development but we can't work miracles.

For example, a girl who is destined to be walking on her first birthday might walk at eleven months if given intensive physiotherapy and encouragement, but no amount of early intervention and bouncing up and down is going to get her on her feet at nine months. Likewise a boy, who is destined to be of average ability at school, when helped by enthusiastic parents and teachers, may rise towards the upper stream, but will never be the top brain in the school. Equally common, unfortunately, is the possibility of a poor environment causing children to fall below their potential. If Dad is an alcoholic and Mum doesn't give a damn, the child of average ability may barely scrape through school, or, for that matter, life itself.

Then there are other attributes. The child with a poor eye for the ball can be coached to play social tennis, but will never go centre-court at Wimbledon. Exercises can help the clumsy, awkward child, but he will never graduate to the Royal Ballet. The impulsive accident-prone schoolboy can become more reliable but would always be a menace in the bomb-disposal squad. No number of lessons can get the tone deaf child into the Royal Opera Company, but they might have a big future in Country and Western.

Development is a product of our genes and the living environment. We can never achieve the impossible but with love, enthusiasm and a stimulating upbringing, we can make a greater difference.

What is normal?

The terms *average* and *normal* can be very confusing. I know lots of *normal* children, but very few who are *average*. The average child sits unaided at six and a half months, walks at twelve and a half months, and will be dry through the night at thirty-three months. At the same time the normal child sits between four and a half months and nine months, walks between nine months and eighteen months and will stay dry at night somewhere between eighteen months and eight years!

We don't need average children, all we need is for our children to be normal. The range of so-called normality is very wide, and even outside these generally accepted limits you can still be normal. Being behind in one or two specific skills is usually quite OK, it's only when a child is behind in a very important skill or many areas that we should start to worry.

Areas of Development

Development is best considered under a number of headings. First there is gross motor, which refers to the big movements of head control, sitting and walking, then fine motor, which is all about hand movements. Next there's self help, which includes feeding and toileting, and after that you've got speech, hearing, seeing, play and general behaviour. (See the tables on page 250 in the Appendix.)

Gross motor (big movements)

Gross motor skills tell us that the movement part of the brain is working well, but tell us little about the child's intelligence. So even if little Willie is up and walking at eight and a half months, he won't necessarily gain university entrance and an Oxbridge Scholarship. There are many animals who move superbly, but don't think too deeply. The greyhound, for example, walks early and runs like a speeding bullet. But let's face it, any animal whose only pursuit in life is the pursuit of a stuffed hare can't be too bright!

To add to the confusion, phrases like, 'Remember, you have to crawl before you can walk' are also quite misleading. Many babies never crawl in their lives. (They're probably too busy thinking about climbing at the time.)

Motor development works like this: first you must learn to control your head before you can learn to sit. You must sit before you can stand. You must stand before you can walk round the furniture. You need to walk round the furniture holding on before you can walk alone. You must be able to walk alone before you can climb stairs. You then have to be able to climb up before you can climb down. That's what gross motor development is all about, starting with the control of the head and spreading like a bushfire throughout the rest of the body.

At birth a baby has absolutely no neck control. If you pull him up to sit, his head will flop back like a rag doll. If he is lying prone and you put a hand under his tummy to lift him up, the head will flop forward. By six weeks, however, the head will be level with the body when you try this and by three months will come up with the body when he is pulled up to sit. At six months there is full head control and almost complete trunk control. In fact a baby can almost sit in a somewhat unsteady and ungraceful fashion, though with one puff of wind he'll fall over!

Having achieved sitting somewhere between six and eight months the rest of the first year is spent getting into an upright position. A little weight can be taken on the legs at six months, but they quickly recoil like springs. Not until the eighth or ninth month can weight be borne reliably and soon he'll be able to pull himself into a standing position.

Just before the first birthday most children will be walking round the furniture, fingering trinkets, pulling off the tablecloths and starting to get into everything. Then one day they will come to the corner of a table, see something across the room that impresses them, forget to hold on and hey presto, they'll be walking unaided.

Once that stage is reached walking soon becomes more sophisticated and in no time at all they are able to stoop, kick and run. Some may go straight into the mountaineer mode and begin climbing everything in sight. With little fear and considerably less sense this can make for a very tense time for parents. They scarcely dare turn their backs for a minute without finding their Edmund Hillary on the bench-top.

By the age of two they can climb the stairs and not long after that they discover how to get down them again. At three they can pedal a tricycle, at four they can graduate to a bicycle with trainer wheels and some ride solo at five. Royal command ballet, league football, 'mean machine' swimming and downhill ski racing come some time later.

Though not impressed by advanced gross motor skills, I do worry about delayed and different patterns. If your baby is floppy, stiff or holds any part of his body in a strange posture, or is abnormally slow to sit or walk, please have an expert check him out – it's best to be sure.

Fine motor (hand movements)

At birth a baby's hands are blocked by the grasp reflex which locks them involuntarily on to anything placed in the palm. This reflex disappears by three months and the hands become free to hold and wave at will. By six months young ones can pick up toys in a somewhat primitive way, using all the finger-tips to close against the palm. Items are passed from hand to hand at this age, and then into the mouth.

Just before the first birthday comes the big breakthrough – the pincer grip. Here the index finger and thumb start to act together as a team and are used for all fine work. Now a marble can be picked up out of a cup and blocks can be put in a container. At eighteen months three blocks can be stacked on top of each other, and at two a pen – perhaps not as mighty as the sword at this stage but rather held more like a dagger – starts to scribble. By age three they can probably hold the pen properly and copy a V and a circle. Scissors can also be used at this stage, though generally not so much for cutting paper as snipping bits off the dog and trimming their hair. At age four buttons can be done up and by five most children can write their own name and tie their own shoelaces.

It is generally thought that fine motor skills are better indicators of intelligence than gross motor ones. However, just having the skill is in itself not enough, you have to be able to do something clever with it. An eighteen-month-old may have the best pincer grip in the country, but if it is used only to bang blocks together or chuck them down the hall, then it's no great help. If, on the other hand, he's already started using the blocks delicately to construct a mini Taj Mahal then that's pretty impressive. Advanced fine motor skills which produce advanced actions are what we really want.

Speech and understanding

Young babies may have no readily understandable speech but they sure do a lot of communicating! One cry says 'I'm hungry', another 'I'm tired', and there's no doubt when it comes to pain. Whole chapters can be written with their eyes and the body language they use.

Babies will experiment with a whole range of various noises in the first months. However it's not generally until about nine months that the first recognisable speech-like sounds are heard. We call this pre-speech babble and it consists of a tuneful rendering of babababa and dadadada. Rather like an orchestra tuning up, this lets us know that the big performance is about to begin.

The first meaningful word slips out at around the first birthday and it has always seemed one of the great injustices of being a mother, who after all devotes more time to Baby than anyone else at that stage, that this first word is usually Dada, or worse still Doggie or ball! It's just that Mmmms are harder to say than Ddddds.

These early words are supposed to be appropriate and meaningful, but it is my experience that Mum often gets called Doggie and Dad called Baba, so there is a degree of confusion still as to the exact meaning of words. Doubtless your baby knows exactly what he means!

Between the ages of one year and eighteen months there is a great variation in the number of words each child uses. Some children can only use one or two words, others may be veritable walking dictionaries. Interestingly the word 'No' is more often picked up before the word 'Yes', which may be a reflection of how we speak to our children. After eighteen months most enter a great speech explosion with their vocabulary mushrooming daily.

By the second birthday two word phrases are being used, the more common being 'Me want' and 'Don't want', and these are closely followed by three-word utterances. By three years old the speech is relatively refined and by four most can debate like a parliamentarian as they justify why they aren't going to do what they know they should be doing.

Of course it can be argued that parrots and mina birds can also be taught to speak clearly and this is no great feat. What separates us from the birds, however, is the use of new appropriate meaningful speech and our comprehension. Intelligent humans do not repeat and echo like parrots. We are also way ahead of our expressive abilities when it comes to understanding what is said. Although there may be no speech at nine months, babies understand the command 'No!' (whether they decide to act on this understanding is another matter!).

Soon after their first birthday babies' comprehension is such that they will close a door or fetch a ball on demand and by eighteen months they can point to various parts of the body if requested, and are interested in pointing to all the cars, dogs and balls when looking at a book. From here comprehension rapidly speeds up, and in no time at all they understand the differentiation between bigger and smaller, now and later, under and over and before you know it they're into generalisation and lateral thinking which is the real intelligence.

Good appropriate speech coupled with good comprehension is by far the most valuable predictor of intelligence. Lack of speech on its own very often means nothing at all, but if associated with delayed comprehension can be a serious sign of slow development. There is also the possibility that **a late talker could be deaf, and if you have the slightest doubt you must get the hearing tested.**

Hearing and seeing

It never ceases to amaze me that even in the most advanced countries deafness in children is rarely diagnosed before the first birthday. It is so easy to show that a young baby can hear but still we don't seem to be very good at spotting the obvious signs of deafness.

Babies begin to hear during the last months of pregnancy and are born with full hearing. The fact that tapes of uterus noises and mothers' heart beats can calm some newborn babies suggests that they have heard those tunes before. It has also been reported that expectant mothers living directly under the flight path of Tokyo's main airport say that their newborns were more restless in the maternity hospital but soon to settle when reunited with the soothing sound of the 747s.

There is no doubt that at birth babies respond to loud noises. If a clumsy nurse drops a tray on the nursery floor twenty newborns will startle in unison. They can also hear quiet sounds. If a baby is crying in his cot he will change the rhythm of the cry if you talk softly and soothingly to him. Even the smallest baby moves his eyes and mouth to show that he is taking in every word his loving parents drool over the cot.

At six months babies will start to turn their heads to locate sounds and it is now you will find that if you walk quietly and unannounced into your baby's room he will turn with surprise and joy when you whisper.

The first words indicate that there is a reasonable amount of hearing, and these usually appear around the first birthday. After this the stubborn toddler may refuse to listen, just to be bloody-minded. Despite this apparent deafness, most can hear the hiss of a Coke bottle open at fifty feet and can quickly turn to words like 'Mars Bar'. If you have any doubts about your baby's hearing, take him to the baby clinic for an opinion or get a specialised hearing centre to examine him.

Unlike many other animals who are born blind, human babies can see right from the moment of birth. As you hold the baby and move your head slowly across his plane of vision, the little eyes will light up and his face will be animated as he follows Mum's gaze. At six months the normal baby is visually insatiable. His interest spreads from close to far as he watches the dog moving round the room and then switches his attention to a far-flying aeroplane.

When it comes to both hearing and vision, please shout for help if you ever have the slightest concern. This world is quite tough enough already without our children being held back by some undiagnosed sensory deficiency.

Self-Help Skills

Self help usually refers to dressing, feeding and toilet training. Of course babies do none of these things, but let's take a sneak preview anyway.

Dressing

You won't find your baby giving you much help with dressing until the end of the first year when his little arms will start coming up in anticipation to help you. Try to build on this by dressing your child in the same order of clothing every day.

At two years old most children can strip off all their clothes, like a streaker at a soccer match. However, they can put absolutely nothing on themselves. At age three many children go to preschool and it is a convenient coincidence that at this age they can take care of their dressing almost unaided. Tight T-shirts, buttons, shoelaces and getting the clothes the right way round all come a bit later.

Feeding

Feeding is a pretty passive affair up until the eighth or ninth month when an attempt will be made to hold a bottle or some finger food. Most one to one-and-a-half-year-olds still like to be spoon-fed, though a few militants will shut up shop if not allowed to hold their own spoon. Independence is an admirable ideal, but where it outstrips technical ability it gets you nowhere. Your child may be able to load the spoon up well but cannot quite stop the cargo shifting on the way to his mouth. The result? Splat goes the food all down his front! Don't fuss however. Go out and buy one of those plastic bibs with a gutter at the bottom which catch any dropped food, leaving it ready to recycle. This allows him to be as independent as he wishes, feeding away while you patiently transfer all the dropped food back to the plate slipping a few spoonfuls into the mouth as you pass.

By two and a half years they can get a drink and pour most of it into a glass. By four and a half they can tackle a knife and fork, or even poke about with chopsticks.

Toilet training

This is not for babies. Despite what your mother-in-law may have told you about her brilliant brood, all trained by six months, you must make allowances for her confusion. There is a world of difference between *toilet training* and *toilet timing*. Training is a deliberate, voluntary action, whilst timing is a mindless reflex which requires nothing more than a full stomach, a potty and an IQ over 10. They sit, the full stomach gives the bowel a reflex 'tweak' and the feel of the potty triggers some action. Success is not guaranteed, but if you sit them on the potty after every meal the law of averages says that you must have a sporting chance of success every so often.

Toilet training is more useful, and more permanent. It's pointless however to start thinking about this until the child is capable of knowing when he is either wet or soiled, a situation not encountered before eighteen months. It is successful somewhere between this and two and a half.

The average child will stay dry at night at thirty-three months, though the 'normal' range is between eighteen months and eight years! Though it may be of little comfort, let me tell you that one in ten of all children is still wetting his bed at the age of five. All you can do is make sure the washing machine is in good order and hope that your baby is in the nine out of ten.

Play

Young babies don't need toys to play with. Everything they need comes already attached: feet and arms to wave and fingers to chew. At six months your baby will grab his first toys. Usually however it's for the rapid transit to his mouth. Not until about one year old will toys become more important. Toy blocks will start to be banged together and posted into a container. Teddy will start to be flung out of the cot, and when you pick it up and put it back, out he will go again. A comedian once claimed that babies throw teddy bears out of their cots because they don't want them in there in the first place. It's a nice thought, but not true. At this age the game of peek-a-boo is as entertaining as a night at the opera. Rearranging the kitchen is another favourite, saucepans and vegetables seemingly giving the utmost pleasure leaving Grandma's sparkling new toys for dead.

It is at two years that the real play break-through is seen. This is generally when imaginative, pretend play starts. Before this a toy car is seen as a fairly dull object with wheels, but now it screeches its way round the house with deafening vrooms and numerous crashes on the way. With the aid of imagination a cardboard box can become a boat and the innards of a toilet roll some super shuttle that keeps blasting noisily into space.

Play in the two-year-old is not very sociable. He likes to be with other children, but playing beside them rather than with them. Working together, sharing and taking turns doesn't come until the preschool years. Team games with rules will not hold any interest until the age of five and even then the game is more important than the code of rules.

Early Milestones and the Prediction of Later Intelligence

There is a great selection of developmental milestones, but when it comes to predicting intelligence they are not all of equal importance.

Obviously you're not going to be greatly impressed at the age the first teeth appear, the time of walking or when your child stays dry at night. These are not pointers to intelligence. Kicking a ball, repeating nursery rhymes and holding a pen are also fairly unreliable and depend a lot on how much the child has been taught.

The one area of high predictive value is speech and language. No child with advanced quality speech is going to be a slow learner, but first make sure that the speech you are hearing is of high quality. Quality means more than just the volume of verbiage. What you should be looking for is new, appropriate, well-constructed communication that is relevant to the matter on hand. A child may say 'good day' with perfect intonation, recite a nursery rhyme faultlessly like the kindergarten parrot, count to 1000 and know all the words to the national anthem, but this may have little relevance to intelligence.

Intelligence can be seen in children who answer questions clearly, cleverly and appropriately, who can use generalisation and lateral thinking. It's not difficult to recite *Three Blind Mice* by rote. It takes cleverness to work out how many tails the farmer's wife cut off! Knowing the numbers 1 to 1000 is all very impressive, but using them to do simple sums is the real skill.

Advanced speech is my favourite milestone, but remember there are some children who are slow to speak yet are still very clever. Einstein was one of these. He seemed to turn out OK, despite his quiet start.

When speech is delayed, focus on your child's comprehension. This is not as easy to test but if he seems to have a good comprehension of words and to understand how to manipulate his environment, then he's fine.

The other milestone I like to use is watching children at play. I like to see children playing with rich, inventive imagination, responding crisply to what is going on around them and showing a great interest in life. In assessing the abilities of a young child it is often these features that tell us most. It's not just what they do, but the way they do it. It's quality that counts. The top horse trainer at the yearling sales decides who will be a future winner not by measurements or horse IQ tests. He looks at the quality of how they move and behave and makes his prediction.

Development – doing the best for our children

If you are the sort of parent who is planning early music lessons, junior gym, swimming lengths by one year old, reading by three years and playing the classics on the violin by four then you will find my ideas a trifle old-fashioned. I believe in the old, well-tried methods. I don't know if the fad for superstimulation helps in the long run nor do I know if it makes children better balanced and happier. Some children are pushed so hard that they seem to miss out on childhood. Many of these must be destined to become just as boring as the parents who push them. Often I worry that all this is designed more for the benefit of the parents' own egos than to help their child to a better life.

Here are a few old-fashioned principles that can make parenting more effective:

- Warm, loving parents create warm, loving children.
- Touch, hold, carry your baby. Be close, be there.
- Talk, chat, and talk some more. Even the tiniest tot needs words and these all help speech development and understanding.
- Horseplay, having physical fun, being roughed up by Dad is worth more than a season ticket to junior gym.
- Education is not just the three Rs, it's also social competence, communication, loving life and those old values like honesty, decency and good manners.
- Parents are a child's main teachers. First, sort yourself out and then teach them as your apprentice.
- Play is not only enjoyable, it's a great way to learn.
- Confident parents do it better. They are more relaxed, more effective and produce more confident children. Get on with your own brand of childrearing, not someone else's. Competitive childcare devastates confidence.
- Parents with a goal and purpose in life have a better chance of producing the same in their children.
- With parenting it is the **quality** not the quantity that counts.

22

Premature Babies

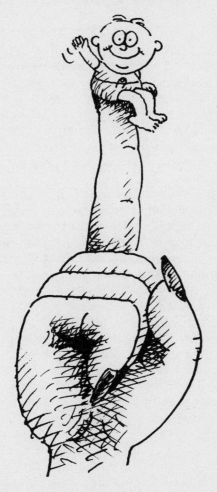

ABOUT 7 per cent of all babies born weigh under 2500 g (5½ lb).
Of these tinies, some came into the world too early, while
others arrived at the ordained time but due to some problem
became rather undernourished along the way.

If a baby is born before the end of the thirty-seventh week of a
normal forty-week gestation period, he is called *premature* or more
correctly *preterm*. When the length of the prematurity is great the
baby will be immature in all his body functions and will need
months of very special care. In this chapter we will be looking at

the problems these babies may have and how parents can hold together while modern technology attempts to sort out the difficulties.

The Preterm or Premature Baby

When I first started in paediatrics, babies weighing under 2500 g (5½ lb) caused us great worry and those under 1500 g (3½ lb) would rarely live. In the last fifteen years, however, all this has changed with the great advances that have been made in the area of newborn intensive care. Nowadays a baby born eight weeks early has about the same chance of survival and future success as any other baby. Babies born between thirty and thirty-two weeks certainly give some cause for concern, though not too great, while those born at twenty-eight weeks still have a reasonably good chance, but it's a long and hazardous haul ahead. (See Appendix on page 252 for dimensions of premature babies.)

If prematurity is between twenty-six and twenty-eight weeks, life becomes extremely hazardous. When they're this small, specialists do not approach resuscitation in a heroic, unthinking way. The amount of medical interference is carefully considered against the likely long-term outcome. Even with this sensible approach some will survive and fare extremely well, while others will have long-term complications which continue to be a big worry.

Caring for these very small babies has become so specialised that it really has to be done in the biggest and best-equipped medical centres. Getting the baby to one of these centres often involves a very special transport service and a highly trained team will fly or drive to another hospital to administer intensive care to the baby and bring him back to base.

Where there is adequate warning of prematurity it is best to plan ahead and move Mum straight to the main maternity centre. The safest form of transport for a very small prem will always be inside Mum's tummy!

Living through the initial stormy weeks after such a baby is born puts a great strain on any family. There is a lot of worry, concern for the future and restrictions of the normal close contact one expects with a newborn baby. Nowadays, however, newborn nurseries not only care for babies, they also care for their families as well. Technology has certainly raced ahead, but happily humanity has managed to keep pace alongside.

Problems of the Very Small

Because premature babies have entered this world ahead of their appointed time, they have immature, unprepared lungs, brains and bodies. The earlier they are born, the greater the problems, but strangely no two babies of the same premature gestation period will have the same severity of difficulties. Some seem to handle prematurity badly, whilst others manage quite well. Let's consider the practical implications.

Breathing

A baby born ten weeks early will have lungs caught in a totally unprepared state. They will try to move sufficient oxygen across the immature membranes but this process will initially be pretty inefficient. If the baby is mildly affected, his breathing will be fast, laboured and will require some extra oxygen. Those who are badly affected will need mechanical ventilation to keep enough oxygen in the blood and for some very small babies this assisted ventilation can go on for months.

The control of respiration is another problem. It's not only the lungs that are immature, so is the brain which sends the messages telling the baby to breathe. Very small babies have a tendency to forget to breath, a condition known as apnoea. During the first weeks these tiny babies are wired up to a monitor that sounds an alarm if the breathing stops. In special care nurseries the staff spend much of their day running around the nursery prodding little ones, reminding them to breathe.

Temperature control

Premature bodies were never designed to survive outside the womb and they find the big world a chilling experience. Initially the prem is nursed in a crib which has its own in-built central heating system linked directly to the baby's temperature monitor. If the baby has to be taken out of the crib, his body temperature is maintained by the use of special heat lights not unlike those that keep the food hot at your local take-away.

Sucking and feeding

When babies are very preterm, they don't know how to suck strongly and, even if they did, very often their gut wouldn't be ready to digest food. In these cases, they are fed through a tube directly into the stomach, or if they are tiny, directly by drip into a vein. Don't panic when you see tubes and drips on a premature baby. They are normal and to be expected and they will disappear as soon as the baby is mature enough to take real food.

Jaundice

The liver of every newborn baby is pretty inefficient and immature. The premature baby, of course, will have even greater problems with it. During the first month, the liver is kept busy processing and cleaning out the body's overload of bile products. Since initially it doesn't always work up to full power, most normal babies tend to have a tint of jaundice and the premature baby is even more vulnerable to this.

The bile products are mostly cleared by the liver, but some can also be broken down by the action of sunlight on the skin. It is quite common for some small prems to have a special bright light shining on their crib. This photo-therapy, as it is called, eases the load on the liver and reduces the risks to the baby of excessive levels of bile in the blood.

The jaundiced prem lies stretched out under the lamp like a sunbather on a nudist beach, but for him it's a bit of reverse sunning – he's trying to lose his tan, not develop it!

Vitamins and iron

Newborn babies arrive in the world with their little bodies filled with reserves of vitamins and iron. These supplies keep them free from anaemia and vitamin deficiency in the first six months until they can start a properly balanced mixed diet. These important stores are transferred across the placenta in the last couple of months of pregnancy, but the premature baby, however, slips his mooring and sails into life without the stores having been loaded aboard. This early embarkation can cause problems so iron and vitamin supplements have to be given for at least the first four months of life.

The special care nursery

The first sight of a special care nursery can be a mind-boggling experience. There laid out before you are so many tiny scraps of humanity amid a mass of electronic gadgetry which would seem more at home in the cockpit of a jumbo jet. But these are friendly skies and the staff manning them are experienced and gentle.

There have to be quite rigorous rules however and first among them is sterility – not the supersterility of the operating theatre, but enough to keep out major infections and germs. Visitors to the nursery will be asked to wear a gown over their clothes, remove their watches, roll up their sleeves and wash their hands and up their arms. If you are suffering from a cold, flu, or any other infection it may be best not to enter and just watch through the glass for a couple of days. If in doubt, the sister in charge will guide you. Wearing a mask might be an equally effective answer.

On your first visit you will be welcomed by one of the staff who will show you round the nursery and explain how they are helping your baby. There may be drips, tubes, alarms, monitors – a whole array of paraphernalia whose purpose will all be explained to you. Don't be daunted, it's only there to keep your baby well, safe and properly monitored. You are there to get to know, love and become attached to your little one, so focus on him and ignore the machinery.

The human touch

These nurseries are not just centres of high technology, they also specialise in great humanity. The staff will know that you are worried and ill at ease in such strange surroundings and will help you overcome your fears. As time goes by they will encourage you to do more and more of the caring and they are always on hand twenty-four hours a day to answer any questions you will have.

Parents' Feelings

At first most parents of premature babies are bound to feel a bit shell-shocked and numb. You never thought that the pregnancy would end like this and you can hardly believe that this is happening to you. As you lie in the postnatal ward you may feel very lonely, knowing that you cannot have your baby with you to nurse and feed. When the time comes to go home it will feel strange leaving without your baby and those treks to the hospital to visit will seem to consume most of your life.

In the early days when a baby's life may hang in the balance it is common to have doubts about just how close to allow yourself to get to a child with such an uncertain future. You cannot deny your feelings however and you just have to let Nature take her course. You will also get all those nagging questions like: What did I do wrong? Is it all my fault? Why can't I produce a normal baby like everyone else? It's also very easy to feel guilty and blame yourself quite incorrectly for not eating a better diet, not stopping smoking, not giving up work earlier or a multitude of other inappropriate causes. And of course there is the most common question of all, 'Why me?'

You may start to feel angry and while you are having a go at yourself, it's not uncommon to kick a few passing heads at the same time. This is very normal human behaviour and acts as a defence mechanism to cope with your confusion.

Another typical problem at times like this is the way in which different people cope. Mum may become completely obsessed with the baby, while Dad distances himself by burying himself in work. Mum may want to talk about it while Dad copes better by trying not to think about it. It's not always easy to remember at times of high tension like these, but different people cope with a crisis in different ways and all you can do is try to understand the other's reaction. Also, try not to forget the other children in the family if you have any. They will feel the tensions and be worried and frightened themselves. I know you probably won't have a great deal of spare emotional energy left, but try and leave a tiny bit for them.

Asking questions and getting answers

The surest way to create confusion in your mind is to ask an opinion of every passer-by from head doctor to the junior cleaner. Make up your mind exactly who you are going to listen to and trust them and confine your questions to them. When you shop around you get conflicting answers which will only confuse you more.

Don't feel a burden if you want to ask a lot of questions. Everyone expects it, even when the same one comes up several times over. When the mind is stressed it sometimes takes more than one answer to sink in. It's not a bad idea to write down questions as you think of them so that you are well-prepared when you next visit your doctor or whoever you are consulting.

Don't be afraid to ask direct questions. The answers may hurt but the sooner you know exactly where you stand the quicker you can make provision for them. Questions like: Will he live? Will he be OK in the future? How long will he have to be in hospital? What caused the problem in the first place? All these need to be answered at some stage but people may be wary of volunteering the answers unless they know that you want to hear them.

Going home

Most prems make it home at about the time they were meant to be born, though those who have had a really rough ride or severe breathing problems may take a little longer. By the time they are well enough to go home, all the problems of temperature control and feeding will have been ironed out and you can treat your baby like any other.

If you have had a lot of worry and the baby has had a long session in special care it's bound to leave its mark. It's hard to stop worrying and overprotecting your little scrap, but nevertheless try to loosen up a bit and start focusing some more of your attention on other members of the family and getting your own life back on the rails. Remember that the doctors wouldn't have let you take your baby home if they didn't think he was perfectly fit to be there, and that you were very capable of taking care of him.

The outlook

The whole science of looking after very small infants is itself in its infancy. Each year new techniques are developed and more and more babies survive at earlier and earlier ages. It's still the really small ones of less than twenty-eight weeks which cause the most worry with other tinies causing significant but much less concern. The year following birth will be one of frequent reviews as your doctors keep a close watch on health and development to check for any complications such as squints, poor vision, hearing difficulties, cerebral palsy, delayed development or residual lung and breathing problems.

When assessing development, allowance has to be made for the baby's prematurity for the first two and a half years. A baby who was two months preterm is not expected therefore to have his six months skills until eight months, his one year skills at fourteen months or his two year skills until twenty-six months. After two and a half they have to forget the past and get on with it like the rest of us. You can't plead prematurity when you're booked for speeding or fail your final year at school. By that time it's all past history and by rights you should be sparking away on all cylinders like anyone else.

23

Twins – Twice the Trouble, Twice the Pleasure

Two for the price of one is a sales gimmick which can usually guarantee a good reaction from the buying public. When it comes to babies, however, one isn't quite sure. Certainly there may be twice the pleasure, but with that comes twice the work and twice the tiredness.

If twins were a more common occurrence I am sure mothers would have been equipped with heavier duty brains, but as it is, it's hard work and takes quite a bit of juggling to keep a firm grip on the situation.

As for triplets, it would take an octopus to keep them all entertained! There simply comes a time when you have to admit you're beaten and call for help. Let's use this chapter to look at what multiple births entail and the sorts of things that worry most parents who are blessed with them.

Twins

Twins occur in about one in ninety births, but if there is a strong family history or Mum has been taking fertility-stimulating drugs then the incidence is much more common. The ratio of identical to non-identical twins is about one-third to two-thirds. Identical twins occur when one egg and one sperm join and then split into two halves, each with an identical genetic make-up and usually fuelled by one cord from one placenta. The non-identical twins come from two separate eggs being released instead of just one. Both of these are fertilised by different sperms and the twins will be just as different as any other two of your children. The only things they will have in common are their parents and their birthday. They can both be boys, or girls, or one of each.

Careful examination of the placenta at birth will give a reliable indication of whether the twins are identical or not but to be completely sure special blood or tissue typing tests are needed. But stop and think before rushing off to have these expensive tests done. You can answer a lot of questions with pure commonsense. It's not rare to see a proud parent with a boy twin in one arm and a girl in the other asking if you think they are identical. You don't need to be a Nobel Prize winner to spot the difference!

The pregnancy

If you are having twins, it is rare nowadays for it not to be diagnosed well before birth. The first suspicions usually come between sixteen and twenty-four weeks when the obstetrician sees you expanding well ahead of prediction. A simple ultrasound test will show you how many babies you have in there. Twin pregnancy has all the discomforts and difficulties of a normal pregnancy but usually to a greater degree. Tiredness is often more of a problem and in the later stages the obstetrician will keep a sharp eye on your blood pressure and if it rises, order rest. In the last weeks the enormity of the situation can become a real trial, especially for the fine-framed mum contending with two front-row forwards locked in a scrum inside her.

Most twins are generally born on time and without any problems, but there is always a slightly greater chance of prematurity and complications around birth. I mention this just so that you may be forewarned – the twins may come a bit early and one or both may have to remain in the hospital nursery for a short while after you go home.

Hospital

With the birth safely over Dad will return triumphantly to work, doubtless to be hailed as the stallion of the year for his prowess in producing not one, but two or possibly even three children. He should enjoy this adulation while he can because it isn't going to take too many nappy changes and sleepless nights to wipe that clever smile from his face.

Meanwhile, back at the hospital Mum is learning how to feed and manage her two babies. Most mums complain that each change of nursing staff brings a different opinion on how they should be coping with the situation. In addition they find that hospitals aren't designed for twins – the chairs aren't wide enough and the beds are too small to hold one mum and two babies in safety for a start. Initially breast-feeding seems like an acrobatic event.

It is usual for the mothers of twins to stay in hospital a couple of extra days just to make sure that feeding, weight gain and day-to-day management has got off to a reasonable start.

Home

When the twins first come home they are greeted as an epic attraction, a real double bill which draws a big audience of admiring friends and neighbours. If you have other children make sure they aren't ignored in the rush. The balance of power is going to be shaky enough as it is with the arrival of twins without well-meaning outsiders disturbing it any further.

Encourage those who are prepared to come bearing gifts of pre-cooked food and then roll up their sleeves and pitch in. Professional spongers and scroungers who see your twins in rather the same light as they view their favourite soap opera should be less welcome. Don't be too proud to accept help when it is offered, you are going to need all the help you can get and if you turn people down they will soon stop asking.

As with any other baby, an easy care existence is what's needed for the first three months. Cooking should be kept simple, housework to a minimum and rest should be snatched at whatever unusual time chance allows. Take your phone off the hook when you are snoozing, and a sign on the door to discourage unannounced bellringers and doorknockers isn't a bad precaution either.

Feeding

Breast-feeding twins is something of a handful to say the least, but most mothers manage it without too much difficulty. If you encounter any problems the maternity hospital, health visitor, National Childbirth Trust, Twins Club or Multiple Births Association will be only too willing to offer help.

Bottle-feeding is slightly more complicated as it takes twice the volume and requires twice as many arms. Successful stereo feeding needs good, roomy seating arrangements and the arms of a spider monkey to ensure that the two bottles both get pointed in the right direction at the right time. Some people perch on a stool with a carry cot on either side, others use two chairs or securely supported bouncer seats which can provide eye-level feeding with relative comfort.

As for the milk supply itself, you will either have to keep an amazing number of bottles or else make up large reserves and create a reservoir in your fridge which you can tap into on a daily basis.

Later when it comes to solids, sitting the children in a bouncer or high chair is best. One plate, one spoon and one hand working in double time in and out like a fiddler's elbow is generally the order of the day and a good deal more effective than two place settings of sparkling sterile silverware.

Clothes

Although you may have twice as many bottoms to cover, most mothers find that one and a half times the usual nappy quota is sufficient. Go for easy care soaking, bulk washing and hanging out in quantity. With twins or triplets you are just going to have to get used to seeing your garden filled with fluttering whiteness not unlike the French fleet after Trafalgar. You can make life a little easier by making sure you fold everything as it comes off the line so that they are ready for action next time. Forget about ironing baby clothes, aim for easy care. Use unisex outfits if your twins are of different sexes. Blue-pink coding may be very smart but you can be sure that you'll get one messy twin and one as pure as the driven snow and end up with piles of unnecessary clothes in reserve.

Make sure that the clothing you buy is simple – the gift giver can provide the fancy show-off outfits. And don't pay any attention to what the amateur psychologists tell you about dressing your twins identically. It doesn't matter what you do, they're both unique little people and as soon as they're old enough they'll very quickly decide the way they want to dress, whatever you may say.

Sleeping

Remember that most young babies sleep so soundly that a crier close by is unlikely to cause any disturbance. This means that it's probably unnecessary to rush in every time you hear a squeak. The noisy one usually won't disturb the sleeping partner.

If after six months one of the twins is proving to be a light sleeper and a sleep programme is being used, then they will have to sleep separately for a week or two until there is success.

Having lived very intimately for the nine months since conception, twins can generally tolerate being pretty close thereafter. They will sleep quite happily top to tail in a single carry cot when you are out visiting and even at home they can sleep top to tail in one cot if you want. They'll soon tell you if they are happier apart.

Mobility

Whereas the mothers of single babies tend to carry their offspring around like a bomb disposal officer nursing a ticking parcel, those with twins find themselves a little shorthanded for such gentleness. Nevertheless their offspring seem to survive and the situation can be greatly helped by using slings, backpacks, frontpacks, prams or pushchairs.

The first necessity will be a pair of car seats for car travel. It is a bit expensive to buy two of these, but they can usually be hired relatively cheaply (see Chapter 8). The only problem is that they are rather too heavy to carry for any great distance. For pedestrian travel an English-style pram is a perfect platform from which to show off your twins. You may be able to buy one second-hand as they are something of an extravagance otherwise, being the Rolls-Royces of infant conveyances. Pushchairs are useful for all babies, a double one being the order of the day for twins, or you can put one in a single buggy and carry the other in a backpack.

Actually mobilising yourself to go out is rather like organising an expedition to climb Mount Everest. At times you feel as though you need a team of Sherpas to carry the stores between camps, but it's well worth it once you are out and the admirers will do wonders for a bruised ego.

Twin differences – can you love them equally?

Although twins share the same birthday most of them are far from identical. It is a mistake to compare the two, though difficult to avoid as you watch them growing up side by side. Milestones will never be identical, they will develop like any two different children in a family, each with their individual strengths and weaknesses.

It's not just the development that differs, so does the temperament and behaviour. This makes it very hard to give absolute equality of love and attention to both parties. Human nature being what it is, the most noisy and demanding half of the duet is bound to get more attention than the quiet one. Although human nature may dictate a certain inequality of attention, this doesn't mean that there is a similar bias in the allocation of love.

Parents who only have one child have little idea what a difference two makes. When they become toddlers they seem to work as a team, perpetually devising ever more ingenious ways of getting up to mischief. If one toddler can stay a step ahead of his parents, imagine what a long way in front two can be!

When it comes to identical twins, some can be so identical that even the parents find it hard to tell them apart. However as you get to know them better you learn to recognise differences and don't have to rely on skin spots or putting nail polish on one of their hands to avoid confusion.

If you feel that coping with two babies is a bit of a handful there's nothing like support from someone who has been through it and understands. Both the Multiple Births Association and The Twins Club have branches all over the country and are only too ready to help you with good ideas and practical support if you feel you may be sinking under the double weight load.

Conclusion

Twins may be double the joy, but also double the trouble. Life can be much easier if you are sensible.

- Don't be too proud. Don't knock back genuine offers of help.
- Organise an easy care routine with easy meals and little housework.
- Try to rest whenever the opportunity presents itself.
- Dress your twin babies in simple clothes and avoid colour-coding them.
- Force yourself to get out even though the preparation may seem to take forever. It's always worth the effort in the end.
- Don't worry about trying to be equally fair to each twin. The attention may not be equal, but the love will be and that's what counts.
- If you feel weighed down, ask for help. The Multiple Births Association and The Twins Club are both always ready to assist.

24

The Special Baby – Birth Defects and Handicaps

I WOULD be a very happy doctor indeed if it were possible to write my baby book without mention of cot death, birth defects and handicaps. Sadly we live in a tough world, one in which children's disabilities are unfortunately all too common.

Some of you reading this will already have first-hand knowledge of the upsets and worries of having a special child. Those of us who are fortunate enough to have healthy children are very privileged parents and should always be thankful.

In this chapter we will take a brief look at some of the more common disabilities that may occur in our babies. Then let's think of the parents and what this does to them, and lastly see how those of us around can help.

Congenital heart disease

The formation of the human heart is one of the great miracles of Nature. In the early weeks it starts as a thin sausage-shaped tube and by birth has become a complex system of channels, chambers and valves. The greatest miracle is the total change of circulation that occurs within seconds of birth. While the baby is in the uterus there is no need for lungs, because all the oxygen needed comes from Mum via the placenta. Half a minute later, now out in the wide world the placenta has become dislodged and the lungs have full responsibility for providing all the oxygen that is needed to preserve life.

At birth the lungs expand, the cord is cut and within seconds channels close, new ones open and an entirely different plumbing system springs into action.

With the complexity of all this it's hardly surprising that sometimes things go wrong – valves don't work, holes stay open and abnormal channels remain. These are the defects that make up congenital heart disease which affects almost one in every 150 babies born. Some of these are simply not compatible with life outside the womb and the baby will become very ill in the early days either with blueness (cyanosis) or with heart failure which shows as rapid breathing and a greatly enlarged liver. A number of these defects are extremely serious and difficult to treat, while other major problems will respond well to surgery. With all the modern techniques, success in heart surgery is now remarkably good.

Some heart defects give no signs or symptoms at birth. Parents find this hard to understand when a problem first comes to attention some time later. A number are so mild that they are diagnosed as a chance finding in an otherwise healthy child, and some of these are small holes in the heart that close themselves with age. The majority of heart problems which are amenable to treatment will cause no barrier to a long, normal and healthy life.

The message therefore is:

- Congenital heart defects are quite common.
- If your baby shows problems of blueness, breathlessness and tiring at feeds and when crying, seek help.
- Not all heart problems can be diagnosed at birth. This is not due to the incompetence of your medical attendants – sometimes there are no signs early on.
- Many problems need only diagnosis, yearly review and little further treatment.
- Surgery, when necessary, is much safer and more successful than parents realise.

Gut blockages

The long tube that makes up the gut of the newborn is often found to have some obstruction along its course. When the stoppage is close to the top end, the problem becomes obvious with the very first feed. When it is further down however it may take a bit longer for its effects to be felt. Occasionally the blockage is only partial and this gives a more confusing picture which appears only days or even weeks down the track.

Surgery will be required for most of these babies and although this may sound hazardous and frightening, with the use of modern children's anaesthesia, even the tiniest premature baby should have a good chance. I feel heartened when I see that the advances in surgery have not just been in technique but also in the human approach to it. Nowadays the smallest scrap of a child will be given the same high standard of treatment and post-operative pain relief as would be offered to the most demanding adult. Gone are the days when it was said 'too small to complain, they can't feel pain!'.

Cleft lip – cleft palate

Cleft lip is where the baby's upper lip is incompletely formed to leave a gap in the centre. Cleft palate is where the roof of the mouth is defective which leaves a small, medium or large gap. It is common for both clefts to occur together and this affects about one in 500 babies.

At birth these defects appear so unsightly that parents can see nothing but disfigurement for life. However it is vital that all involved keep an optimistic and positive outlook right from the start. This is justified as the prognosis is extremely good. Most major hospitals reassure the parents with an album of before and after surgery shots which can show convincingly that, though the present may not look any too rosy, the future promises well.

Surgery to repair the lip is performed at about three months, while the palate is left until later in the first year.

A large cleft will obviously make feeding difficult, but with special teats and other techniques most of the food can be channelled in the right direction. Once surgery is over speech therapists move in to make sure that the voice develops normally and with a good quality tone.

Talipes – clubfoot

At birth many completely normal babies hold their feet in a strange posture. This is not due to some dreadful foot deformity, but rather is a result of the lack of space to stretch out in the uterus.

Clubfoot, however, is different. Here the foot is fixed in an inturned and abnormal position. Unless this is treated, the child would eventually walk on a foot so twisted that it would be the outside of the little toe that touched the ground. This affects about one child in every 100 born but over half of these will regain a normal foot position without anything more than physiotherapy, home exercises and splints. For the remainder, corrective surgery is needed and is almost always successful.

Hydrocephalus

The human brain is not a solid mass of cells, it has a fluid-filled middle. This inside is made up of a series of connecting lakes called ventricles. The fluid that fills these is manufactured centrally, then flows from chamber to chamber before squeezing through a narrow channel to be absorbed outside the brain.

Hydrocephalus (or water on the brain as it used to be called) occurs when this narrow exit is obstructed and dams up the fluid flow. When this happens the central lakes overfill, expand and force the soft skull to enlarge. Sometimes hydrocephalus is an isolated finding but usually it is associated with the abnormality of the spinal cord, spina bifida. By itself, hydrocephalus is relatively benign, but when associated with spina bifida, the double disability is more serious.

Once the channels are obstructed, they are blocked for good and no surgery can reopen them. To ease the pressure and prevent damage to the developing brain, a small tube is inserted into one of the overfilled ventricles which then drains the fluid outside to be absorbed in another part of the body. This is called a shunt and is remarkably effective. Once the shunt is in place and working, it is usually required for life and keeps the fluid flow under control. Once the pressure is eased, brain growth can once again develop normally. Periodic readjustments of the tubing will be needed as plastic tubes unfortunately do not grow longer as the child grows with age.

The diagnosis of hydrocephalus is made initially by the simplest of methods, a tape measure. When the baby's head is found to be expanding too quickly, then an ultrasound scan or special head x-ray will be arranged to confirm the diagnosis.

Spina bifida

Spina bifida is a congenital deficiency of the bony arch that protects the spinal cord at the back. If this deficiency is limited to the bony structure then it is called spina bifida occulta and is benign. If, however, both the bony arch and the spinal cord which runs through it are affected then a serious disability will result.

The damaged area on the back will be obvious at birth and comes as a great shock to both the parents and obstetrician. If the baby's legs move well then one hopes that the spinal cord is pretty intact. If the spinal cord is seriously involved then there will be a major paralysis of the legs as well as problems of bladder control and kidney damage. Hydrocephalus will also occur in about 80 per cent of babies born with spina bifida.

Spina bifida has always confused medical researchers who have never been able to understand why the incidence varies so much from district to district in certain countries. For example parts of Wales, Scotland and Ireland have exceptionally high numbers of babies born with the condition. No-one has been able to decide whether this has anything to do with racial factors or whether it is some feature of the environment.

What we do know is that spina bifida and hydrocephalus have a definite genetic link. Where parents have had one child born with the condition the risk of a second is greatly increased. For such families a prenatal diagnostic test is now available. A useful, but not entirely reliable, blood screening test is sometimes offered to parents at the sixteenth week of pregnancy. If the result is suspicious, a high quality ultrasound scan gives a much more accurate level of diagnosis.

Recent research has shown that the naturally occurring vitamin folic acid taken two months before conception and in the first three months of pregnancy greatly reduces the risk of spina bifida.

Cerebral palsy

The brain is made up of many different parts, each one of them in charge of a particular function. When the area that controls the movement and body posture of the baby is damaged, then you have what is called cerebral palsy. Though occasionally caused by extreme prematurity, infection or birth complications, this condition usually appears out of the blue for no apparent reason. It is exceptionally rare for it to be caused by breech births, the use of forceps or other obstetric techniques despite what is often claimed by smooth-talking lawyers.

The words cerebral palsy used alone tell us little. The condition has many subtypes, each of which can occur with varying grades of severity. There are three major forms of cerebral palsy – the *spastic* type, the *athetoid* and the *ataxic*.

Spastic is often seen as a term of abuse but in medical language it means nothing more than the muscles are stiff due to a defect in that part of the brain that controls movement. When this stiffness is isolated to one side of the body it is known as *spastic hemiplegia*, if only the legs are affected, it is called *spastic diplegia*, and if the whole body is affected, *spastic quadriplegia*. The most minor cases often go undetected for the first year, while the most major are devastating right from birth.

Athetosis results in very floppy muscles and many involuntary movements, while ataxia causes unsteadiness, co-ordination problems and poor balance.

Despite these physical difficulties children with cerebral palsy are generally of normal intelligence. The public need to be constantly reminded that they must never underestimate the intellectual abilities of those with a physical handicap.

It is not always easy to diagnose cerebral palsy in the very young baby, but there are certain tell-tale signs which worry those of us who work in this area:

- If the muscle tone is too tight or too floppy.
- If the baby doesn't 'feel right' to the experienced mother.
- If motor development seems unacceptably delayed.
- If sucking or spoon-feeding seems to be an unexpected struggle.
- If there is an unusual tightness in the hips or ankles.
- If the head or any other part of the body is held in an unusual position.
- If the baby keeps his fists tightly clenched.
- If one side seems to be used more than the other.

Once cerebral palsy has been diagnosed it is important that physiotherapy commence to loosen up the tight muscles and remove unwanted postures. Occupational and speech therapy may also be required at a later stage. How a child with cerebral palsy will progress depends on the severity of the problem, the amount of therapy, and the determination of both parents and child to overcome the disability.

Down's syndrome

Down's syndrome affects almost one in every 600 children born and is the result of a chromosome abnormality in the baby. At birth the features can be spotted immediately, although it may take several weeks before the results of the confirming blood tests are available. Initially there may be few obvious differences in the baby other than a characteristic facial appearance and muscles which seem a bit floppy.

Every normal baby is born with forty-six chromosomes in each cell which line up in pairs, one half (twenty-three) originating from the father, the other half from the mother. These chromosomes carry all our genetic information and are responsible for the uniqueness and family characteristics of every child. In Down's syndrome the baby is conceived with a forty-seventh chromosome. This is a genetic mistake which occurred when the egg was being manufactured, which gave it twenty-four chromosomes rather than the twenty-three that were expected.

The main concern with Down's syndrome is the mental retardation that accompanies it. This is usually of mild or moderate severity. In the old days heart defects coupled with a susceptibility to infection greatly reduced life expectancy in such children, but nowadays with the aid of antibiotics, surgery and good home care, the lifespan will be close to that of any other.

In the dark age of paediatrics, many parents of a child with Down's syndrome were advised to 'put their child straight in a home'. This is certainly not the case these days and most of the Down's syndrome children are firmly established in their own homes and thriving in the care of their families.

We now believe in getting these babies started on an **early intervention programme** as young as possible. Therapy will get underway soon after diagnosis and many will still have almost normal development at one year with a number now going on to integrate into regular school settings. However, a word of caution, if I may. Treatment should certainly always be optimistic, but kept within the bounds of reality. Despite the zeal of some evangelical early interventionists, the child cannot be remade, just helped to achieve his full, but usually limited potential. I am certainly a believer in early therapy, but I see that the greatest power to help any child comes from the stimulation of being **in the home with a loving family**.

When the dust starts to settle and therapy gets underway, the parents are going to need an awful lot of support. They often feel numb, shattered and unsure if they are celebrating a birth or mourning a loss. They are confused about their feelings and about the future. If they give too much time to the new baby they ignore others in the family, if they give too little they start to feel guilty. Then there are all the stories of miracle cures which are told to them by well-meaning friends and the popular press. They hear of the benefits of hours of exercises, the benefits of injecting foetal sheep cells or gigantic doses of vitamins. Most of these claims have been thoroughly investigated and disproved, but it doesn't seem to halt their promotion in the press.

With Down's syndrome, as with many disabilities, the important thing is to give your love, try to remain patient and hopeful, and remember that there are other members of your family who deserve equal attention as well.

The risk of a mother giving birth to a live Down's syndrome baby is about one in 600 or 700 but this is much higher when the mother is over thirty-five. (See the Appendix on page 248 for information about this.)

Parents Matter – So Do their Feelings!

When a serious illness or handicap is diagnosed it is as though the parents have been hit by a thunderbolt. They are left stunned, numb and disbelieving. Gradually this passes, leaving them to weave their way slowly through a grief reaction. It is as though they have lost the normal child they expected and subconsciously they mourn this loss.

The human brain is not suited to sudden emotional shocks but Nature in her wisdom combats this with a series of protective defences which help keep us on the rails. We defend by *denial*, by *activity* and even by *anger*. These defences partially protect us from becoming overwhelmed by the stress and unhappiness of the situation.

Denial

This is the most important defence each one of us uses for our day-to-day survival in this worrying world. We know there are famines, fights, nuclear stockpiles and terrible injustices, but we cope best when we put these to the back of our minds. Of course, we are aware that the problems exist but a bit of denial keeps us sane and stops us worrying ourselves into a mental home.

Denial is a much needed defence when we are told our baby has a major disability. At first it is more comfortable to deny the full story than digest it all and consider its implications. It is tempting to deny the opinion you have been given and shop around from doctor to doctor in the vain hope of securing a more favourable diagnosis. It is less painful if we do not accept the harsh reality of the situation, instead search far and wide for the elusive miracle cure.

Denial is normal, natural and keeps all thinking humans sane. Time eases in the acceptance and then denial becomes unnecessary.

Activity

Keeping minds busy and bodies active lifts the spirits of all worrying adults. When you sit alone in quiet self pity your problems magnify as does your sadness. Parents with a disabled child do best when they keep active. They do even better when life goes forward with a purpose and towards a goal. Activity is useful but it must not become overdone and a large chunk of this energy must be directed towards all our family members.

Anger

This is a strange defence that causes great confusion in those who are looking on. When angry at Fate, it's hard to be angry with the one responsible, so instead you take out your upset on some innocent person close to hand.

This is what happens when your team loses the cup final. You stomp home and kick the dog. Now it's hardly that poor pooch's fault that the referee disallowed the final try, but it certainly makes you feel a whole lot better.

Parents who are upset with what has happened to their baby may feel angry at nurses, doctors, neighbours and even those they dearly love. Be warned, many of us may find ourselves at the receiving end of all this. Anger should be handled gently, the flames not fanned but slowly smothered. With this approach, it soon passes.

So what does this mean?

- Parents with a child who is disabled have a right to grieve.
- Parents may deny, be angry and keep unexpectedly busy.
- Defences have a healing role. They are not to be dismantled by meddlesome medicos.
- With time, talk and the help of good friends, soon these defences will no longer be needed.

What friends can do to help

When parents are having a tough time, it helps to have a good friend close by. You are there to provide a shoulder to cry on and an ear to listen.

When the baby is first born you are confused whether to send a card of congratulations, one of sympathy or none at all. Of course, you don't send one of sympathy, but why not a short letter to let them know you are thinking of them. One of my mums got a nice note which said simply 'Love you – love your baby'. What more could you say?

When you visit, acknowledge that the baby has been born. If you pretend they don't exist it's particularly hurtful. Remember that all parents differ in how much they want to talk. Please be sensitive in how you read the signs. Talk may upset you but it is probably therapeutic for the parents.

As you talk, watch your words and say nothing that could destabilise the situation. You have your own views but don't use them to create doubts or dispute the diagnosis. Be particularly careful never to undermine the opinion and efforts of the professionals they trust.

Parents are allowed to deny. Friends and relatives must accept this but not collude with them to turn this denial into an immovable blockage to acceptance. When anger is about to blast off, stay cool, stay impartial and use this position of neutrality as a platform from which to gently hose the flames.

When you don't know what to do, get on with something of practical help, such as shopping, some cleaning, providing a meal or looking after the other children. Real friends listen and help.

When it comes to counselling, although you are not trained as a psychologist or social worker, you can still be very powerful. Loosen up, talk, listen, rake gently through the embers and give quiet reassurance.

Attitudes and sadness will change. It is a slow process, but time and good friends can work wonders.

Conclusion

Sadly, there will always be babies born who have birth defects. Not only do these disable the child but they cause grief to the parents. Families mourn the perfect child they had hoped for, which is both a normal and natural thing to do. Time is the great healer, and with good friends and relatives there for support, this will speed the process along.

25

Sudden Infant Death Syndrome (S.I.D.S.)

Sudden infant death syndrome (S.I.D.S. – cot death) is a subject that all of us would prefer not to think about. It is a terrifying prospect that a healthy young child can die unexpectedly in his sleep and all without any warning or any apparent cause.

Unfortunately about one in 800 of our babies die in this way. In this chapter we will look at what happens, the theories about S.I.D.S., how parents and siblings are affected and, finally, possible prevention.

What happens

A perfectly healthy baby is put down to sleep and without any apparent reason is later found to be dead. This is possible any time in the first two years of life, but 90 per cent will occur in the first six months, with the greatest incidence between two and five months.

When I say 'perfectly healthy', in hindsight about 40 per cent of parents will describe some trivial difference, such as a slightly stuffy nose, but these changes are so minor at the time that they are not thought to be relevant. At later examinations no infection, poison, abnormality or other possible cause can be found.

Although night-time is the usual time for death to occur, it can also happen during the day. It can happen after many hours of sleep or within five minutes of going down. There are no warning signs and no sounds of struggle or choking. This means that cot death, if it is going to happen, will do so whether the baby is sleeping near your bed or in a distant bedroom.

Occasionally a baby is discovered in the middle of an attack and is able to be resuscitated. This is termed failed or near miss S.I.D.S.

The cause

What causes S.I.D.S.? The simple answer is that no-one knows. Theories come and theories go, and most of them turn out to be unlikely, however one theory which has stood up well to the test of time is the apnoea-anoxia theory. Apnoea means stopping breathing, while anoxia refers to lack of oxygen.

The most consistent finding at post-mortems has been evidence of anoxia in the tissues of the body. It seems that in many of these babies, death was due to oxygen starvation and they just stopped breathing. Primitive breathing movements are first detected when the baby is still in the womb at about twenty weeks' gestation. By thirty weeks they are regular but prone to periods of forgetfulness and failure. We know this is so with premature babies who often need to be reminded to breathe.

The apnoea theory suggests that the reliable regulation of respiration is slow to mature in certain babies, which will make them more prone to forget to breathe and in certain situations this can cause death. This idea has not been proven, but it certainly sounds most plausible. It would certainly explain the anoxic changes and why death is so quiet. It would also explain why it is slightly more common in premature babies whose regulating systems we know to be immature. It could account for the higher risk in those with colds and infections, as this would be the last straw that tipped the balance.

There are of course many other theories. One of the oldest was the idea of suffocation in a soft pillow or smothering when rolled on in the parents' bed. We are always cautious with sleep in the parents' bed and the use of pillows for the very young, but neither of these theories is now accepted as being the cause.

Starvation at night was another theory which sounded plausible for a while, until it was discovered that most of the babies who die still have milk in their stomachs. Could this milk then have been regurgitated and inhaled? Choking could certainly cause Baby to turn blue, but this is quite different from S.I.D.S. It is a noisy experience anyway which is quickly resolved by a good splutter.

A defect in the conduction of electrical messages round the heart is another possibility that the medical profession has considered. If the rhythm of the heart were to change dramatically, death by anoxia would follow. This has been well researched but though an interesting possibility, there appears to be little evidence to support it.

We know that these deaths are slightly more common during the winter months. Could they therefore be attributable to cold and hypothermia? The answer again is no, since S.I.D.S. can occur in the best-heated houses. It is probably the increase in infections during winter which lifts these figures and overheating appears of greater concern than underheating.

Poisoning has a good Sherlock Holmes ring to it, but once again there is no evidence to support this theory. For years now the blood of these babies has been subjected to minuscule measurements in a search for chemicals, poisons and pollutants. Nothing abnormal has so far been found.

Though we do not know the cause, or causes, of S.I.D.S., we now know ways to reduce the risk. This reduction has been most dramatic in extreme high incidence areas e.g. parts of South New Zealand, where the previous 1:200 risk has more than halved.

The main breakthrough came with changing the popular, tummy down sleeping posture, to lie infants on their backs or sides. Overheating also seems to play a part and care is now taken to reduce excessive clothes and wrapping. Reducing the exposure to cigarette smoke and encouraging more breast-feeding also appears to bring a slight reduction.

It is uncertain why sleep posture is so important. It is possible that the face down position reduces air to the nose and also decreases the usual heat loss from the face.

At the time of writing most researchers believe that an infant is for some reason created to be susceptible to S.I.D.S., then sleep posture and other factors tip the balance. Of course, infants can play on their tummies when awake, but we must try hard to get the sleep position right.

The parents

S.I.D.S. delivers an incredibly cruel blow to the parents. It is not just that their baby has died, but there is all the uncertainty and soul-searching that surrounds the event and which serves to deepen their grief.

There are some legal formalities which have to be gone through. The police are obliged to interview the parents and the law requires that a post mortem examination be carried out and the coroner informed. This all happens extremely quickly so that the parents can be reassured that nothing amiss was to blame.

At the end of the enquiries the police, coroner and doctors are very sure that nothing more could have been done, but the parents still find it less easy to convince themselves of this. Their minds are full of 'if onlys'. If only we had gone in to check . . . If only we had given a midnight feed . . . If only the cot had been beside our bed . . . If only I had breast-fed longer . . . If only . . . If only . . .

'How could something like this have happened to us?' they ask. It seems hard to understand how one so innocent and perfect should just die like that. Many will question life itself, wondering what there is left to believe in when events like this are allowed to happen.

Anger is always a normal response and this may be directed at family, friends, doctors, God or just life in general. Who wouldn't feel angry in a situation like this?

Grieving goes on for a long time and the parents need a lot of understanding and help. Most large cities have their Sudden Infant Death support groups who always like to get involved early with every family. In counselling, the parents need reassurance that:

- This was not caused by any form of inferior parenting.
- This could not have been avoided.
- This has not been some subtle form of poisoning.
- This is not suffocation.
- This is not starvation.
- This is called S.I.D.S. which descends out of the blue for no known reason and is certainly not the fault of the parents nor anyone else.

Brothers and sisters

I am often asked how to explain to an unhappy little child the idea that their brother or sister has died. Parents tell me that their child is disturbed, insecure and asks endless questions. They believe that the child cannot accept the death.

I am not sure that the parents have quite got this right though. The child wonders what is going on, so quite innocently he asks copious questions. He is a bit confused and it's not easy to explain the intricacies of life and death to a three-year-old, when we often find them pretty hard to comprehend ourselves.

I may be simplistic in my views, but I feel that little children can accept almost anything as long as their parents are equally well adjusted. The questions, behaviours and clinginess are not of the child's making, they are symptoms of living in a stressed environment. Once parents are able to warm up and talk comfortably about it, the questions and clingy behaviour will evaporate.

Can cot death be prevented?

The short answer is yes, but to a limited degree. The trouble is that the onset is so symptom-free and silent that we are given no warning.

Home monitors are available, but unless there is some major indication, such as a previous cot death or failed cot death, they are not usually advised. These monitors register movements of respiration and when there is no movement an alarm goes off. These may give some sense of security, but even they are not 100 per cent reliable and you do get frequent false alarms.

Some parents keep their little babies close by their bed at night. They then attempt sleep with one ear switched on, trying to monitor the slightest grunt or change of respiratory rhythm. This can occasionally help prevent a death, but more often than not will only result in excessive wear and tear to nerves. This leaves all focus on the four risk reduction factors.

Minimising the risk of S.I.D.S.

Four recommendations are currently promoted to reduce the risk of S.I.D.S. Of these, sleep posture appears the most important. It must be emphasised that these are risk factors, they do not cause S.I.D.S. By following these recommendations, we can minimise the risk, but can not guarantee prevention.

- Sleep your baby on his back or side. (There is some evidence that the back position is safer than the side.)
- Do not let the baby get too hot – avoid overwrapping or a too warm room.
- Avoid smoking when pregnant and keep your baby in a smoke-free environment.
- Breast-feed your baby if possible.

26
Working Mothers

Today, about one-third of all mothers with young children will be found back in the work force. The decision to return is not easy as mums always feel pangs of guilt as they leave their young. This is made considerably worse by the stirring of the anti-work activists, who criticise and convince even the very best mum that she is short-changing her children.

As you will see these criticisms are not warranted.

Do working mothers damage their children?

The simple answer has to be, no! Despite the views of the anti-work lobby, studies that have followed the children of working mothers have not been able to show any long-term problems.

My personal view is that mothers should be allowed to work if they wish and certainly not to be criticised or made to feel guilty by others. However, if all things were equal, I suppose I would secretly prefer to see mums at home with their little preschoolers. These early years flash past in what seems like the blink of an eye and once missed there are no re-runs.

I worry when mums return to full-time work in those early months after birth. I do not believe any newly delivered mother is physically fit for this. This is a stage of chronic tiredness and befuddled brains where there is already little enough energy for childcare let alone taking on extra work.

Often there is no option

Whether we like it or not, there are a number of mums who just have to work. There are those who have invested such a large chunk of their lives in establishing a career that they cannot afford to see it lost. Then there are very many who must work out of pure economic necessity. It's strange, isn't it, how we apparently clever people manage to plan our lives so poorly? Most of us seem to conceive at that time of our lives when we are under the greatest financial stress. Here we are with heads just above water on two incomes and when there is just one, the figures don't add up. Perhaps we should plan more carefully, lower our material sights or adopt the long-term view where we accept four lean years but know it will come right in the future.

Many mothers are simply not cut out to be twenty-four-hour-a-day parents. After a few months at home with a much loved infant, they feel trapped, isolated and ill at ease mentally. With the return to work they refind their identity and with it their sanity. For them, work is no luxury, it is a necessity which is best for them and best for their children.

A fair go for mothers!

I believe few fathers have any idea of the amount of work and tiredness of motherhood. With working mums, they now have at least three jobs to do, that of mum, house manager, as well as paid work, often only for half of a decent wage. If you think of it, there is not a union boss in the country that would accept these conditions for his members.

Wouldn't it be nice if we could go back to those starry-eyed days before marriage to set down a few firm ground rules? That is the time to ask, do both partners want children? Will the mother be expected to work after the baby is born? If Mum does go back to work, will there be an equal division of the labour of childcare and housework? This is the time to decide who will

215

do what, while the novelty is there and before the relationship gets stuck in a rut.

A fair go for children!

After work you pick up excited little ones from care. Toddlers in particular are all revved up wanting to catch up on some fun with their parents, but mums are tired, have a meal to cook and have to get the house into some form of order. This split in roles makes working parents feel extremely guilty. The most caring always feel no matter how much they do they are still short-changing their children. There is no easy answer to this. Just be aware and always try to give a little extra. While a meal is being cooked, ideally one parent should be allocated to entertain. Then weekends must be for the family and not spent asleep or in the company of the vacuum cleaner and washing machine. When working there may be fewer hours together with our children, but let's be sure to make the best use of what we have got.

Choosing childcare

There are a number of options when it comes to choosing childcare, ranging from crèches, long day care and family day care through to Granny or the kind lady across the street. In reality, however, many parents don't have any choice, they have to accept anything they can get.

If available, grandparents, relatives or close friends are a good idea but if you have to decide on outside carers then the choice becomes difficult.

Try to choose somewhere that has one consistent carer, as little children like to know that the same people will be there every day. When you first enter don't be fooled by the quality of the decor or the number of new Fisher Price toys on the shelf. What is important is how it feels. If you can feel the warmth then sign up, but if all you get is a feeling of cool indifference, keep on looking.

When children are sick this really taxes the working mother. Group carers don't want ill infants and even if they did mothers often feel guilty about leaving their children when they need them most. Most mothers manage by taking sick leave. Employers sometimes view these mothers as unhealthy and unreliable, and in the end they have no leave left, when it's needed for themselves. There is no easy answer to this though a return to the old extended family would certainly help.

Separation and anxiety

Be prepared! No matter how good the childcare may be, some children are going to protest wildly when left. This is not a reflection on either you or the centre, nor is it a sign of emotional disturbance in the child. This is a perfectly normal stage of child development. (See Chapter 20.)

Babies in the first six months separate well, but soon after that they start to get a real crush on Mum and close family members. When you leave them with someone else they will exhibit separation anxiety which will usually peak at about one year of age and wane gradually over the next two years.

Don't be surprised if you leave for work amid a flood of tears and return at pick-up time to find more tears. It might appear as though the crying has been non-stop, but that is very rarely the case. If you are at all worried, a quick telephone call from work will reassure you.

Make sure that in the first week you allow enough time to help settle your child in. Don't just dump him and run. Remember that all children are different. Some are as independent as Superman, while others are of the clinging vine variety. The truth of it is that most children are as happy as Larry in childcare once they've got used to it.

Conclusion

Be reassured. Science is on the side of the working mother, who must be encouraged to do what she wants and not be made to feel guilty by the antics of ill-informed critics. Personally I believe that mums should try not to return to work in the first few months and if all else is equal, not to be in too much of a rush thereafter.

With working parents, it's not the amount of time we spend together, but how we use that time that really matters.

27

Grandparents – A Valuable Natural Resource

THERE is no doubt in my mind that one of the greatest and least utilised natural resources is the grandparent. It is a sad fact of life that grandparents seem to have become a casualty in the march of progress and it would appear that the close-knit extended family of the pre-war years is largely a thing of the past.

In this chapter we'll look at some of the benefits – and some of the drawbacks – of having an extended family.

The Benefits

If parents are the tightrope performers in the circus of life, then good grandparents must surely be the safety net. We don't expect them to do quite the same acrobatics as we are prepared to do, but they are always there to support us when we most need it.

With the break-up of the close-knit family has come an isolation which is one of the great scourges of modern-day society. Thousands of people live together in close geographical proximity, but are millions of miles apart emotionally and are incapable of giving much needed mutual support. When you are isolated, problems, which normally might seem insignificant, can be blown out of all proportion and become major hassles. Many of the childcare worries that I am called on to handle would never exist if the parents had a sensible granny close by to provide advice and support.

I believe that many of the older generation have a magic way with little children. Maybe it's because they approach life at a more sensible pace and view today's fashions with an experienced eye, having watched to many come and go. When it comes to making a fuss of the little one, grandparents are certainly top of the premier division. They provide an attentive audience for long-winded toddlers, appear ever interested and rarely pass judgement. Good grandparents are a child's confidantes, counsellors and personal therapists. They boost a child's self-confidence and make the child feel important when the parents are too busy to notice.

In the case of a newborn baby, grandparents can be of great help. They can provide babysitting facilities for your other children and care for you when you become exhausted. They can give a great deal of practical experience if you are willing to listen to them. They can also play a vital part in helping other children in the family adjust to the newcomer, by affording them the time that understandably the mother of a newborn doesn't have.

Unfortunately some people see the older generation as being out of touch and old-fashioned, which is a bit odd considering that Granny or Grandpa is probably a lot younger (and more sensible) than many of the world's most powerful leaders. Rusty they may be, but out of touch? – unlikely.

I'm not pretending that all grandparents are wonderful assets to the family. There are of course those who don't want to get involved, who want to be in the action, but only to offer advice and disappear in a puff of smoke whenever it is time to offer practical help. They are the ones who had little enough time for their own families or who successfully mismanaged their own children and are now straining on the sidelines waiting to have a go at the next generation. But leaving these aside, most grandparents are a wonderful help particularly when a new child is born. They should be encouraged to become involved.

Parents and Grandparents – Keeping the Peace

Despite the fact that parents and grandparents are adults, it is a constant source of amazement to me how they can still behave at times with all the self-centredness and insensitivity of a two-year-old. It really is up to grandparents to use the diplomacy and wisdom that befits their age and up to parents to exercise restraint and learn not to be so prickly when advice is given.

Let's see how relationships might be improved in the four main areas of potential strife.

Interfering

Goodness knows what comedians would have done for a gag if there had never been such a person as the mother-in-law! Listen to them and the central theme is usually one of interfering. Admittedly it's very hard to stand by and watch your children making all the same mistakes you made twenty years earlier. The skill required is not to tell people what they should do but to influence and advise with great subtlety. I firmly believe that most original ideas attributed to the famous and powerful were in fact seeded subtly into their minds by clever advisers.

Everyone likes to think they have had the great ideas and in this respect parents are no different. Instead of trying to enforce their ideas on someone else, the trick for grandparents is to drop hints that are sooner or later adopted as original thoughts. For example, try the indirect approach, e.g. 'I heard on the radio last week, that two was a good time to start toilet training'. This is going to be far more effective in the long run than a head-on directive along the lines of 'That child of yours should have been toilet trained months ago, why haven't you started?'.

From the parents' point of view advice should be taken in the spirit in which it is given. Accept it graciously. It is futile to fight about such things. You must always accept it with thanks, but it's up to you whether you intend to act on it or not.

Taking over

When a new baby is born some grandparents march into the home like Hitler marched into Poland. They set up camp, declare a sort of martial law and start to tell the residents what they can and cannot do. Others arrive with offers of help that are very selective and not always too useful. They monopolise the baby, but are of no help when it comes to sharing the cooking, cleaning, shopping and other chores.

Grandparents must never take over. They may produce a very efficient interim government, but unless the parents are in charge from the start they will never gain the confidence to cope once the occupying forces have left.

Grandparents who really want to help should be prepared to help in all areas, not just a few of the choice tasks.

Discipline

Parents and grandparents can spend a lot of time arguing about discipline. Parents, for example, may be strict, allow no food treats and expect impeccable manners. Grandparents, on the other hand, may consider this too tough on a young child and set up a crash course in overindulgence whenever they are in charge. The result? An unwinable argument which alienates both sides.

There are many ways to bring up children, the best way being the one that feels right and works for you. Little ones are quite capable of coping with different sets of rules in different venues. What they can't take are squabbles, inconsistencies and disputes between their carers.

Parents often tell me that they find it hard to discipline their children, because all their good work is undone when the child goes to Granny's. This is a feeble excuse. As the parent you are the 95 per cent care-giver and as such have the ability to give 95 per cent of the discipline and example. You cannot blame the 5 per cent of time that the child spends with someone else for your failings.

My recommendation for peace is that when the child is with the grandparents, leave them in charge and accept the way they do things without criticism. The converse should also hold true, and the grandparents should never criticise your way of handling the child either. Easy to write, I know, and perhaps not so easy to do, but please give it a try.

Upset Relationships

Most family relationships are complex and delicate at the best of times. When a marriage is rock solid it can withstand a lot of outside interference, but when it is a bit shaky and the partners are a little insecure, then sparks can fly far more easily.

Take the visit of Grandma as an example. Dad now has two roles to play, husband to his wife and son to his mother. If Grandma tries to make demands on his time and repossess him without consideration for his other role, this is bound to cause an upset. If Grandma and Dad huddle in a corner and chat cosily together, this can raise the paranoia level in the insecure excluded partner. Where Grandma becomes spokeswoman for her son and issues joint statements on the running of the home, this too is a sure recipe for unrest.

The secret for both parents and grandparents is to be tolerant, gentle and patient in equal doses. Grandparents should be careful to go out of their way to ensure they don't cause conflict in a marriage. They may be unhappy about the way their daughter-in-law carries on, but should bite their tongues

221

and say nothing. For a start it's none of their business, and secondly they're bound to start an unwinable war.

Parents, on the other hand, should learn to turn a deaf ear to comments that were best left unsaid. Be sure that any anger which you may display towards Grandma over her interference isn't your own insecurity and paranoia breaking through.

The rule for both sides is simply this: tread carefully lest you tread on each other.

28
Getting Back into Shape

THE first thing to come to terms with when you are pregnant is
that your body is going to change shape. The ligaments loosen
in preparation for delivery, your size increases and as it does your
fitness begins to fade. This is not a cause for despair however.
What you are going through is only a temporary stage and it only
takes about twelve weeks after birth to get your poor battered body

back into some sort of physiological balance and a further twelve weeks to get your full strength back.

In this chapter we'll look at fitness, fatness, stretches and sags, and see how best you can retain and maintain your shape.

Weight and diet

I don't wish to appear a killjoy, but it is so much easier to avoid putting on that extra weight during pregnancy than it is trying to lose it after the event. Don't listen to all that rubbish about having to eat for two, all that does is give you twice the problem!

The extreme tiredness most new mums feel is mostly mental, and unfortunately mental activity doesn't seem to burn off any kilojoules. Breast-feeding will cause weight loss in some mums, but for many the weight gain still seems to continue. To achieve weight loss after the event, don't go on some spectacular fast, but rather be gentle with yourself, changing the balance of your diet.

Eat most	Cereals, bread, vegetables, fruit.
Eat with moderation	Lean meat, fish, low fat milk, low fat cheese, low fat yoghurt.
Eat very little	Nuts, raisins, fried foods, sweet drinks, butter, margarine, cakes, sweets, honey, sugar, sweet cordials.

Here are some other useful points about diet which should help you:

- Fatty foods have twice the kilojoules of the sweetest sugary foods, i.e. fat makes you fatter than sugar.
- Breads, cereals and vegetables are all excellent and contain relatively few kilojoules as long as you don't add butter or sugar to them.
- Sweetened drinks can add lots of kilojoules to the diet. So watch out for sweetened cordials, milk and fruit drinks. A glass of orange juice contains about four oranges. Each orange may be low in kilojoules but take the four at one time and it starts to add up.
- Low fat milk, cutting down (or out) butter and margarine, and changing from fried to steamed food will also make a big difference.
- Watch out for constant snacking as this is an efficient way to heap the weight on.
- All of us have different bodies which metabolise food in a different way. Some people will always stay thin however much they eat, whilst others have only to smell a chocolate eclair to pile on the kilograms. For those who put on weight easily, I'm afraid diet is a life sentence. You may take it off but it will always be a recurring problem unless you continue to watch what you eat.

Exercise

It is unrealistic to expect that a body which was way out of shape before conception will miraculously fall into shape after birth. In pregnancy the aim is for the fit to retain their fitness and the unfit to try and lift their act a bit.

In the months before birth, the body's ligaments are loosened by the action of hormones in preparation for the expansion to allow the baby through the birth canal. It takes these ligaments about another three months to tighten up again. These hormones are not selective and as they work on all joints this can cause some pain and instability if heavy exercise is started too soon after birth.

For the best results try and follow this exercise plan:

- Following birth, start basic exercises which strengthen the greatly stretched pelvic and abdominal muscles. The physiotherapist at your maternity hospital will get these started the first day after delivery. They will be painful at first, but you should do them.

- On returning home, tiredness becomes such a part of life that the thought of expending any extra energy on exercise where little or no energy exists is almost unthinkable. Nevertheless you should try and walk and even swim if you can, and give some thought to a gentle, progressive exercise programme.

- By three months the body will have settled down to near normal and you can start doing more strenuous exercise, always assuming that

225

you have a baby that leaves you with some energy to spare! The sporting enthusiasts can now start training, but it will be at least another three months before you are anywhere near full strength.

Breast shape

It is widely believed that breast-feeding damages the shape of your breasts. This is not true. Any damage that may occur takes place during pregnancy, not as a result of breast-feeding. That nine months of enlargement, when the breasts are being bombarded by hormones, stretches and alters the anatomy whether you breast-feed later or not. So be warned – if you've stocked up on canned milk in a bid to save that prenatal model figure, you may be in for a disappointment.

Just how much pregnancy affects the breasts varies in every mum. For most there will be no change whatsoever, while others may find that they waste away or even get bigger. All this is predestined by that great model-maker in the sky, however with a bit of simple care you can do something to protect your interests.

For a start, stretching can be avoided by using a good supporting bra. A well-fitting one by day and a light one at night. Remember also that excessive fat deposits often land on the breasts so excess weight will cause more stretching.

Stretch marks on the skin of the breasts are another common complaint. Once again all that can be done is to provide proper support and avoid excess weight gain.

Stretch marks

Our skin is a flexible cover to our bodies which allows us to move easily and change shape without more than a few wrinkles developing. All this is due to the elastic fibres in the skin which allow the body all this flexibility.

Each of us has a genetically predetermined tolerance to stretching of our skin and whilst some people can take great stretching, others seem to snap the elastic all too easily. When this happens it causes stretch marks, often found over the abdomen or breasts.

There's little you can do about them than watch your diet and ensure that you wear the proper supporting garments. There are a great many creams and lotions advertised which claim to stop wrinkles and stretch marks. These feel good massaged into the skin and although they leave you all soft and sweet smelling, I'm afraid they will do absolutely nothing about stopping your elastic snapping.

Skin pigmentation

Our skin contains lots of little pigment cells which turn brown as you lie sizzling on the beach. During pregnancy the body was running high in oestrogens and these stimulated the pigment cells to work overtime in certain places.

The most noticeable pigment occurs on the face, over the cheek bones and around the eyes. This is called 'the mask of pregnancy' and can look a little strange when it is severe. Of course it will fade and totally disappear sometime after the hormone levels go down.

If you wish to avoid this mask, during pregnancy, you should use a wide-brimmed sun hat and lots of sun cream. Remember that in a sunny climate you don't have to lie around sunbathing to catch the sun, you can get it as easily out shopping or just going about your daily business.

Husbands and wives – shaping up for the future

The birth of a baby is a major landmark in the lives of all good parents. Landmarks such as these are good opportunities to take stock of your lifestyle and see how you can perhaps increase your general fitness, health, purpose and family strength.

Now is a good time for both parents to put the breaks on smoking and excessive drinking. Exercising should become a part of both parents' daily lives and both parties can share a sensible diet. I'm not suggesting that you approach these things with the fanatical zeal of Ayatollah Khomeni, but just take things gently in hand.

Your aim should be to keep up with your children as they grow and become more active and hopefully there will still be a bit of bounce left in the old body when the grandchildren arrive.

29
Relationships Matter – Most

I LOVE YOU

IN many aspects of our modern lives we have lost sight of what really matters. With childcare we may spend hours worrying whether we should cuddle our baby at birth, wean him first on to rice or wheat cereal, or whether or not to breast- or bottle-feed him. However, all that pales into insignificance when we consider whether or not we have a happy home environment.

Today's harsh reality is that we live in a community where between one-quarter and one-third of all our children will be part of a single-parent family some time before they finish school and many more live in unhappy, two-parent homes. Just think of the enormity of all that disruption which we parents have brought to **a quarter or more of an entire generation of our children.**

It's not separation or single parenthood that does the harm it's the conflict. Don't fool yourself for a moment. Tension and conflict can never be hidden from children. They may not hear the raised voices but they are painfully aware of the unhappy atmosphere.

Children are ever so sensitive to their parents' sulking, quarrels, messy break-ups and downright disrespect for each other.

I believe that happy families produce the happiest children. I think it is about time that **those of us who work in childcare should lift our eyes from the small print trivia we preach and make a strong statement on what really matters.** I make no apology for giving over this last and special chapter to relationships. If it's a child's emotional wellbeing you are interested in, this contains the most important message of the entire book.

Modern-day misdirections

We live a life of quite unrealistic expectations, forced on us from our earliest years by the media and the misrepresentations of many glossy magazines. We bust ourselves in our quest for the perfection they promise – the perfect white wash, the perfectly balanced breakfast cereal, perfect sexual fulfilment and of course the perfect marriage.

In the world I inhabit there is little perfection. Life is a compromise where we give of our best, try to be flexible, and have to accept that nothing is as consistently good as it seems. Those whom we admire for having the perfect lifestyle are generally showing us their perfect public face.

Our society seems to be moving ever more towards the *Me* mentality. We expect a lot of satisfaction, fulfilment and pleasure for ourselves. An admirable goal possibly, but too much of the *Me* mentality is incompatible with the generous giving needed to sustain a strong relationship.

We also live in a world of easy outs. If we want sex and no children, there is reliable contraception. If pregnancy doesn't suit, there may be termination. If marriage does not live up to expectations, we can always walk away from it and get a divorce. It's easy to slip in and out of many situations without any strong commitment to see them through. Easy outs may suit us adults but they don't always impress our children.

In my more reflective moods I often wonder if arranged marriages work just as well as those which have been 'forged in love' because of the in-built commitment which goes with them. Partners in an arranged marriage enter it knowing exactly what the rules and expectations are, and knowing where they stand go at it with a strong determination to make it work.

My reflections may be a dream, but the word *commitment* is no dream. It is the mainstay of every successful relationship.

Strong relationships don't just happen

Successful relationships don't just happen. They need a commitment to make them work, not just today or tomorrow, but in the long-term. They need to be maintained with care, especially while our children are with us.

229

The first flush of love fades for all of us as the pressures of day-to-day life edges us into a monotonous rut. We could all benefit from some marriage guidance. Not the sort given when the relationship has hit the rocks and is sinking, but some sound advice before we set out together. Perhaps it's guidelines not guidance that are needed.

Let's look at some sensible expectations of marriage and try to spot a few potential landmines. Then let's give some basic thought to how to stop sliding into a rut and keeping our relationships alive. I don't wish to patronise or lecture, I mention what I have found useful for myself and the families in my care.

Sensible expectations and common stumbling blocks

- No relationship is ever going to be 100 per cent smooth and happy all the time, no matter how good it may appear to those who look on from the outside.

- All relationships have bumpy patches, times of tension and crises. These are normal. Please try to ease, not escalate these bumps.

- All of us who can communicate with our partners will have arguments and disputes. Unresolved conflict tends to fester. The old saying that 'the sun should not be allowed to set on an unresolved quarrel' still holds a lot of wisdom. Let's go for dispute settling, not point scoring. Let's be big enough to apologise when we are wrong and make it easy for others to apologise without loss of face.

- Beware of passive aggression, that poisonous wrecker of any relationship. Not one unpleasant word ever leaves the lips but such is the icy tone and manner that all in your path feel bitter, angry and hurt. Sulking, holding grudges and this non-verbal cold shoulder brings unhappiness to many families. This behaviour is for school kids – not intelligent adults.

- While money should not be allowed to rule our lives, it is important to recognise how financial stress can destroy many a good marriage. Babies are often conceived when parents can ill afford to live on just one income. When the accounts cease to balance, tension rises and rifts develop. We have the ability to plan our baby, so bit more thought will never go amiss. Contraception requires an active decision while conception is often by a non-decision. It would be more sensible if we made sure these were both active decisions.

- Having children rattles the equilibrium of the most stable relationship. Having a baby in an attempt to save a faltering marriage is rarely a success.

- Respect and equality are important in any worthwhile relationship. Where one partner behaves as though he or she is superior or worth a larger cut of the family funds, there will never be warmth and stability. It seems pointless for us to lobby for equality of the sexes while in the meantime our children see little respect and equality in the lives of their parents.

Keeping relationships ALIVE

I was once chatting about life to a mature young teenager when he came out with a great piece of wisdom. 'Love,' he said, 'is something that you don't appreciate or know you have had until you have lost it.' This is so very true for most of us. In our busy lives, we tend to take our greatest possessions such as health and loving relationships for granted, much of the time never realising how important they are until they are going or have gone. The outside world sees our best face, with all our worst behaviour often reserved for those we care for most. It doesn't have to be like this, we can smarten up our act now! It may not be easy to get those we love to change, but if we make the first move, others often follow.

Relationships must not be allowed to get into a rut. They must be worked at to keep them fresh and alive. Partners must be **noticed, encouraged and appreciated**. Kind thoughts, acts and unexpected little gifts all keep richness in a relationship.

Time together is not a luxury, it is a necessity. Some couples find that once the children leave home, they have forgotten how to talk to each other.

Cuddles and all those non-verbal 'I love yous' are great. The marriage vows talk of cherishing and we all need to be cherished. It may sound old-fashioned, but gosh it keeps things alive.

I am not asking for a major change or miracles, just a gentle move to protect and strengthen what matters most to us and our children.

The message

Let's finish this book fired up with a new commitment to those who matter most in our lives, and never take them for granted. We should actively work to keep our relationships alive and strong. Let's give, let's forgive, let's notice and appreciate and, above all, let's cherish. Love may not pay the bills, cook the meals or wash the nappies, but it sure helps our children.

Peace and happiness at home is the aim. It seems to me pointless holding prayer vigils for peace in the world when many of us are quite unprepared to lift a finger towards bringing any form of peace to our own home. This family goal is at least attainable. Once achieved, we may then address the more difficult problems of the world.

Being kind to each other is the kindest thing we can do for our children.

Appendices

Drugs, Lotions and Potions

A selection of the most frequently used remedies

Pain/fever

- Calpol (paracetamol)
- Disprol (paracetamol)
- Note that aspirin is not recommended for children

Antibiotics
- Bactrim (co-trimoxazole)
- Septrin (co-trimoxazole)
- Amoxil (Amoxycillin)

Skin softeners
- Glycerine in sorbolene cream
- Bath oils
- Oatmeal in the bath water (in a stocking – otherwise it's bathing in porridge)
- Numerous other trade name products

Nappy area protection
- Zinc and castor oil cream
- Trade name products e.g. Sudocrem
- Vitamin E creams

Nappy rash
- Hydrozole cream (hydrocortisone with the antifungal clotrimazole) – requires prescription

Oral thrush (monilia)
- Nystatin oral drops – needs prescription

Cradle cap
- Olive oil or baby oil following bath – comb and shampoo after some hours
- Trade name products e.g. Cradocap, Dentinox shampoo

Colic preparations
- Infacol-C
- Herbal remedies e.g. camomile tea

Sedatives (use caution)
- Medosed (paracetamol and sedative)
- Phenergan
- Vallergan – needs prescription

Gastro-enteritis
- Clear fluids e.g. diluted (1 part to 4 parts water) lemonade, cola or cordial
- Electrolyte – sugar rehydration sachets when major, e.g. Dioralyte
- Note – antibiotics and other medicines should not be used

Constipation
- Fruit juices – 100 per cent
- Extra water
- Maltogen
- Coloxyl drops
- Glycerine suppositories

Oesophageal reflux
- Carobel feed thickener or cornflour to thicken feeds
- Mylanta (antacid)
- Gaviscon
- Maxolon

Fluoride
- As drops

How to Fold a Nappy

The triangle (for small babies)

1   Fold the nappy in half to make triangle.

2   Fold triangle in half again to make a smaller triangle.

3   Place the baby on the folded nappy and join the three corners with a pin,

pinned inside the first fold. This will stop the pin sticking into the baby if it comes undone. Make sure the pin runs across the baby's tummy and not up and down as otherwise it could poke into the tummy.

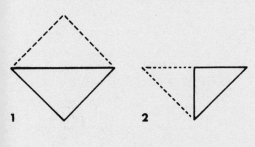
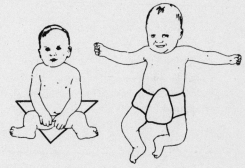

The triangle (for older babies)

1   Fold the nappy in half to make a triangle.

2   Fold down the top edge, adjusting the size to suit your baby.

3   Place the baby on the folded nappy and join the three corners with a pin.

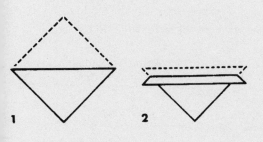
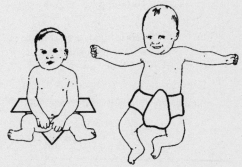

The rectangle (for small babies)

1   Fold the nappy in half to make a rectangle.

2   Fold the top third down for a girl and the bottom third up for a boy.

3   Place the baby on the folded nappy and join the corners on each side with a pin.

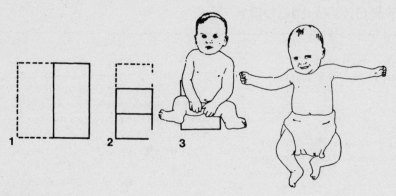

The kite

1 Spread out the nappy in a diamond shape.

2 Fold the left and right-hand corners into the middle.

3 Fold down the top corner and form an elongated triangle.

4 Take the bottom corner up to meet the top corner.

5 Place the baby on the folded nappy and join the corners of each side with a pin.

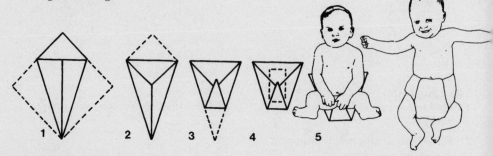

The neat nappy

1 Spread out the nappy in a diamond shape.

2 Fold up the bottom corner so that the corner is level with the other corners of the diamond.

3 Fold down the top corner so that it just crosses over the bottom corner.

4 Fold in the left corner so that the top edge is level with the top fold.

5 Fold the right corner in the same way.

6 Place the baby on the folded nappy and join the corners of each side with a pin.

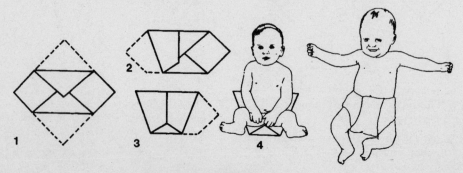

The Chinese nappy (good for origami experts)

1 Spread out the nappy in a square shape.

2 Fold in half from the top to bottom to form a rectangle.

3 Fold in half again from right to left. There should now be two double folds along the top.

4 With your left hand, hold down the bottom three layers of the lower left-hand corner.

5 With your right hand, pick up the fourth lower left-hand corner on the top layer and pull it across to the right as far as it will go.

6 You should now have a square with a triangle attached.

7 Turn the nappy over so that the longest edge of the nappy is at the top.

8 Take the top two layers on the left and fold them over three times from left to right. Leave the triangle underneath.

9 You should now have a long thick rectangle in the middle and two triangles on either side.

10 Place the baby on the folded nappy with the centre rectangle between his legs.

11 Fold the corners of the two triangles over the rectangle and join with a pin.

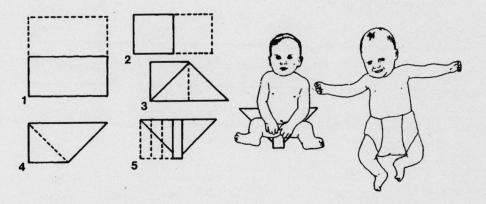

Milestones in Development

From birth until two years
Please, please remember that these are
average levels, the range of normal is
very wide.

At birth

- Tends to lie on his tummy with knees drawn up underneath.
- When lifted, his head flops forwards and backwards like a rag doll.
- Hands are usually closed, but not fisted tightly.
- Hands close involuntarily in the grasp reflex. (Place your finger in his palm and his hand clasps tightly on to it.)
- Startles at any loud sound.
- When asleep he is generally oblivious to disturbance around.
- When a face moves slowly across his line of vision, he may briefly focus and follow.
- No other social interaction obvious.
- Almost continuous drowsiness.
- May show a primitive type of walking reflex which soon disappears.

At six weeks

- Lies in a more relaxed, less flexed posture.
- When held in the prone position, his head raises slightly to be on the same plane as the rest of his body. But still has no head control when pulled forward to sit.
- The grasp reflex continues.
- Hands do not voluntarily hold objects.
- When mother's and baby's eyes meet you are rewarded by a big smile.
- Responds to a comforting voice with facial movements and by altering the rhythm of breathing.
- Sleeps most of the time when not being fed or handled.

At three months

- Lies on tummy propped up on forearms with head up and looking around.
- When held upright his head has reasonable control.
- When pulled up to sit his head does not flop back.
- Grasp reflex disappears.
- Hands kept open most of the time.
- Will not pick up a toy but waves a rattle put in his hand aimlessly.
- Fascinated to watch and play with his own fingers.
- Quietens when hears an unexpected sound.
- Smiles when hears a friendly voice.
- Excited when sees food coming.
- Eyes are bright and alert.

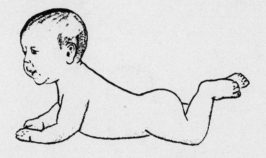

At six months

- Head control complete and strong.
- Just about able to sit alone.
- Can roll easily from front to back, but back to front is more difficult.
- Can take weight briefly when held upon feet.
- Can reach for a toy he wants.
- Toys moved from hand to hand.
- At this stage everything seems to end up in his mouth.
- Turns decisively to the side, to locate a noise.
- Laughs, squeals, chuckles.
- Very interested in everything around – visually insatiable.
- First teeth appear – ouch!
- Still separates easily and is friendly to complete strangers.

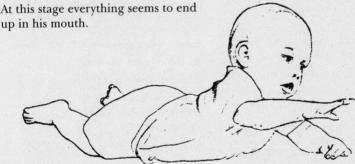

At nine months

- Can sit securely and lean forward to pick up a toy.
- Needs some help to get himself up to sit.
- Can hold on to furniture and pull himself up to stand.
- Makes walking movements when held standing.

- Squirms around floor.
- Some are now crawling, but at first this is backwards.
- Pokes at objects with index finger.
- Starts to hold small objects between thumb and index finger.
- Begins to be able to release things from hand, intentionally.
- Keenly interested in what is happening around him.
- Babbles away – dadadada . . . babababa . . .

- Understands the word no!, and obeys it sometimes.
- Plays peek-a-boo.
- Starts to hold bottle by himself.
- Feeds himself with a biscuit and can now chew lumpy food.
- Less dribbling.
- Likes to be close to the family, fear of strangers usually strong.
- Starts to throw body back in protest – this, I am afraid, is the earliest start of toddlerhood.

At one year
- Walks around the furniture with competence.
- Many can now walk alone (range nine months to eighteen months).
- May walk around the floor on arms and feet – like a bear.
- Drops from walk to sit with a poorly controlled bump.
- Picks up small items with a good pincer grip (between index finger and thumb).
- Gives and takes objects to and from spectator.
- Puts small blocks into a container.
- Turfs toys out of cot to gain attention.
- Now has much tuneful babble.

- Usually says first two meaningful words.
- Turns when own name called.
- Starts to point to things he wants.
- Starts to show an interest in pictures.
- If a toy is hidden under a cup as he watches, he now knows where to look to find it.
- Dribbling usually stops except when teething or with a cold.
- Holds arms up to help dressing.
- Starts to discover that he has great power to wind up Mum.
- A proportion start to be fussy, stubborn feeders.

240

At fifteen months

- Usually walks alone with a broad-based, high-stepping gait.
- Can crawl upstairs.
- Plays with wooden blocks. Enjoys posting them into an open container and may be able to pile two.
- Still enjoys throwing toys.
- Uses two to six words with meaning.
- Babbles away in what sounds like a foreign language.
- Some hold spoon and make a very messy attempt to feed.
- Much less mouthing and chewing of toys.

- Often starts to climb.
- Explores environment with no sense or idea of danger.
- Often frightened by loud noises.
- Usually clingy and likes to be close to familiar family.
- Now eats a cut-up version of the family dinner.
- Some start to show a dislike of wet nappies.
- May be pretty acrobatic when you attempt to change nappy.
- Starts to lose puppy fat, legs lengthen and muscles appear.

At eighteen months

- Walks well, with feet close together and some flow of movement in his arms.
- Runs.
- Throws a ball without overbalancing.
- Builds a tower of three wooden blocks.
- Holds a pen like a dagger and scribbles.
- First signs of hand dominance may start to appear.
- Uses between six and twenty appropriate words.
- Understands many more words than he can say.
- Points to four body parts on demand.
- Points to named items in a picture book.
- Starts to enjoy nursery rhymes.
- Demands what he wants by pointing.
- Extremely impatient.
- Doesn't quite know what he wants but must have it immediately.
- Kicks off shoes and socks.
- Likes to play at putting objects in and out of a container.
- Pushes wheeled toys around.
- Explores, climbs and gets into mischief.
- Usually clingy and likes to be close to family.
- Starts to imitate household tasks like brushing the floor.
- A few start to toilet train.

At two years

- Holds on and walks upstairs quite reliably.
- Comes down again with difficulty.
- Kicks a ball without overbalancing.
- Rides along on a push car (no pedals).
- Turns the pages of a book, singly.
- Can do a simple three separate piece puzzle.
- Builds tower of six to seven blocks.
- Can do circular scribble and copy a vertical line.

- Talks non-stop.
- Constantly asks questions.
- Refers to self by name.
- Uses words I, me and you.
- Puts two words together usually 'me want' or 'don't want'.
- Plays beside, not with other children.
- No idea of sharing, turns or rules.

- A very little sense is now appearing.
- Start of pretend/imaginative play.
- Toilet training usually underway by day.
- For half – behaviour is not bad. For the rest – welcome to the terrible twos.

Teeth

Babies have twenty teeth. They appear as follows:

Teeth	Appear – months
Lower central incisors	6-10 months
Upper central incisors	7-10 months
Upper lateral incisors	8-10 months
Lower lateral incisors	12-18 months
First molar	12-18 months
Canine	16-20 months
Second molar	20-30 months

Permanent teeth
The first permanent teeth appear at six years of age and the last by the age of twenty with the arrival of the third molars (wisdom teeth).

The benefits of fluoride
Fluoride is extremely beneficial in the care of teeth. It reduces cavities by about half and is considered safe.

If the local water is not fluoridated, fluoride drops can be obtained from your chemist. Your health visitor or dentist can advise on the appropriate dosage.

Care of teeth
It might seem strange, but you should start to think about the care of the teeth before they arrive.

Here are some important points to remember:

- Avoid putting very sweet drinks in the bottle, e.g. some of the high vitamin C, 'unhealthy-health' drinks.
- Don't encourage a toddler to suck on a bottle of milk or juice all night.
- Try to establish a diet with variety – one that is not too sweet.
- Remember 'health foods' such as honey, glucose and raisins, rot teeth just as effectively as chocolate.
- Apples, cheese and such snacks are reasonably kind to teeth.
- Try to introduce a soft, small toothbrush at about two years. It will need to be guided around the mouth for at least another five years.
- Introduce the toothbrush just after a meal, or when playing in the bath. At first, a bit of movement around the mouth is all one can expect.
- At first use no toothpaste, and later just a little.
- It's good to get preschoolers used to visiting the dentist. It may cost you money but it's a good long-term investment.
- I have no objection to thumb-sucking in the early years. I see no problems until the permanent teeth are through.
- Remember for the future – if a tooth is accidentally knocked out, keep the tooth, soak it in a little milk and go straight to your dentist. Often these can be re-implanted.

Immunisation for Babies

Polio, diphtheria, tetanus, whooping cough and measles are unpleasant illnesses that can kill. There is no need for this to happen nowadays if we take the trouble to have our children vaccinated.

Most recommended vaccines are effective and safe, though there are some concerns with the product for whooping cough. (See below.)

Polio
This viral disease often causes permanent paralysis. It is still common in many overseas countries which experience the devastating problems that were seen here before a safe vaccine was available. Polio immunisation is easy. All you do is put a drop of oral vaccine on the tongue. This is safe, painless and gives good protection.

Diphtheria
These nasty bacteria set up a focus of infection in the throat which sometimes causes a sudden obstruction to breathing which can be fatal. The infection also releases poisons which can cause paralysis or heart failure. Luckily it has become very rare since immunisation has been widely available. Diphtheria vaccine is given by injection. It is well tried and very safe.

Tetanus

Tetanus, or lockjaw, comes from an organism which is frequently found in the dirt of our streets, paddocks and gardens. It enters the body through a dirty wound, later to release poisons which cause severe spasms and eventual respiratory failure. Every child who plays outside or is likely to have the usual cuts and scratches should be vaccinated.

A booster injection should be taken every ten years or so after the course is complete – this goes for adults too.

Whooping cough

This illness is unpleasant although usually not fatal. Those at greatest risk are little babies who seem to get almost no immunity across the placenta from their mothers. This is why vaccination now starts at two months of life.

The Chinese talk of whooping cough as 'the cough of 100 days'. It is not usually that severe but it can go on and on. The child gets into a spasm of coughing, loses breath, whoops as he tries to get air into the lungs, spasms again and often ends up by vomiting. It is all extremely distressing for the child, to say nothing for the parent watching.

Whooping cough vaccine is the least liked preparation by doctors. It only gives complete protection to between 80 and 90 per cent of those who are vaccinated. Almost 50 per cent will also get a mild reaction which causes slight fever or a little irritability. This is usually nothing to worry about and will be put right with a small dose of paracetamol.

The main concern with the whooping cough vaccine debate is the much publicised danger of permanent brain damage. This is *exceptionally rare*, occurring only in about three per million children but it is still of great concern to the medical profession and all childcare workers.

It is important to see the whooping cough vaccine in its proper perspective. If the vaccine is not given, the majority of children will have natural whooping cough. For most this will be a really unpleasant and long illness. For a few there is a risk of residual brain damage or even death. The chances of these serious complications alone are at least 100 times greater than the risk of problems due to the vaccine.

Measles

This is just about the most infective of all childhood illnesses. Without vaccination almost everyone will catch it. Measles is more than a rash, it causes children to have high fever, be very sick, have a nasty cough, sore eyes and feel very sorry for themselves. In third world countries, where nutrition is poor, it is a much feared illness. Children who contract measles in this country become extremely sick and only very occasionally are there long-term serious complications.

Babies are born with high antibody levels, which have come across the placenta from Mum. These gradually wane in the first year and give sufficient protection for vaccination not to be advised until after the first birthday. Vaccination is by simple injection and usually without side effects. A few children (10 to 15 per cent) will suffer with a slight fever about ten days after the injection when the vaccine takes hold. Some of these may even have a mild measles-like rash. In these instances, it's best to give paracetamol.

Mumps

For many years there was debate whether to add mumps vaccine to the current immunisation protocol. It was argued that this was a relatively mild condition and not worth the expense of routine vaccination.

Following successful programmes in the United States and Canada, it is now believed to be worthwhile and is given at the same time as the measles vaccination. Also given by injection it is simple and safe.

Common questions

Q What medicine do you give for a child with fever following immunisation?
A Paracetamol.

Q If the baby has a cold or flu, should he be immunised?
A No, not until he has recovered.

Q If you believe there has been a major illness or reaction to a particular vaccine, is further immunisation to be given?
A Any major reactions must be reported to your family doctor. If these fit certain criteria, it is likely that next time the same vaccines will be given, but the whooping cough part will be omitted.

Q When do premature babies get their vaccines?
A If they are healthy, immunisation should start at the same time after birth as it would for any other child.

Q If I miss one vaccine do I need to start all over again?
A No! You need no extra shots. Start where you left off and continue at the original spacing.

Q If the vaccines are commenced at an older age than suggested, do you use the same spacing?
A Yes.

Q If a young child has a bad cut or is bitten by a dog, does he need a tetanus shot?
A Not if he has had a tetanus immunisation in the previous two years.

Q If a child has been sick with measles in his first year of life, does this mean that no measles vaccine should be given?
A Studies show that most rashes diagnosed as measles in the first year of life are, in fact, misdiagnoses. There is no harm giving the vaccine to a child who has already had measles, so if in doubt, please vaccinate.

Q What ever happened to smallpox and tuberculosis vaccinations that many of us were given as children?
A A worldwide vaccination programme for smallpox seems to have eradicated the disease and so it is no longer needed. Tuberculosis vaccine is only given in special instances where there is a risk of contracting TB from someone close to your family who is known to have the condition.

Q If a child is allergic to eggs, should the measles vaccine (which is egg cultured) be given?
A There is some dispute about this, but most doctors would now say, yes, but with care.

Immunisation Schedules for Children in the U.K.

(Recommended by the Department of Health and current at the time of publication.)

At two months   Injection of diphtheria, tetanus, whooping cough and meningitis Hib (Haemophilus influenzae type b) vaccine, plus oral polio vaccine.

At three months	Injection of diphtheria, tetanus, whooping cough and Hib vaccine plus oral polio vaccine.
At four months	Injection of diphtheria, tetanus, whooping cough and Hib vaccine, plus oral polio vaccine.
At twelve to fifteen months	Injection of MMR – measles, mumps and rubella (German Measles) vaccine.
At three and half to five years, prior to school entry	Injection of diphtheria, tetanus, plus oral polio vaccine.
At eleven years	Injection of BCG (tuberculosis) vaccine.
At eleven years (only girls who did not have MMR)	Injection of German measles (rubella) vaccine.
At sixteen years	Injection of booster tetanus and booster polio vaccine.

Allowances and Legal Responsibilities

Registration of birth

All babies must be registered within six weeks in England and Wales and three weeks in Scotland from the date of their birth. The local Health Services Department is notified within 36 hours, and this is usually done by the doctor, midwife or hospital administration. Some hospitals arrange for the local registrar to visit the maternity ward, otherwise you or your husband will have to visit the registrar in person.

In the case of unmarried mothers, the baby is registered in the name of the mother although, with appropriate paperwork, the father's name may be used. No details of the father will appear on the birth certificate unless a request for this is specifically signed by him or he registers the baby with the mother.

Child Benefit

Child Benefit is a tax-free sum, payable whatever your income, for each child up to the age of sixteen (and in some cases beyond). It is not means tested and is usually paid direct to the mother every four weeks in arrears.

You will need a claim form, available from the local registrar or Social Security office, which is supplied with a post-free, addressed, envelope. The claim form needs to be sent with the original of your baby's birth certificate (not a photocopy), which will be returned. It is best not to delay your claim application as your benefit can only be backdated for a limited period.

Attendance Allowance

This allowance provides the extra funds required to care for someone with a major disability. This is not to be seen as a form of compensation for parental distress, it is money to help provide the extra expenses needed to help a special child get a better deal. It is available as a weekly amount to anyone over the age of two years who has a physical or mental disability. It is tax-free, not means tested and is paid in addition to any other benefits received. Parents making a claim will need to complete a form available from the Social Security office, after which a doctor's assessment is made before the allowance is granted.

Family Credit
Families on low incomes may be helped by this supplement which may be small but very worthwhile when funds are tight. If you think you might be eligible, discuss your situation with the local Social Security office. Application forms are often also available from your local registrar.

If a baby dies
If a baby shows any signs of life prior to death, regardless of the gestation period, then registration must take place and a burial or cremation certificate has to be issued by the registrar or coroner. Any registered baby who dies requires a funeral and all expenses for this are the responsibility of the parents. Hospital staff will of course help at this difficult time and assistance can be arranged where there is financial hardship.

With a stillbirth of 28 weeks or more gestation, registration must take place and a death certificate has to be issued by the registrar. With a stillbirth of less than 28 weeks gestation, registration is not required and cannot be made even if it is the parents' wish.

Older Mothers – Special Problems

Today there is a move towards later pregnancy in many women. Careers seem to take up the twenties then babies arrive in the mid to late thirties. With this trend have come special concerns over *birth defects, lack of energy* to cope and the *difficulty of adapting* to such a drastic change in one's life when entrenched in one's ways.

Birth defects – the risks
Probably the ideal time for conception is in the years between eighteen and twenty-six. These will be the times of greatest physical fitness and conceiving health. As the years move on things start to get more difficult, but having little babies can still be very safe and satisfying right up to the forties.

The great fear of the older mum is having a baby with Down's syndrome. The risk of any mother giving birth to a live born Down's syndrome baby is about 1:600 to 1:700. Note the words 'live born'. Most major abnormalities are lost early on through miscarriage, with Nature policing pregnancy and stopping many abnormal foetuses from continuing. Even between sixteen weeks' and forty weeks' gestation, there is a natural loss of 30 per cent of all those with Down's syndrome.

Figures taken from amniocentesis results at sixteen weeks are therefore 30 per cent greater than live birth figures.

Risk of Down's syndrome at sixteen weeks' gestation by maternal age

35 years – 1:263 – (birth figure about 1:384)
37 years – 1:158 – (birth figure about 1:242)
38 years – 1:123
39 years – 1: 96
40 years – 1: 75
41 years – 1: 59
42 years – 1: 46 – (birth figure about 1:65)
43 years – 1: 36
44 years – 1: 28
45 years – 1: 22

Reference: – Ferguson-Smith et al, *Prenatal Diagnosis*, 1984, vol. 4, pp. 5-44.
– Cuckle et al, *British Journal Obstetrics & Gynaecology*, 1987, vol. 94, pp. 387-402.

These figures are a bit alarming, but the risks can be removed if prenatal diagnosis is accepted and its recommendations are prepared to be acted upon.

Mothers who are thirty-seven years or over (preferably thirty-five and over) are recommended to have either the chorionic villous sampling test or amniocentesis, either of which will diagnose Down's syndrome with accuracy.

Having excluded the possibility of Down's syndrome, the risk for these mothers is now equal to that carried by any mother of a younger age.

Remember that medical science is able to exclude some specific defects, e.g. Down's syndrome and spina bifida, but no test or investigation can ever guarantee that an unborn baby will be completely normal. Nothing in life is that certain.

Energy fade

Thank God for menopause. Without it babies would continue to be delivered in our geriatric years. As we leave our overactive teens and twenties it becomes obvious that our energy reserves are starting to fade. This is no problem when the baby we get is easy, sleeps well and is an angel. It becomes living hell if you have an irritable, demanding non-sleeping baby.

Those who are following careers now, who plan to have their families later, must concentrate on a healthy lifestyle and fitness. You want to be able to enjoy your children and keep up with them right through all the sport and activity of the school years.

Entrenched lifestyle

It is hard to teach an old dog new tricks. After all the freedom, with years of an utterly self-centred, entrenched lifestyle it is no easy matter to adapt to a baby. When new babies come they bring a revolution with them.

The super-successful career mother usually gets hit hardest. For years she has floated through life just clicking her fingers to get people jumping. It is unfortunate that babies and toddlers are not that controllable.

Weight from Birth to Toddler

	Weight in kg from birth – 2 years boys (girls)					
Age (months)	Average weight kg		Upper average weight (3% will be heavier) (97% will be lighter)		Lower average weight (3% will be lighter) (97% will be heavier)	
0	3.3	(3.2)	4.2	(3.9)	2.5	(2.3)
1	4.3	(4.0)	5.6	(5.0)	3.0	(2.9)
2	5.2	(4.7)	6.7	(6.0)	3.6	(3.4)
3	6.0	(5.4)	7.6	(6.9)	4.2	(4.0)
4	6.7	(6.0)	8.4	(7.6)	4.8	(4.6)
5	7.3	(6.7)	9.1	(8.3)	5.4	(5.1)
6	7.8	(7.2)	9.7	(8.9)	6.0	(5.6)
7	8.3	(7.7)	10.2	(9.5)	6.5	(6.0)
8	8.8	(8.2)	10.7	(10.0)	7.0	(6.4)
9	9.2	(8.6)	11.1	(10.4)	7.4	(6.7)
10	9.5	(8.9)	11.5	(10.8)	7.7	(7.0)
11	9.9	(9.2)	11.9	(11.2)	8.0	(7.3)
12	10.2	(9.5)	12.2	(11.5)	8.2	(7.6)
13	10.4	(9.8)	12.5	(11.8)	8.5	(7.8)
14	10.7	(10.0)	12.8	(12.0)	8.7	(8.0)
15	10.9	(10.2)	13.1	(12.3)	8.8	(8.1)
16	11.1	(10.4)	13.3	(12.5)	9.0	(8.3)
17	11.3	(10.6)	13.6	(12.7)	9.1	(8.5)
18	11.5	(10.8)	13.8	(13.0)	9.3	(8.6)
19	11.7	(11.0)	14.0	(13.2)	9.4	(8.8)
20	11.8	(11.2)	14.2	(13.4)	9.5	(8.9)
21	12.0	(11.4)	14.4	(13.6)	9.7	(9.1)
22	12.2	(11.5)	14.6	(13.9)	9.8	(9.3)
23	12.4	(11.7)	14.8	(14.1)	9.9	(9.4)
24	12.6	(11.9)	15.0	(14.3)	10.1	(9.6)

Reference: World Health Organisation Standards
Note: The ideal relationship of height and weight is to be in proportion, e.g. if the child is of low average weight, then he should also be of low average height.

How to weigh a baby
You will find baby scales at hospitals and baby clinics. Scales can even be hired – see the yellow pages telephone book. At home, the easiest but a less accurate method is to weigh yourself, then weigh yourself holding the baby. The difference will be the baby's weight.

Length from Birth to Toddler

Length in cm from birth – 2 years boys (girls)					
Age (months)	Average length cm		Upper average length (3% will be longer) (97% will be shorter)		Lower average length (3% will be shorter) (97% will be longer)
0	50.5	(49.9)	54.8	(53.9)	46.2	(45.8)
1	54.6	(53.5)	59.1	(57.9)	49.9	(49.2)
2	58.1	(56.8)	62.9	(61.3)	53.2	(52.2)
3	61.1	(59.5)	66.1	(64.2)	56.1	(54.9)
4	63.7	(62.0)	68.7	(66.8)	58.6	(57.2)
5	65.9	(64.1)	71.0	(69.0)	60.8	(59.2)
6	67.8	(65.9)	72.9	(70.9)	62.8	(61.0)
7	69.5	(67.6)	74.5	(72.6)	64.5	(62.5)
8	71.0	(69.1)	76.0	(74.2)	66.0	(64.0)
9	72.3	(70.4)	77.3	(75.6)	67.4	(65.3)
10	73.6	(71.8)	78.6	(77.0)	68.7	(66.6)
11	74.9	(73.1)	79.9	(78.3)	69.9	(67.8)
12	76.1	(74.3)	81.2	(79.6)	71.0	(69.0)
13	77.2	(75.5)	82.4	(80.9)	72.1	(70.1)
14	78.3	(76.7)	83.6	(82.1)	73.1	(71.2)
15	79.4	(77.8)	84.8	(83.3)	74.1	(72.2)
16	80.4	(78.9)	85.9	(84.5)	75.0	(73.2)
17	81.4	(79.9)	87.0	(85.6)	75.9	(74.2)
18	82.4	(80.9)	88.1	(86.7)	76.7	(75.1)
19	83.3	(81.9)	89.2	(87.8)	77.5	(76.1)
20	84.2	(82.9)	90.2	(88.8)	78.3	(77.0)
21	85.1	(83.8)	91.2	(89.8)	79.1	(77.8)
22	86.0	(84.7)	92.2	(90.8)	79.8	(78.7)
23	86.8	(85.6)	93.1	(91.7)	80.6	(79.5)
24	87.6	(86.5)	94.0	(92.6)	81.3	(80.3)

Reference: World Health Organisation Standards
Note: The ideal relationship of height and weight is to be in proportion, e.g. if the child is of low average height, then he should also be of low average weight.

Average Dimensions of the Premature Baby

Length in cm	Weight in g
26 weeks (14 weeks early) 34 cm	700 g
28 weeks (12 weeks early) 37 cm	900 g
30 weeks (10 weeks early) 40 cm	1250 g
32 weeks (8 weeks early) 43 cm	1700 g
34 weeks (6 weeks early) 46 cm	2000 g
36 weeks (4 weeks early) 47.5 cm	2500 g
38 weeks (2 weeks early) 49 cm	3000 g
40 weeks (on time) 50 cm	3300 g

Normal pregnancy lasts forty weeks from the last period. Babies of twenty-six or twenty-seven weeks may survive. See Chapter 22 for more information.

Measurement Conversion Tables

Centimetres – inches/inches – centimetres
(Inches expressed as decimals, i.e. inches and tenths of inches)

	1 cm = 0.3937 inches		1 inch = 2.54 cm		
cm	inches	cm	inches	cm	inches
40	15.75	57	22.4	74	29.1
41	16.15	58	22.8	75	29.5
42	16.5	59	23.2	76	29.9
43	16.9	60	23.6	77	30.3
44	17.3	61	24	78	30.7
45	17.7	62	24.4	79	31.1
46	18.1	63	24.8	80	31.5
47	18.5	64	25.2	81	31.8
48	18.9	65	25.5	82	32.2
49	19.25	66	25.9	83	32.6
50	19.65	67	26.3	84	33
51	20	68	26.7	85	33.4
52	20.4	69	27.1	86	33.8
53	20.8	70	27.5	87	34.2
54	21.2	71	27.9	88	34.6
55	21.6	72	28.2	89	35
56	22	73	28.6	90	35.4

lb/oz to g – g to lb/oz
1 kg = 2.2 lb 1 lb = 0.45 kg

	5 lb	6 lb	7 lb	8 lb	9 lb	10 lb	11 lb	12 lb	13 lb
0 oz	2270	2720	3175	3630	4080	4535	4990	5445	5895
1 oz	2295	2750	3205	3655	4110	4565	5020	5470	5925
2 oz	2325	2780	3230	3685	4140	4595	5075	5500	5955
3 oz	2355	2805	3260	3715	4165	4620	5075	5530	5980
4 oz	2380	2835	3290	3740	4195	4650	5105	5555	6010
5 oz	2410	2865	3215	3770	4225	4680	5130	5585	6040
6 oz	2440	2890	3245	3800	4250	4705	5160	5515	6065
7 oz	2465	2920	3375	3825	4280	4735	5190	5640	6095
8 oz	2495	2950	3400	3855	4310	4765	5215	5670	6125
9 oz	2525	2975	3430	3885	4340	4790	5245	5700	6150
10 oz	2550	3005	3460	3910	4365	4820	5275	5730	6180
11 oz	2580	3035	3485	3940	4395	4850	5300	5755	6210
12 oz	2610	3060	3515	3970	4425	4875	5330	5790	6240
13 oz	2635	3090	3545	3995	4450	4905	5360	5810	6265
14 oz	2665	3120	3570	4025	4480	4935	5385	5840	6295
15 oz	2695	3145	3600	4055	4510	4960	5415	5870	6320

	14 lb	15 lb	16 lb	17 lb	18 lb	19 lb	20 lb	21 lb	22 lb
0 oz	6350	6805	7255	7710	8165	8620	9070	9525	9980
1 oz	6380	6830	7285	7740	8195	8645	9100	9555	10005
2 oz	6405	6860	7315	7770	8220	8675	9130	9580	10035
3 oz	6435	6890	7340	7795	8256	8705	9155	9610	10065
4 oz	6465	6915	7370	7825	8280	8730	9190	9640	10090
5 oz	6490	6945	7400	7850	8305	8760	9215	9665	10120
6 oz	6520	6975	7430	7880	8335	8790	9240	9695	10150
7 oz	6550	7000	7455	7910	8365	8815	9270	9725	10175
8 oz	6575	7030	7485	7940	8390	8845	9300	9750	10205
9 oz	6605	7060	7510	7965	8420	8875	9330	9780	10235
10 oz	6635	7085	7540	7995	8450	8900	9355	9810	10260
11 oz	6660	7115	7570	8025	8475	8930	9385	9835	10290
12 oz	6690	7145	7595	8050	8505	8960	9410	9865	10320
13 oz	6720	7170	7625	8080	8535	8985	9440	9895	10345
14 oz	6745	7200	7655	8110	8560	9015	9470	9920	10375
15 oz	6775	7230	7680	8135	8590	9045	9495	9950	10405

Temperatures

°F	°C	°F	°C
96	35.6	101	38.3
97	36.1	102	38.9
98	36.7	103	39.4
99	37.2	104	40.0
100	37.8		

Volumes of fluids

1 litre	= 1.76 pints
1 pint	= 0.57 litres
1000 cc	= 1 litre
28.4 cc	= 1 oz
20 oz	= 1 pint

The normal body temperature is 98.4°F or
37°C. 104°F or 40°C is extremely high.

Where to Get Help

Helping organisations

Check your telephone directory for the local addresses of the following:

* **Baby health clinic** – your health visitor is the first point of contact for almost all baby care worries.

* **Family doctor** – contact your doctor when sickness is suspected. For behaviour and management problems, most are good at this, but some are not.

* **The maternity hospital** – in the weeks after discharge from hospital, most will answer questions and give advice over the telephone.

* **Your local children's hospital** – if living in a major city, help is available at your children's hospital.

* **National Childbirth Trust**, Alexandra House, Oldham Terrace, London W3 6NH (0181-992 8637) – this organisation has trained counsellors who are second to none when it comes to concerns over breast-feeding. Their advice is extremely practical. Be aware that their philosophy is to keep breast-feeding going if this is at all possible, even when others might decide to call it a day.

* **Pre-school Playgroups Association** – there are playgroups in most cities, towns and country areas. They provide some educational play for young children as well as good parent support for the mothers.

* **Multiple Births Association**, Queen Charlotte's and Chelsea Hospital, Goldhawk Road, London W6 0XG (0181-748 4666) – this organisation gives counselling, support and advice to parents with twins and all multiple births.

* **Twins and Multiple Births Association (Twins Club)**, P.O. Box 30, Little Sutton, South Wirral L66 1TH (0151-348 0020) – support group for parents of twins, triplets or more. It runs Twins Clubs throughout the country.

* **Foundation for the Study of Infant Deaths**, 14 Halkin Street, London SW1X 7DP (0171-235 0965) – good support and counselling for parents. Their 24-hour helpline is 0171-235 1721.

* **Postnatal depression groups** – these are just being set up in a number of centres throughout the U.K. Information on your nearest group can be obtained from your health visitor.

* **Parents Anonymous**, Manor Gardens Centre, 8 Manor Gardens, London N7 6LA (0171-263 8918) – offers confidential counselling and help, including over the phone. Parents who fear they are being driven towards the brink with their children should phone for support.

Notes

1 Klaus & Kennell, *Developmental-Behavioural Paediatrics*, Saunders, 1983, pp. 64-80.
2 Chess, *Temperament and Development*, Bruner Mazel, New York, 1977.
3 Rutter, *Child Psychiatry – Modern Approaches*, Blackwell, 1985.

Index